Battering of Women

Battering of Women

The Failure of Intervention and the Case for Prevention

Larry L. Tifft

CENTRAL MICHIGAN UNIVERSITY

Westview Press

BOULDER • SAN FRANCISCO • OXFORD

Copyright © 1993 by Westview Press, Inc.

Published in 1993 in the United States of America by Westview Press, Inc., 5500 Central Avenue, Boulder, Colorado 80301-2877, and in the United Kingdom by Westview Press, 36 Lonsdale Road, Summertown, Oxford OX2 7EW

Library of Congress Cataloging-in-Publication Data
Tifft, Larry.
    Battering of women : the failure of intervention and the case for
prevention / Larry L. Tifft.
        p. cm.
    Includes bibliographical references and index.
    ISBN 0-8133-1390-2. — ISBN 0-8133-1391-0 (pbk.)
    1. Abused women—United States.   2. Wife abuse—United States—
Prevention.   3. Abusive men—Counseling of—United States.
4. Abusive men—Rehabilitation—United States.   I. Title.
HV6626.2.T54   1993
362.82'927'0973—dc20   93-18313
                                                                                                            CIP

Printed and bound in the United States of America

        The paper used in this publication meets the requirements
        of the American National Standard for Permanence of Paper
        for Printed Library Materials Z39.48-1984.

10   9   8   7   6   5   4

Contents

Preface

Violence against women, and, indeed, violence in our society, is a social problem of enormous magnitude. This book is an attempt to understand battering, specifically, the battering of women, as a social phenomenon. It is an attempt to develop a needs-based, primary prevention, social structural approach to battering. Consequently, I present the context and decision-making processes that lead men to choose to batter their intimate partners and the meanings these experiences have for these men. At the same time, I explore the meanings and effects of these experiences for women who are battered so as to understand the context and the decision-making processes that lead them to choose different coping, resisting, and survival actions. In contrast with research that has focused primarily on intervention and empowerment programs for women who have experienced and survived battering, this book systematically focuses on men, assesses and critiques intervention programs for men who have chosen to batter, and analyzes the failure of these programs.

Whereas others have conceptualized battering as one among many forms of interpersonal violence, this book explores battering from both social structural and interpersonal perspectives. Prevention of battering requires the recognition that battering is fundamentally a social structural problem.

Battering has its genesis in a set of specific social arrangements that simultaneously foster a high prevalence and incidence of battering and significantly thwart the development of both individual and collective human potential. Acts of violence between intimates, which are often part of a system of battering, may range far beyond physical violence to include sexual, psychological, emotional, and spiritual violence. They may involve an attempt to annihilate the partner's voice and presence, to erode or deconstruct her sense of self and reality. Acts of *interpersonal violence* are, however, conditioned by and creative of social arrangements that obstruct human development and therefore constitute *structural violence.* Interpersonal violence often reflects structurally violent conditions in the workplace and in other institutional arrangements within our society. It is only in the wider context of institutional or structural violence that the dynamics of battering on an interpersonal level can be understood. It is within structurally violent arrangements that many intimates experience violence and create or learn the motivations, meanings, explanations, attributions, and accounts for their violent actions.

Battering an intimate partner essentially involves one person attempting to control the thoughts, beliefs, realities, and/or conduct of another. Battering most often occurs within a context of hierarchical power arrangements, and the battering of women by men is located in specific gender, economic, and decision-making structures. It is symptomatic of women's structurally denied access to collective resources and opportunities for development, participation, dignity, and respect. The battering of women is also directly related to the ideological and institutionalized strength of specific hierarchical arrangements and has varied with different modes of production and participation within specific historical periods. Its prevalence becomes more understandable when we acknowledge that many persons in our society are handsomely rewarded for controlling the realities and life choices of others and accept violence as a legitimate means for resolving conflict, creating dependency, and establishing dominance.

This book synthesizes the social structural context within which battering occurs and the individual experiential and interactional dimensions of battering to explore the meanings and consequences of differing battering patterns, the interpersonal dynamics and responses to these patterns, and the developmental stages of the battering process. Battering as a social phenomenon is thus specifically located in both the social structural and cultural dynamics of our society and in the social organizational and interpersonal dynamics of the family. In addition, this analysis integrates our knowledge of similar phenomena in the literature on family crises, the social organization of the family, and social deviance.

Finally, this book presents a theoretical framework that places interpersonal and structural violence in context and suggests how the cycle of violence might be broken. The book articulates some of the personal, organizational, and cultural changes we must make if we are to live in a world much more supportive of our essential needs and our individual and collective potentialities. I have tried to present a primary prevention strategy that might greatly decrease battering, violence in all its forms, and the acceptance of violence in our society. In this sense my work is an act of resistance to structural violence and the structural sources of interpersonal violence that both pervade the culture and social organization of our society and jeopardize our collective survival.

Writing this book has been both an individual and a collective endeavor. Therefore, I want to acknowledge the influences, support, and help I have received. Most importantly, I thank Lyn. Markham for working on the manuscript with me, listening to my frustration and excitement along the way, and encouraging me to enter the 1990s by giving up my manual typewriter. My framework for attempting to better understand battering and violence has been most influenced by the writings of Peter Kropotkin, David Gil, Bernard Farber, Norman Denzin, Elaine Scarry, Carl Rogers, Ellen Pence, and Dennis Sullivan—who is in spirit, thought, and deed always an inspiration. Dick Fox and Jim Owens, counselor education teachers, generously shared their insights and provided a learning environment for me. Many critical comments and perceptions were provided by Jan Kristiansson, whose copyediting has made this a much more understandable book. I wish to thank Bernard M. Meltzer for editing an earlier version and the following colleagues and friends for their support: Hal Pepinsky, Richard Quinney, Jim Julian, Larry Reynolds, E. G., Sasha, Slim, Mark Grant, Leela Towler, Susan Caulfield, Colleen Tifft, Quinten, Brandy, Love, Skye, Bart, and The Legend and Friends. Rick Messick, my friend and librarian at Central Michigan University, helped enormously, as did Henry Mendelson, librarian at the State University of New York at Albany. Financial support during my 1990–1991 sabbatical leave was provided by Central Michigan University and the generosity of the Central Michigan University Faculty Creative Endeavors Committee. Finally, I want to thank Ellen Williams, Nancy Carlston, and Martha Robbins at Westview Press for their professionalism and humor and for being "the human side" of publishing.

Larry L. Tifft

Text Credits

Permission to reprint excerpts from the following publications is gratefully acknowledged. Page numbers given are the original page numbers of the excerpted material.

Dennis A. Bagarozzi and C. Winter Giddings, "Conjugal Violence: A Critical Review of Current Research and Clinical Practices," *American Journal of Family Therapy* 11, no. 1 (1983): 9 and 11–12.

Anne Flitcraft and Evan Stark, "Notes on the Social Construction of Battering," *Antipode: A Radical Journal of Geography* 10 (1978): 82–83.

Viktor E. Frankl, *The Doctor and the Soul* (New York: Knopf, 1965), pp. 70–71; copyright © 1955, 1965 by Alfred A. Knopf, Inc. Reprinted by permission of Random House, Inc., Alfred A. Knopf, Inc., and Souvenir Press.

Edward W. Gondolf and David Russell, "The Case Against Anger Control Treatment Programs for Batterers," *Response to the Victimization of Women and Children* 9, no. 3 (1986): 3–5.

L. Kevin Hamberger and James Hastings, "Characteristics of Male Spouse Abusers Consistent with Personality Disorders," *Hospital and Community Psychiatry* 39, no. 7 (1988): 765–766 and 769–770; copyright © 1988 by the American Psychiatric Association. Reprinted by permission.

Gayla Margolin, Linda Gorin Sibner, and Lisa Gleberman, "Wife Battering," in Vincent B. Van Hasselt et al., eds., *Handbook of Family Violence* (New York: Plenum, 1988), pp. 104–106.

Suzanne Pharr, "The Connection Between Homophobia and Violence Against Women," *Aegis* 41 (1986): 35–37. Reprinted with compliments from Suzanne Pharr and the Women's Project, 2224 Main, Little Rock, AR 72206.

1

The Essence of Battering

In our most intimate relationships we expect and are expected to love, nurture, and empower one another. Yet violence and violent interaction patterns are generally accepted and thoroughly woven into the fabric of these intimate relationships. The prevalence of child abuse, sexual abuse and incest, battering, marital rape, and abuse of elderly parents indicates that violence is, and has been a fundamental and pervasive pattern of experience among family members in the United States (Oppenlander, 1981; Nadelhaft, 1987; Pleck, 1987; Gordon, 1988; Van Hasselt et al., 1988; Pagelow, 1988). We are much more likely to be victimized both emotionally and physically by an intimate family member than by a stranger (Straus, Gelles, and Smith, 1990).[1]

Moreover, assaults by an intimate family member are more dangerous for victims than are assaults by a stranger (U.S. Department of Justice, 1980). Many couples in the United States experience violence at some point in their relationships or marriages, and most parents believe, in accord with their legal rights, that they have a *moral obligation* to use physical punishment (e.g., spank or slap) in raising "their" children (Carson, 1986). In fact, a vast majority of parents report that they have acted violently in the course of "caring" for their children (Straus, Gelles, and Steinmetz, 1980). Based on parent admissions, data from the National Family Violence Surveys indicate that more than 90 percent of the parents of three-year-olds use physical punishment. One in four parents starts hitting children before they are one year of age (Straus and Smith, 1990:509). This chilling reality makes it clear that certain patterns of family life actually foster and maintain violence and that these actions can be understood only in the context of our society's general acceptance of violence as a normative and legitimate means of resolving conflict, creating dependency, and establishing dominance.[2]

The battering of women by men can be understood within a historical context in which men established social approval for controlling their wives and a legal right to do so.[3] Anglo-American cultural doctrines such as "coverture" held that a husband and wife were a single entity at law. A wife could not take her husband to court for most causes of action, nor could she testify against him. At the same time, a husband could be held legally liable, at least in principle, for his wife's acts. Consequently, according to coverture, a husband was entitled to discipline his wife to ensure that she would behave properly and that he would not have to answer for her. The only protections a wife had against her husband's disciplinary actions were a few statutes that limited their extent and severity. The most noted of these was the reformist "rule of thumb" that legalized the use of a stick no thicker than the husband's thumb (Fleming, 1979; Archer, 1989).

Although most of the formal laws supporting a husband's right to physically discipline and punish his wife have been abolished in the United States (Saline, 1984:82), traditions of male entitlement and hierarchy linger. They are ceremonially embedded in the promise to "honor and obey" and are concretely rooted in economic and gender structures that diminish and marginalize women. To continue these traditions of entitlement, many men use that amount of force and coercion necessary to establish and maintain dominance over their partners (Schechter, 1982; Pagelow and Johnson, 1988; Ptacek, 1988a, 1988b).

Recognizing the Reality of Battered Women

The prevalence and incidence of battering are difficult to discover primarily because battering has remained relatively invisible as an interpersonal and a social phenomenon and because there is a dissensus over what actions, with what meanings, constitute battering.[4] Nevertheless, one cannot overstate the importance of counting acts of violence against women because doing so indicates, at least symbolically, that women are important. Without prevalence and incidence estimates, it would be impossible to justify either serious public attention or an allocation of resources and relief for this violence. Until recently, violence against women has not been counted (nor, for example, has toxic waste dumping or death as a result of corporate or state policy).

Acts of physical aggression by husbands against wives are underreported in both official reports and victimization surveys. In the United States, national victimization surveys indicate that 16 percent of married couples report one or more acts of physical wife assault during the twelve months prior to the data collection. Estimates of violence over the course of marital relationships indicate that as many as 27–50 percent of women are physically assaulted by their husbands.[5] Couples who are dating but not living together (Arias, Samios, and O'Leary, 1987; Carlson, 1987), couples who are unmarried and living together, and couples in "remarried families" (Kalmuss and Seltzer, 1986) appear to experience much higher rates of physical violence (Morrell, 1984; Smith and Straus, 1988; Stets and Straus, 1989; Pirog-Good and Stets, 1989; Ellis, 1989).[6] Additionally, some research indicates that physical violence among young couples is initiated early in their relationships (often prior to marriage) and is associated with serious marital discord (O'Leary et al., 1989).

Cross-cultural research on violence against women and family violence places violence and battering in a structural context.[7] This research indicates the following:

1. Intrafamily violence is associated with societal violence.[8]
2. Violence in one family relationship is associated with violence in other family relationships (e.g., rare or infrequent wife beating is associated with rare or infrequent physical punishment of children [Levinson, 1983]).
3. Intrafamily violence is associated with specific family organizational arrangements (e.g., child abuse occurs infrequently when there are multiple adult alternative caregivers; wife battering occurs less frequently when partners have a high degree of consensus regarding power, share household and financial decision-making, and have little status inconsistency.[9]
4. Male-dominance patterns maintained through violence are associated with specific cultural circumstances (e.g., wife beating is infrequent in cultures where other cultural and normative practices severely control women and keep them in an inferior position [Campbell, 1985:183]; violence undertaken to assert male dominance is frequently precipitated by real or perceived challenges to the male batterer's possessions, authority, or control [Dobash and Dobash, 1983]).

Not surprisingly, the battering of women has only recently received public recognition as a *social problem* in the United States (Schechter, 1982; Davis, 1987; Davis, 1988). This recognition has been met with considerable resistance (Davis, 1988) and cooptation (Davis, 1987) because it means acknowledging that our society's core values and interaction patterns—hierarchy, gender superiority, property possession, and domination—regularly generate, legitimize, and reinforce the battering of women.[10]

As a public policy issue the recognition of battering is further impeded by an idealized or romanticized view of family life, proscriptions against state intervention into the alleged sanctity of the home, and the belief that if battering exists, it is either episodic or the result of individual pathology (Pagelow, 1984; Pleck, 1987; Davis, 1987). Most centrally, however, denying the reality of battering and not recognizing it as a social problem reflect gender stratification and gender politics (Gordon, 1988; Pence, 1989).

Women are the most frequent and seriously injured victims of recurring episodes and patterns of battering. Perhaps as much as 20 percent of emergency medical services provided to women result from battering (Flitcraft and Stark, 1984). The National Woman Abuse Prevention Project (1988) reports that woman abuse results in more physical injuries that require medical treatment than do rape, car accidents, and muggings combined (Cahn and Lerman, 1991:97). Violence against women is often generally defined as a private matter or "personal trouble," as a psychological problem of one person, as a transaction of individuals within a dysfunctional family system, as mutual combat, or as the transmission of behavior across generations. Each of these definitions maintains the illusion that our cultural beliefs do not support and our social arrangements do not embody power imbalance (Gondolf, 1990:8; Pence, 1989).

This decontextualization of battering places responsibility solely on individual family members while minimizing the impact of historical conditions, cultural traditions, and current institutional arrangements that maintain battering just as they maintain dominance generally and the subordination of women to men specifically. It is not surprising, then, that battering has become an issue of public policy largely through the consciousness-raising, organizing, and lobbying efforts of women.[11]

Blaming Women

Responses by persons outside the women's movement to battering have frequently isolated and blamed those who have been battered, have mystified the structural sources of battering, and have advocated the maintenance of the traditional patriarchal family and a hierarchical order based on gender (Dobash and Dobash, 1988). Even though men who batter subject their partners to physical, emotional, and spiritual terrors, women who manifest resultant sequelae, resist, fight back, or escape are labeled "provocateurs," man-haters, whores, drunks, failures, enablers, or codependent partners by both batterers and colluding officials.[12] Theories that view battering solely as the result of specific attributes of the batterer, the relationship, or the survivor have promoted intervention strategies that do not challenge or attempt to alter the societal power arrangements underlying battering behavior (Pence, 1989:2).

Fifteen years of empirical research focused on the characteristics of women who have been battered have yielded few risk markers (Hotaling and Sugarman, 1986, 1990). Like other persons or groups at the bottom of oppressive and structurally violent social hierarchies, battered women have been generally perceived as causing their own suffering. Explanations for why women are battered, whether given by therapists, academicians, or men who batter, sound alike—battered women lack certain skills, attitudes, and experiences. In a postbattered state, survivors have been compared by researchers to nonbattered women and the differences between the two groups judged to be the causes or correlates of battering (Pence, 1988a:15). Like the peoples of invaded nations, battered women are perceived by the general culture as the cause of their own invasion, torture, and anguish (Tifft and Markham, 1991).

Although until recently there had been a lull in blaming battered women for their victimization, the battering of women is again being psychologized. Individual and family interventions are once more favored and funded over interventions that seek to change social structural and community-coordinated responses to battering and violence (Davis, 1987; Davis, 1988; Currie, 1990; Osmundson, 1992). Even though women are now less likely to be overtly blamed, battering continues to be interpreted in ways that tacitly reinforce notions of women's complicity in the violence (Adams, Jackson, and Lauby, 1988:15). It has again become popular to blame women for their inappropriate attachment to men (Schaef, 1986; Norwood, 1985). "At-risk" factors are confused with sequelae of the battering experience. For example, women's "codependency," "enabler" role, low self-esteem or lack of assertiveness, and histories of sexual abuse are themes commonly found in "at-risk" research. These characteristics are infrequently recognized as a consequence of women's experiences of violence. This confusion implies that women who are battered need therapy more than they need support, advocacy, and justice.

The currently preferred methods of family violence research directly support these inferences. These methods are highly skewed in the direction of quantitative empirical research techniques. They are also misleading in that they isolate acts of physical violence from the interpersonal biographies of the participants and from the specific relational contexts in which battering occurs—relational contexts that have their own emergence, history, duration, and meaning (Pence, 1987:22; Johnson and Ferraro, 1988:183–184; Mayer and Johnson, 1988; Williams and Hawkins, 1989a). Inasmuch as this research has simply counted acts of physical violence, it has failed to recognize the power context and the real differences in meaning, action sequence, intent, and effects that "similar behaviors" may have for different persons (e.g., those who batter, those who are battered) during an episode of battering (Breines and Gordon, 1983). In addition, those researchers using the Physical Aggression Subscale of the Conflict Tactics Scale count as equivalent the act of a woman pushing a man once in the chest during a single episode, causing no physical injury, and the act of a man pushing a woman many times during a single episode that resulted in serious physical injury—they both pushed their partner "once" within the previous year.

Although it is imperative to count acts of violence to convince others that this violence, and all violence against women, is important and requires a political response, the data garnered utilizing these methodologies have been interpreted and presented by some researchers as indicating that women are as (or more) physically violent as men in their intimate relationships (e.g., Arias, Samios, and O'Leary, 1987; O'Leary and Arias, 1988a). Drawing on this research, some academics, policymakers, and media have even attempted to shift the focus of violence to "mutual violence," to "violent women," or to "violence undertaken by women" (McNeely and Robinson-Simpson, 1987; Arias and Johnson, 1989:306). Others have attempted to create the perception that there is a "battered husband syndrome" (Langley and Levy, 1977; Steinmetz, 1978) of a magnitude equal to that experienced by battered wives[13]—an assertion that has been strongly refuted (Pleck et al., 1978).

Research with these seriously limiting and flawed methodologies is blind to gender and to the biographic, historically dynamic aspects of this violence. This research ignores multiple meanings and intents and neglects the differential effects of physical, emotional, sexual, and spiritual violence.[14] Although the methodological limitations, flawed inferences, and negative impact of this research have all been vigorously aired, similar research continues unmodified (Adams, Jackson, and Lauby, 1988:15–16; Kurz, 1989). Sometimes these issues are mentioned as cautionary stipulations for interpreting results (O'Leary et al., 1989:267), but in general policymakers have accepted this research as the basis for their responses to battered women.

Nonetheless, most researchers agree that public policy responses ought to focus primarily on battered women. This response is based on the consensus that

1. Typically, husbands repeat their violence and inflict the more physically injurious forms of violence (Makepeace, 1983; Kurz, 1987).
2. Battered women are more likely to suffer stress and serious psychological distress (e.g., headaches, depression).
3. Battered women are less commonly reported as having initiated violence—their violence is more often defined as self-defense (Saunders, 1988) and is evaluated as less negative than male violence (Arias and Johnson, 1989:303).
4. Within our current cultural and social structural context, women's needs for empowerment and safety are much greater—sex equality is a central dynamic in the primary prevention of battering.

Focusing on women and/or blaming women for being battered has led many psychologists, counselors, social workers, and physicians to respond to battering on an isolating case-by-case basis. Often these professionals have transformed battered women into "mentally disturbed women." In disbelief, many battered women have faced the accusation that they were battered "because they had deficiencies" (Flitcraft and Stark, 1978) or "had asked for it." Or they have been told that their injuries and bouts with depression were the result of interpersonal disputes, with one or both persons to blame. Many of these professionals have intervened in the belief that by doing so they could "restore harmony" in the relationship and preserve the family (Martin, 1981:190). "Restoring harmony," however, has frequently meant asking these women to accept relational inferiority and the social arrangements that would likely continue to foster their feelings of injustice, dependency, and repression (McGrath, 1979:16). Such interventions have clearly failed to either reduce victimization or generate harmony.

Since the early 1980s most states have enacted domestic violence legislation (Lengyel, 1990) but have not designated domestic violence or partner abuse as a specific criminal offense (Lerman, Livingston, and Jackson, 1983). Decision-makers within the criminal justice system have typically defined these batteries as "civil matters," "mutual violence," or private matters (Cahn and Lerman, 1991).[15] In spite of some recent legislation requiring police officers to give "battery victims" affirmative notice of their rights and authorizing officers to make warrantless probable cause misdemeanor arrests in domestic violence cases (Lengyel, 1990; Law Enforcement Training Project, 1989), the police have regularly not arrested assailants. Customarily, they have discouraged women from pressing charges and have held on to the belief, clearly unsubstantiated by research, that legal action would either serve no useful purpose or increase the likelihood of future battering (Dunford, Huizinga, and Elliott, 1990; Buzawa, 1988; Goolkasian, 1986). Similarly, prosecutors have conventionally viewed battering "cases" as inappropriate for criminal prosecution (U.S. Commission on Civil Rights, 1982; Cahn and Lerman, 1991), thereby permitting the partner who battered to escape the criminalization process. In accord with this perspective, some states have enacted diversion legislation. Moreover, the cases that currently give guidance as to how the courts should interpret legislation indicate that domestic abuse legislation is "civil in nature" (Lengyel, 1990:75–76).

In spite of the vitality of this legislation, in practice the culture of hierarchy and domination has been reinforced (Martin, 1981a:194), male power expectations and relations have been "normalized," and the battering of women has been denied both a social structural and a political context (Dobash and Dobash, 1988). Some men batter to control or gain the submission of their partners, in part because it is "normal" in this culture for some individuals to dominate others, for some people to be perceived as existing for others' use, and for some tactics to be necessary to ensure hierarchical power (Pence, 1987:56).

The recurrently asked question "Why do women stay in violent marriages or relationships?" is consistent with the tendency to "blame the victim" (i.e., hold the battered woman responsible for the violence inflicted on her). This question seems to imply that battered women have an ethical obligation to leave these relationships and consequently that they ought to prove that they are deserving victims—worthy of our assistance or even our sympathy—if they do not leave (Okun, 1988:107–108; Loseke and Cahill, 1984:297–298). Furthermore, battered women and their relationships with their partners have been portrayed by experts almost exclusively in terms of how different from others they are. As a result, experts have frequently characterized battered women as little more than "victims" (Loseke and Cahill, 1984:304), failing to note how they are similar to other women who do or do not leave their partners and how their relationships are similar to or different from those of other couples (Blumstein and Schwartz, 1983; Kurdek and Schmitt, 1986). The question of why some women do, while others do not, leave relationships that contain violence may elicit important information for understanding and counseling survivors and for creating options and opportunities for them to better meet their needs within or outside these relationships.

But we should be asking the public policy question "What is it about the way we have defined and organized marital or intimate relationships and our society that places and entraps women in relationships that they define as deconstructively violent?" (Martin, 1981a:195–196).[16] The evidence suggests that most women who are battered take a variety of active and strong steps to improve their lives and that this often means leaving partners who batter them (Schwartz, 1988a).

The historically asserted and generally accepted beliefs that some types of violence are legitimate and that women are the property of their husbands or at least subject to the authority and control of men certainly contribute to entrapment and developmental oppression. Both public policies and private-sector practices have made alternative living arrangements for women insufficiently available, unaffordable, and extraordinarily tenuous. Moreover, gender socialization is extraordinarily difficult to transcend. Indeed, gender inequality is institutionalized as natural in our culture's philosophy, science, morality, and law (Martin, 1981a:196; Brock-Utne, 1985; Stanko, 1985). As a consequence, most young persons are socialized to act out the culture's sex-based power (control) and responsibility "scripts" and are therefore likely to encounter work and school arrangements that reinforce the reality and acceptability of battering behavior in intimate relationships.

Individual and Relational Sources of Battering

Research designed to discover the relational correlates of battering indicates that "official," physically violent battering typically occurs in an interpersonal context characterized by considerable stress (Lloyd, 1990) and traditional sex-role and gender expectations but with only fragile resources to maintain the dominance inherent in them (Dutton and Browning, 1988a; Peterson, 1991; Goode, 1971; Gondolf and Hanneken, 1987), and a problem-solving or disputing style that often fails to resolve conflict (Margolin, Sibner, and Gleberman, 1988). Official, physically violent battering also commonly occurs within a family context of social isolation, lack of community affiliation, and low access to outside resources. Some women become literally imprisoned within their households and communities (Feyen, 1989), terrorized with fear for their safety and that of "their" children.

In these isolating and dehumanizing circumstances and as a consequence of battering, many women develop high levels of psychological distress

(Gelles and Harrop, 1989), depression, anxiety, somatic disorders, and other related health problems (Gelles and Straus, 1988). Although in their strategies of surviving most women display considerable creativity and strength, many also develop a variety of self-deconstructing psychological sequelae, "forms of psychological suicide," or "social death" (e.g., self-trivialization, horizontal hostility, approval seeking, and misplaced compassion) (Kelly, 1988a; Walker, 1983; Johnson, 1988; Pence, 1987:42–43, 1989; Rich, 1979). Often they experience low energy levels characterized by considerable individual stress and relational distress, and they feel or learn that they are unable to control or prevent their partners' violent behavior (Walker, 1979). Like other victims of violence, their sense of meaning, of reality, is disturbed and distorted; they are uncertain about what is happening to them. Their vision of themselves as autonomous individuals in a safe and understandable world is shattered, and the sense of trust they had in relating with others is violated (Kelly, 1988a; Zehr, 1990:29).

Many victims of battering need to make sense of their experience and secure safety and justice. For healing and self-restoration to begin, each woman must understand at least the following issues (Zehr, 1990:26–27):

What really happened?
Why did this happen to me?
Why did I act as I did?
Why have I reacted as I have since then?
What if this happens again?
What does this battering mean for me, for my vision of the world, for my
  marriage, for my future?

Women who survive repeated battering episodes alternate between hoping that their situation will improve and feeling that they can do nothing about it. As time goes on they become convinced that they are to blame for whatever problems anyone in the family experiences. Consequently, they try harder to please, help, or act as a buffer between their partners and the outside world. In time, the battered woman's focus in life becomes her partner; her identity, her existence, her fate, and her needs become defined in his terms. Even her attempts to leave seem dominated by the powerful hook that "he needs her" and that she is "the only one who will ever be able to understand him" (Wetzel and Ross, 1983:425). In the context of social isolation, identity focus on the partner, misplaced compassion, self-denial, self-deconstruction, and few perceived and real options, many battered women agonizingly acquiesce to the terror and to their own, often accurate, dread and fear that attempting to separate would make their circumstances even more dangerous and violence-filled.

Barriers to escaping this imprisonment are erected by isolation, gender socialization, and the absence of tenable redefining catalysts (Ferraro and Johnson, 1983; Peterson-Lewis, Turner, and Adams, 1988). They are further reinforced by sexism in the wages market and the denial of access to opportunities for prior skills and talent development. A battered woman's sense of entrapment is fortified by the emotional difficulties of uncoupling, the disquieting experience of depriving the children of a father, the financial burdens of child care, and religious condemnation.[17]

Research designed to discover the individual correlates of men who batter women indicates that these men have difficulty forming close relationships and are often emotionally dependent in their intimate relationships.[18] Commonly, they express negative emotion through anger and possess diminished self-esteem (Pagelow, 1984). They tend to hold patriarchal, sex-stereotyped values; subscribe to rigid sex-role definitions; and believe that society sanctions controlling women and keeping them in a position subordinate to men (Watts and Courtois, 1981:246). Moreover, these men hold a set of attitudes supportive of violence against wives who violate, or who are perceived as violating, the ideals of familial patriarchy (Smith, 1990). They consistently express jealousy, do not recognize the real effects of their violence, and have often been exposed to violence as children (either as witnesses of parental violence or as victims of child abuse).[19]

According to some researchers, these men are likely to demonstrate severe stress reactions when pressured by work, family, or financial matters (Watts and Courtois, 1981:248; Sonkin, Martin, and Walker, 1985:42–46; Newman, 1979:145–146; Hotaling and Sugarman, 1986; Farrington, 1986). Perhaps, as L. Kevin Hamberger and James Hastings (1986a) suggest, they have difficulty with stress in intimate relationships because they fear intimacy and have a high need for control and power without the appropriate means (e.g., verbal assertiveness skills and emotional expressiveness) of satisfying these needs.

This list of descriptive correlates has, however, been derived from research incapable of determining whether these "attributes" are the antecedents, concomitants, or sequelae of battering. Furthermore, some research suggests that many of these correlates are descriptive of men and women in highly distressed or discordant relationships, regardless of whether battering is present (Margolin, Sibner, and Gleberman, 1988: Lloyd, 1990), or in family climates (Resick and Reese, 1986) wherein conflicts are responded to with withdrawal, anger, and verbal attack and are rarely resolved. These correlates are also descriptive of those experiencing the effects of relational discord (e.g., low self-esteem, low comparative assertiveness, high stress, inadequate and ineffective communication skills) (Gondolf, 1985; Roy, 1982; Coleman, 1980; Neidig, Friedman, and Collins, 1985).

More critically, men who batter women do not fit stereotypical description. Because battering is multidimensional, men who batter women may exhibit differing patterns of battering in response to different contexts. They may also be located in differing stages of "ethical" development (Gondolf, 1987). Considering all this research, Daniel Sonkin (1988:70) and Evan Stark and Anne Flitcraft (1988:307) conclude that the attributes of men who batter women appear to be descriptive of men in the United States *generally*, rather than of men who batter women or of "violent men" specifically.

In summary, individual correlates research on the "different and strange" men who batter, much like the research on the distinctive, individual attributes of women who are battered, seems directed to discovering how these individuals are defective rather than to elucidating the relationship between their consciousness and their environment (Pence, 1987:41; Margolin, Sibner, and Gleberman, 1988; Resick and Reese, 1986; Lloyd, 1990). Consequently, this research deflects attention from the extensive structural contexts within which battering is undertaken and divorces these men and their behaviors from their interrelational meaning contexts.[20] Correlates research does not tell us why so much violence by men is directed toward a selected specific "target"—women/intimate partners—within a specific selected context—the household (Schechter, 1982:210–211; Goolkasian, 1986:4; Fagan and Wexler, 1987).

Correlates research indicating that batterers are under stress, involved in substance abuse, angry, out of control, emotionally inarticulate, fearful of intimacy, or unable to communicate their needs serves to deny that many men handle stress and anger in other ways (Schechter, 1982; Farrington, 1986; Ptacek, 1988a, 1988b; Seltzer and Kalmuss, 1988; MacEwen and Barling, 1988). Furthermore, this research serves to decouple batterers from responsibility for their acts and deny that men who batter consciously know what they are choosing to do (Martin, 1981:197; Ptacek, 1988a, 1988b; Adams, 1989; Stets, 1988). So, in fact, do those women who batter their intimate partners. Battered lesbians report that many of their battering partners are both excellent communicators of needs and skillful "terrorists" who choose violence as a tactic to control and secure partner compliance (Hart, 1986:24; Lobel, 1986:5).

Structural Sources of Battering

That battering is a chosen behavior occurring within a larger structural context is a fact often denied by those whose research has taken an individual or interpersonal focus. A structural approach, in contrast, asserts that most often battering is behavior chosen within the context of hierarchical *power* arrangements that refuse women the tools for self-development.[21] The prevalence of battering is directly related to the ideological and institutionalized strength of these arrangements.[22] Relatively high rates of battering are associated with decision-making and economic arrangements that foster hierarchical nonparticipation, severely restrict access to collective resources, and deemphasize collective accomplishment and responsibility. Relatively low rates of battering accompany decision-making and economic arrangements that foster voluntary and democratic participation, decentralized and relatively open access to collective resources, individual and collective accomplishment (the development of both individual and collective human potential [Gil, 1977, 1986, 1989]), and individual and collective responsibility (Tifft and Sullivan, 1980; Tifft and Stevenson, 1985; Tifft, 1979). (See Figure 1.1.)

Physical violence frequently operates to maintain and reestablish power relations. When men physically batter their partners, this behavior serves as an enforcer of men's exercise of institutional and personal power. Whether frequent or sporadic, physical violence tends to reinforce and to be reinforced by other tactics of battering—screaming in her face, criticizing her ideas, refusing to talk with her, denying her presence, interrupting her (controlling her voice), attacking her personhood, undermining her sense of self-worth, getting her to question her perceptions and judgments, threatening to take the children, coercing sex acts, controlling her contact with others, and withholding approval (Tolman, 1989:163). Physical violence tends to make these alternative modes more effective in enforcing compliance and to imprint them as symbolic and real reminders of physical violence (Pence, 1988a:12). The similarity of the behavior of batterers (briefly detailed here) and the techniques utilized in torture and in brainwashing prisoners of both civil and international war should be recognized (Russell, 1982; NiCarthy, 1986; Tolman, 1989; Amnesty International, 1973; Nadelhaft, 1987; Romero, 1985; Boulette and Andersen, 1985).

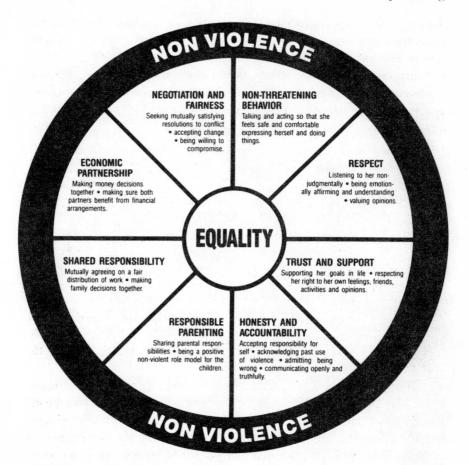

FIGURE 1.1   The Equality Wheel
Source: Domestic Abuse Intervention Project, 206 West Fourth Street, Duluth, Minnesota 55806; (218) 722-4134.

    The presence of accepted male violence within intimate relationships and within the international and organizational relations of our society has come to mean that male hostility or anger, male criticism, and male disapproval serve as reminders of male physical violence and power (Dworkin, 1983). Men who rape, men who batter, men who execute and imprison, and men who terrorize and declare war are the shock troopers of a violent male-dominant society. Because some men rape, all women must become conscious of the power and presence of men; must consider limiting their spatial, developmental, and psychic mobility; and must generally restrict their interactions with others, especially men (Brownmiller, 1975; Adams, 1989:67). Because some men batter, all women must become conscious and wary of male control, hostility, and anger and fearful of confronting male "authority." "Violent men do not exist in a vacuum. Wittingly or unwittingly, their behavior reinforces (and is reinforced by) patriarchal social norms and plays an integral part in the overall system of male dominance" (Adams, 1989:69), thereby serving to keep women in their subordinate place (Leidig, 1981, 1992).

Some authors have asserted that violence against women has always been an instrumental foundation of men's power. Based on some combination of male physical difference ("superiority") and propensity for aggressiveness (Check, 1988), these writers argue that violence against women has been as pervasive, unchanging, and omnipresent as patriarchy itself. This perspective, however, implies that women are the victims of a "sick sex" (males) and perpetuates the falsehood that patriarchy, male dominance, and domination are immutable. Furthermore, it fails to explore how male violence contributes to the processes of domination and fails to recognize that the economic, religious, legal, sexual, ideological, and physical mechanisms of men's control of women have operated variously both historically and cross-culturally (Oppenlander, 1981; Pleck, 1987; Nadelhaft, 1987; McGrath, 1979:19; NiCarthy, 1989).

Today, the family in the United States has lost many of its prior functions. It has become a rarefied emotional environment primarily concerned with consumption, "emotional restoration," companionship, and initial child care. Greatly affected by capitalist economic transformation, the globalization of economic arrangements, and their own conscious activity, women's experience and identity are no longer fully constrained and privatized within the family. The stereotypical family with an employed father and a nonemployed mother at home caring for children now constitutes only 12 percent of households. In nearly 50 percent of all married couples, both partners are employed (Lein, 1986:33). Drawn into the market economy, women have to some degree challenged patriarchal dominance and enhanced their legal and economic independence (McGrath, 1979).

But in spite of women's increased participation in the labor force, enhanced level of education and technical training, and entry into previously exclusively male occupations, women's opportunities continue to be limited by job discrimination, sex stereotyping, and sexual harassment. Women earn substantially less than men, even for the same or commensurate work (Lein, 1986:34). Furthermore, many women in dual-earner or single-headed households have little time to devote to the extra responsibilities or training required in some careers.

Women's limited opportunities and earnings and the stress of combining extrafamily work with household work clearly affect the quality of family life. Women's waged labor conflicts with traditional demands on women's time, attention, and work in the home and calls into question both divisions of labor based on sex and the prerogative of male superiority (Flitcraft and Stark, 1978; McGrath, 1979; Lein, 1986). In those families where the woman's income is essential to maintaining the family's standard of living, or where it is the only income, many partners tend to believe that the responsibility for family routines and fiscal support can no longer be defined as either women's work or men's work (Lein, 1986:40). This reality is often not so easily negotiated and accepted, however. Confronted with the failure of social institutions to uphold many forms of male dominance, and the anxiety engendered by changing sex roles, some men attempt to reconstitute their power, control, "authority," and sense of self through battering.

The contexts in which battering frequently occurs suggest its social significance, its relationship to sex-based divisions of labor, and the changed situation of the family. Battering episodes frequently occur in places that are isolated from outside intervention (McGrath, 1979:21–22; Stets, 1988; Denzin, 1984). They regularly involve conflicting expectations of what women should think and do, and they cluster around "women's work" both outside and within the family (e.g., pregnancy, child care, financial expenditures, career, housework, and sexual activity [Flitcraft and Stark, 1978:80]). Moreover, battering often results in injury to a woman's mouth (Coates and Leong, 1988)—to silence her voice—and to her face, breasts, and abdomen. What is at issue, however, is a woman's freedom of choice, autonomy, and the chance to develop as a fully unique human being (Pharr, 1986).

Theoretical perspectives and intervention strategies derived from the women's shelter movement provide insight into how some processes of domination based on gender operate in our society. If we are to end violence against women, we will have to work for equality and equal participation on all fronts. We will have to recognize that sex inequality is culturally generated and perpetuated by institutional structures and gender socialization (Brock-Utne, 1985; Pence, 1987, 1988a; "Surgeon General's Workshop on Violence and Public Health," 1985; Gil, 1977, 1986; Stanko, 1985). Two most significant components of these latter processes are homophobia (fear and hatred of homosexuality) and heterosexism (the use of sexual identity for dominance and privilege) (Pharr, 1986a). Suzanne Pharr has insightfully elaborated these processes:

> From the time we are very young, we are taught that there are different proper behaviors expected from each sex, and though the women's movement has worked hard to raise consciousness about these differences, these behaviors are still enforced in a child's life. We still see young boys encouraged to be directive, self-asserting, career-oriented, and young girls taught to be accommodating, pleasing, indirect, and family-oriented (with perhaps a career thrown in on the side).
>
> Women are taught that to be directive, self-assertive, career-oriented is not to be womanly, feminine, acceptable to men—and therefore they might lose what little power and privilege that has been granted them. The myth is that for a woman to maintain roles—to be a pleaser, a giver, a nurturer, a supporter who demands little for herself—is to be repaid with a man to provide authority over her life, financial security, decision-making, and direction. To eschew roles is to be cut adrift, to be without order, to be out of proper boundaries, to be someone who gets in the way of the flow of society and the acceptable routined order of relationships. The person who thinks that she should be able to accomplish whatever she is capable of instead of what is expected of her is a threat to society; she has stepped out of line. To know no artificial sense of boundaries gives a heady sense of freedom, a sense of release, of joy, and once one knows it, she has to be intimidated if she's to get back in line again; she must be controlled. She must be taught that she will suffer significant losses if she stays out there in those free, open spaces. ...
>
> It is not by chance that when children approach puberty and increased sexual awareness that they begin to taunt each other by calling these names: "queer," "faggot," "pervert." Children know what we have taught them, and we have given clear messages that those who deviate from standard expectations are to be made to get back in line. The best controlling tactic at puberty is to be treated as an outsider, to be ostracized at the time when it feels most vital to conform. Those who are different must be made to suffer loss. It is also at puberty that misogyny begins to be more apparent, and girls are pressured to conform to societal norms that do not permit them to realize their full potential. ...
>
> To be a lesbian is to be perceived as someone who has stepped out of line, who has moved out of sexual/economic dependence on men, who is woman-identified. A lesbian is perceived as someone who can live without men, who is therefore (however illogically) against men. A lesbian is perceived as being outside the acceptable routinized order of things. A lesbian is perceived as someone who has no societal institutions to protect her and who is not privileged to the protection of individual males. A lesbian is perceived as someone who

stands in contradiction to the sacrifice heterosexual women have made. A lesbian is perceived as a threat.

Lesbian-baiting is an attempt to control women by calling them lesbians because their behavior is not acceptable, that is, when they are being independent, going their own way, fighting for their rights, demanding equal pay, saying no to violence, being self-assertive, bonding with and loving the company of women, assuming the right to their bodies, insisting upon their own authority, making changes that include them in society's decision-making; lesbian-baiting occurs when women are called lesbians because they have stepped out of line. It is successful when women in their fear jump back in line, dance whatever dance is necessary for acceptability. ...

Homophobia keeps us from stepping out of line, getting into the movement for freedom. ... It is used to disempower women and keep us vulnerable to violence and abuse. To work against homophobia and heterosexism is to work against violence against all women. (1986:35–37)

Homophobia, heterosexism, rape and rape "myths," battering, and violence against women must be seen as a system of strategies used to disempower women, to control women's freedom. They regularly accompany hierarchical organizational structures and male socialization patterns that encourage men to reject all that they define as "feminine" in themselves. Men are expected to devalue, marginalize, and objectify the women in their lives and, at the extreme, to relegate them to a status of commodity, sex object, violence object, or servant (Leonard, 1983; Everett, 1988).

The Fundamental Nature of Battering

The recent literature on lesbian battering shatters the sufficiency of the male character and patriarchy perspectives on violence against women.[23] Male dominance is only one form of dominance (Pence, 1987:18); the battering of women by men is only one form of battering (Pence, 1988a; Tifft and Markham, 1991). Battering within intimate lesbian relationships turns our focus to *battering as a social phenomenon,* whether it involves persons of the same or different sex.[24] The literature on lesbian battering directs our attention to the acceptance of hierarchy, superiority, dominance, and inequality and the social arrangements and interaction patterns that embody and enforce these relationships (Lobel, 1986). According to Barbara Hart:[25]

Battering is a pattern of violent and coercive behaviors whereby [one person] seeks to control the thoughts, beliefs or conduct of [an] intimate partner or to punish the intimate for resisting [this control].

Individual acts of physical violence, by this definition, do not constitute ... battering. Physical violence is not battering unless it results in the enhanced control of the batterer over the [person battered]. If the [battered] partner becomes fearful of the [batterer], if [this partner] modifies behavior in response to the assault or to avoid future abuse, or if [this partner] intentionally maintains a particular consciousness or behavioral repertoire to avoid violence, despite the preference not to do so, [that person] is battered.

The physical violence utilized by ... batterers may include personal assaults, sexual abuse, property destruction, violence directed at friends, family, or pets or threats thereof. Physical violence may involve the use of weapons. It [may be] coupled with non-physical abuse, including homophobic attacks on the victim, economic exploitation, and psychological abuse.

A [person] who finds [perself] controlled by the partner because of fear of violence may be battered even if [that person] has not been physically assaulted. If [the] intimate has threatened [per] with physical violence or if [the] partner is aware that merely menacing gestures intimidate [per] because of a past history as a primary or secondary victim of violence, [this person] is battered. [The person] is battered who is controlled or lives in fear of the intimate because of these threats or gestures.

In determining whether ... violence is ... battering, the number of assaults need not be telling. The frequency of the acts of violence may not be conclusive. The severity of the violence may also not be determinative. ...

Battering is the pattern of intimidation, coercion, terrorism or violence, the sum of all past acts of violence and the promises of future violence that achieves enhanced power and control for the [batterer] over [the] partner. (1986:19)

Rather than extracting violent acts from their sequences and histories, Hart's conceptualization suggests that we focus on the meanings and consequences that specific behaviors have in both the relational and structural context. She and others (e.g., Pence, 1987, 1989) assert that the scope and tactics involved in battering form a *system* of behaviors ranging far beyond physical violence to include sexual violence; mental or psychological violence; emotional violence; isolation, degradation, and intimidation; and a variety of interlocking combinations.[26] Different modes of battering are difficult to separate (see Figure 1.2 [Pence, 1989:40]). Batterers rarely use physical violence, within a single episode or recurring episodes, to the exclusion of other tactics (Pence, 1988a:12).

This conceptualization indicates that distinct multitactical patterns or systems of battering (Pence, 1987:33) may well be associated with differing motivations (e.g., displaying power and control, countering dependency, expressing anger, and validating self). They may also be connected with

FIGURE 1.2   The Power and Control Wheel
Source: Domestic Abuse Intervention Project, 206 West Fourth Street, Duluth, Minnesota
55806; (218) 722-4134.

differing "causal" dimensions.[27] Moreover, distinct battering patterns may
be correlated with diverse intimate relations (e.g., noncohabiting couples,
married couples, cohabiting couples, lesbian or gay couples within different
living arrangement circumstances) that are differently situated in the class
and ethnic structures of our society.[28]

As this and other similar conceptualizations indicate, battering is most often conscious and intentional. The tactics shown in Figure 1.2 and similar actions are used not only by men or women who batter their partners, but also
by many decision-makers who act to maintain their positions of power and
control over other individuals and groups (Pence, 1987:57–58; Tifft and

Markham, 1991). Moreover, some men who are physically violent or who exhibit battering patterns are violent only with their partners, while others are (Dutton and Browning, 1988a; Shields, McCall, and Hanneke, 1988; Hastings and Hamberger, 1988) violent in interactions outside the partner relationship as well or only in those interactions. Identifying differing batterers' behavioral and "target" patterns provides a context for discerning the meaning that specific acts or episodes of violence have for the participants. It also provides a context for understanding the full impact that specific acts or episodes of violence have on those persons subjected to this violence (Denzin, 1984; Lobel, 1986; Tolman, 1989).

Like men who batter women, many women who batter women have learned violence from the heterosexual, male-dominated world in which they have grown up (Pharr, 1988:78). They seek to achieve, maintain, and demonstrate power over their partners to meet and further their own needs and desires. Although there is some evidence that committed lesbian couples experience greater shared decision-making (Blumstein and Schwartz, 1983; Kurdek and Schmitt, 1986) and are less materially or financially dependent on each other (Marie, 1984) when compared to other couples, many lesbian couples experience problems of power, attachment-autonomy, emotional dependency, and fusion (Blumstein and Schwartz, 1983; Kurdek and Schmitt, 1986; Marie, 1984; Krestan and Bepko, 1980). Unique problems resulting from socialization, identity formation, and isolation-rejection in heterosexual society are critical issues affecting lesbian couples (Vargo, 1987; Pearlman, 1987; Renzetti, 1988, 1989). Lesbians have even greater reason to experience low self-esteem than heterosexual women for they suffer at the hands of both sexism and homophobia. Consequently, internalized homophobia has a significant role in lesbians' responses to being battered (Pharr, 1988:78).

Lesbians who batter their intimate partners often do so because they perceive violence as an immediately effective method for gaining power and control (Goolkasian, 1986:4; Hart, 1986:20; Lobel, 1986; Stets, 1988; Ptacek, 1988a).[29] These women, like others who batter, desire control over the resources and decision-making processes that power exercise brings, and that violence can assure, when control is resisted. At some level of consciousness the lesbian who batters is aware that her battering behaviors are intended to change how her partner acts, what her partner thinks and feels, and who her partner is (Pence, 1988a:17–18).

The same elements of hierarchy, power, privilege, entitlement, and control that exist in many nonlesbian relationships exist in some lesbian relationships. Like men who batter women, some women who batter women have learned that battering "works" in achieving partner compliance (Hart, 1986a; Marie, 1984). But they have also learned that compliance does not engender peace, personal development, or a healthy emotional commitment in these relationships. Moreover, many lesbian communities within our society have not fully developed cultural and social arrangement alternatives to hierarchy, privilege, and superiority that would more effectively foster peace and initiate strategies for conflict resolution (Lobel, 1986; Dietrich, 1986; Pearlman, 1987; Engelhardt and Triantafillou, 1987; Rainone, 1987).

To conclude, battering is rooted in and reflects specific social-organizational contexts. Battering behaviors and tactics are intended to change who the partner is. Battering deconstructs the partner's self and reality and obstructs the spontaneous unfolding of her human potential. Battering, a chosen behavior, is premised on the following beliefs:

1. Those who choose to batter believe that they are entitled to control their partner and that the partner is obligated to acquiesce in this practice.
2. Those who choose to batter believe that violence is permissible (and conclude that they are ethical/moral persons even if they choose violence against their partner).
3. Those who choose to batter believe that this "violence will produce the desired effect or minimize a more negative occurrence."
4. Those who choose to batter believe that this "violence will not unduly endanger" them. (They believe that they "will neither sustain physical harm nor suffer legal, economic, or personal consequences that will outweigh the benefit achieved through the violence.") (Hart, 1986:25)

Understanding the structural contexts and processes of domination that foster battering underscores our collective involvement in violence-producing values and patterns of interaction. Our social and cultural structures generate violence and must be changed if we are to reduce the amount of pain and suffering in our lives. Working with those who batter and those who are battered must be combined with designing strategies to alter the values and arrangements that stimulate violent behavior and the acceptance of battering (Benedek, 1989; McCall and Shields, 1986; Pence, 1987, 1988a, 1989; "Surgeon General's Workshop on Violence and Public Health," 1985; Tifft and Markham, 1991).[30]

2

The Structural Dynamics
of Battering

Battering, like any form of violence within a society, can be best understood when situated within specific social-organizational and interpersonal contexts. These include (1) the constraints and resources specific to a society's history, ecology, and geopolitics; (2) the specific social-organizational arrangements that have evolved as a result (e.g., the "technico-economic," distributive, and participatory adaptations); (3) the location of the family in this social organization; and (4) the interactions between individuals "socialized" within these arrangements who are actively engaged in regenerating, redefining, and transcending them.[1]

The scope and limits of self- and collective development and the satisfaction of human needs unfold within these contexts. The degree to which people's needs and development are obstructed by these social-organizational arrangements constitutes the degree to which these arrangements are *structurally violent* (Gil, 1977:16). The degree to which an individual's needs and development are obstructed by another's actions is the degree to which these actions are *interpersonally violent*. (See Chapter 11 for a comprehensive cycle of violence theory.)

Acts of violence that occur among family members violate the "natural growth" (Lewin, 1986) of these family members. Acts that form a pattern of battering are conditioned by, responsive to, and creative of structurally violent conditions at the institutional and structural level of organization in our society. Battering, then, is rooted in and reflects the degree to which society's organizational arrangements foster or obstruct the spontaneous unfolding of innate human potential—the inherent human propensity toward development and self-actualization.

For many couples, violent battering episodes form a significant feature of their relationships. Among couples with one or both members working outside the home, these incidents most often occur at the end of the work week and in the late-evening or early-morning hours (Dobash and Dobash, 1984:278). Although there may be considerable time passage between these experiences, they are intense and memorable because of the deep and painful meanings they have for each partner. In this sense battering experiences do not have a clear ending and may assume a presence that not only dominates the daily life of each partner but that also plays a crucial part in framing subsequent violent encounters and the development of the couple's overall relationship (Dobash and Dobash, 1984:269). To fully comprehend this dynamic symbolic process, we need to know exactly what goes on in each battering experience, the circumstances surrounding it, the meanings and motives involved, and the changes that occur in these experiences over time.

A thorough understanding of battering requires an examination of at least three important facets of these incidents: their nature, their dynamic development, and their location within a wider social context. The nature of a battering episode includes the sources of conflict; the type of violence present; the time, location, and duration of the experience; and the presence and reactions of others. The dynamic development consists of the overall unfolding of the process, from the emergence of violent verbal or physical actions to their cessation, either through escape from the battering partner or through the elimination of his violent behavior (Denzin, 1984, 1984a; Mayer and Johnson, 1988; Dobash and Dobash, 1984). Locating these incidents in a wider social context minimally involves relating them to the structure of political, economic, and legal arrangements and the structure of emotional relationships between intimates. This situating of battering episodes identifies the sources of violence and describes the realities within which individuals choose their behavior and create motivations, meanings, and explanations for these choices. It is only in this context that battering episodes and the responses of others to them can be analyzed (Oppenlander, 1981; Pleck, 1987; Nadelhaft, 1987; Davis, 1987; Davis, 1988).

Before carefully exploring the interactive dynamics of battering (Chapter 3), I want to fully delineate the milieu both within and outside the family, specifically the social organization of work, wherein battering processes develop and are perpetuated. Violence in one context or relationship often spills over to others and tends to evoke reactive violence, reflective-imitative violence, or both (Glaser, 1986:6).

For many adults, work and family life are linked through considerable psychological, spiritual, and emotional spillover (Kanter, 1977; Crouter, 1984; Liou, Sylvia, and Brunk, 1990). Those who are experiencing a loving, satisfying, and mutually empowering intimate relationship are likely to bring their positive mood with them to work. Those who are distressed by a child's serious illness, who are experiencing a life crisis or serious relational problem at home (e.g., battering), or who have an "unhappy marriage" are equally likely to bring these feelings, worries, and problems with them to work.

The work of battered women whose partners have not prevented them from working outside the home may be seriously impaired by battering experiences. Low energy, turmoil, and preoccupation with self may lead to on-the-job injury and an inability to concentrate on work or listen to and relate with others. These women may fear that when they go to work their partners might move out or make good on threats to take the children. This fear, physical injuries, pain, and depression may force these women to miss work (Shepard and Pence, 1988).

Reciprocally, when working family members "come home," they bring with them a panoply of psychological and spiritual spillover. The nature of their work, the meanings they attach to it (Barling and Rosenbaum, 1986), and the manner in which the work is organized, including the degree to which they participate in creating its organization, may significantly affect their mood (Gil, 1989; Lein, 1986:38; Crouter, 1984). This seems especially true for men, who quite often derive their sense of self from their work. Their feelings of self-worth, interpretive framework, worldview, relational expectations, and energy level can all be affected by conditions at work. Their stress level may affect their attentiveness and degree of patience and tolerance for others or others' actions at home. The degree to which they attempt to define and control the nature of their intimate relationships may be affected by, and may be a means of compensating for, dissatisfying, deconstructive, nonparticipatory, or structurally violent conditions at work. Paradoxically, the unemployed, the nonworking, and the unable-to-work are subjected to even harsher societal-level structural violence.

The cybernetic elimination of work opportunities and economic changes affecting participation in the work force have each had a notable effect on the social composition of the family and on the escalation of violence in interpersonal relationships. Traditional expectations for women in the home and in intimate relationships have been challenged by the rise and leveling off of women's work force participation (at 45 percent) (Lein, 1986) and the development of the single-parent (usually female) household. Concurrently, the globalization of capital and consequent domestic plant closings, unemployment, underemployment, dislocation, and relocation have transformed feelings of security, lifestyle choices, and future expectations for both self and intimate relationships. These developments have significantly altered the level of commitment perceived as feasible and desirable in intimate relationships and the level of both personal and interpersonal stress and violence experienced in them.

Extrafamily Social Organization and Battering

Institutions such as schools, hospitals, welfare agencies, and places of work (including the household) may through their organization, policies, and practices obstruct and violate individuals' developmental requirements. Simultaneously, these institutions may reward individuals for this obstruction and violation. Moreover, these institutions are located within social structures that enable some groups and individuals to meet their needs and develop their human potential while inhibiting or thwarting others in doing so.

Within our society, hierarchical control of resources, nondemocratic decision-making processes, and the arrangements for production and distribution establish and legitimate abundant opportunity for a few to develop their potential, meet their needs, and, in fact, pursue their whims. These specific arrangements, however, prevent the need satisfaction, restrict the participation, and obstruct the developmental potential of most persons in our society. They create stratification arrangements that place many people in positions of high risk for malnutrition, disease specific to impoverishment, developmental discrimination based on color and sex, occupational injury, and early death. These arrangements create structural violence.

Structural Violence

In our society, structural violence is commonly accepted as normal and is believed by some to be inevitable (Gil, 1987:9). Structural violence constitutes the context for interpersonal violence. Although interpersonal violence transgresses specific interpersonal expectations, structural violence and interpersonal violence compose an interlocking, holistic reality of the same values, social arrangements, consciousness, and dynamics (Gil, 1977).

The tactics chosen by men who batter mirror those employed by many people in positions of power (e.g., low-intensity warfare, withholding of access to survival goods, state-sponsored terrorism) to sustain racism, ageism, heterosexism, anti-Semitism, economic control, and gender hierarchy, and

other forms of group domination (Pence, 1988a:12, 1987:57). Men who batter women customarily learn these tactics in their families of origin and in
their experiences of the dominant culture. They, like many of us, are im-
mersed in the consciousness of oppression, which is rooted in the assumption that some people have the legitimate right to control others.

Many accept this power relationship as beneficial to those who exercise
control and to those who are "guided by" (i.e., subjected to) it. Afrikaners
claim that their technologically advanced Euro-African political economy
has resulted from ethnic superiority and from the institutionalization of
apartheid. Euro-American "whites" in the United States proclaim color seg-
regation and institutionalized racism to be God's plan carried out in the interests of everyone, even oppressed African Americans. The decision-makers of superpower (i.e., superior power) nation-states arrange the invasion of
other peoples and nations (to bring "democracy," development, a "free-mar-
ket" economy, or "communism") for the alleged "benefit" of those invaded.
Elaborate systems of ideology and propaganda legitimize relationships of
mastery and control by, among other means, obtaining acceptance of the
premises that hierarchy is natural and that those who occupy the lowest positions are there because of their own deficiencies, defects, inferiorities, or actions. Of course, those who rule and control do so because of their talents,
skills, and superiorities (Pence, 1988a:13).

Our cultural and social arrangements encourage us to define our personal
and collective power as our ability *to control.* The extent to which we are able
to influence events, to acquire and control resources, and to govern the
behavior and actions of others is the measure of our collective power and, in
many instances, of our personal power and self-esteem. Many of those who
intervene in the lives of others as agents for nation-states, as institutional policymakers, as corporate directors, as therapists, or as persons who batter
their intimate partners share this cultural perspective (Pence, 1988a).

Structural violence and the ideological processes that justify it tend to initiate interpersonal violence, thereby forming a cycle of pain infliction. Some
arrangements and acts through which pain is inflicted are highly accepted;
some are not. Each initiates the creation of language to explain, normalize,
or make sense of this abuse, and each reinforces the cultural acceptability of
inflicting pain. Organizational arrangements that obstruct the unfolding of
an individual's potential are a source for reactive and imitative violence. In
reaction or imitation, those who experience structural violence tend to inflict
pain on themselves or others. To illustrate, many people find that work obstructs the development of their talents, excludes their participation, and at-

tacks their autonomy and positive sense of self. In retaliation for the deep well of pain that results, these individuals may hurt themselves or others. In doing so, they may be attempting to recover what they have lost at work, or they may simply be replicating the organizational patterns they have experienced at work.

Not only do interpersonal and intrapersonal violence feed back into collective attitudes that reinforce structural violence; they may also initiate *collective* pain-infliction processes. For example, penal sanctions explicitly and emphatically affirm that the collective is justified in inflicting pain, especially when an individual's actions violate "accepted" social arrangements. This affirmation holds even if the accepted arrangements are themselves violent in that they have obstructed the development of those who violate these social arrangements.

Reflections on Family Social Organization

According to David Gil (1977:15), whenever interpersonal violence and submission to structural violence are "normal" aspects of adult life, many sources of socialization (e.g., U.S. foreign policy, criminal justice or penal policy, formal educational processes, television programming, music, and other components of popular culture) serve as witting or unwitting agents of structural violence. Children learn "violent tendencies and capacities" and the language for justifying them through individually competitive and violent games and sports and through individually rewarding and punishing cognitive learning experiences. Most critically, they learn these tendencies from their family culture, division of labor, and decision-making arrangements.

Frequently, family culture mirrors ideas supported in other social institutions. Cultural acceptance of violence is encouraged by corporal punishment in the home and classroom and by capital punishment, imprisonment, military invasion, and low-intensity warfare in the nation-state. Cultural sanction of these and other forms of violence not only condones such behavior but also provides a model for it. "The progression of learning is obvious: the state provides a model for the family, the family provides a model for the child" (Beredek, 1989:10).

Mirroring the state and other extrafamily organizational arrangements, many adults create within their families child care arrangements based on sex and divisions of labor based on age and sex. They tend to establish nonparticipatory, hierarchical decision-making arrangements. Often such patterns are enforced through arbitrarily imposed discipline and punishment, including corporal punishment and emotional pain. Ironically, these practices transmit to many children the attitudes and learned capacities they will need as adults to participate in arrangements permeated with structural violence (Gil, 1977:17). Children in these families learn that those who love them most are also those who hit them and who claim a legitimate entitlement to do so. Children also learn that when an issue is important, those who say so justify the use of physical force to obtain acquiescence or control (Gelles and Straus, 1979). Early experiences with these "lessons" tend to lay a groundwork for normative justification of control and violence and help shape a framework for both intimacy and authority relationships.

Family Social Organization and Battering

Paradoxically, individuals in these patterned family relationships, while inflicting their own versions of organized violence and power, expect one another to have the desire, emotional energy, and affective commitment to restore what has been lost in extrafamily contexts. The vast majority of workers have little power over their work environment, work space, schedules, or tasks (Lein, 1986:38–39). Women in particular commonly have little control over their work schedules and are placed in great conflict when family emergencies and the daily needs of children require attention. Whereas some jobs require considerable high-risk decision-making, others require little thought. When workers are treated as organization "personnel" (without attention to each as a specific person) within nonparticipatory work settings, they often feel they are "not themselves" and cannot "be themselves" in their work or at their place of work. Even though most take pride in their work, many feel that their work is unnecessary or meaningless. Even if others perceive them as successful (Johnston, 1988), they may feel they cannot achieve their goals at work, and they may be disappointed in their careers, if they have them.

Many individuals ("workers") return to their families with feelings of insult, anger, frustration, and both emotional and physical pain (e.g., headaches, stress reactions). They may bring home a need to reassert their self-worth or self-importance or vent their feelings of impotence and frustration at being unable to affect their work environment. Many individuals emerge from work not in a mood for parenting and not in a mood for being an intimate's emotional restorer. Perhaps especially, but not by any means exclusively, working-class men (Schwartz, 1988) commonly replicate the processes of pain infliction and violence that they experience as a result of their own obstructed development and loss of voice at work or from not working. The patriarchal power and control patterns they establish within the household often serve as a vital-to-self-esteem defense against the self-destructive effects of the work environment (Lewis, 1983:86; Everett, 1988:137). Those men who do not control others in the workplace and those whose self-concept and self-esteem are attached to controlling others (e.g., having subordinates) in order to "be somebody" may perceive the "private" realm of the household as their only "safe" arena for establishing a sense of self-in-control or self-in-control-of-others. Much less successfully, some men act these needs out violently in public spheres (Ferraro, 1988:127).

The Context for "Safe Violence"

Most people do not express their pain at work, first, because they do not see their coworkers or immediate supervisors as the organizers of this pain and, second, because to do so, especially as interpersonal violence, would be unsafe. They might be arrested and subjected to more pain. Or they might be reprimanded or lose their jobs and as a consequence inflict pain on family members by, among other effects, altering the family's economic circumstance—reducing the degree to which family members can meet their physical, psychological, and social needs. Consequently, most people who work in these structures of violence tend to hold their loss of self and pain within, waiting to express or act to dissipate these feelings with intimates. Some, however, express pain and loss by taking them out on family members who can be subjected to "safe violence."

Some who experience structurally violent work arrangements organize similarly violent home lives through which to express their feelings. They become the persons with the position of power and privilege. Others (e.g., partnered, working women) come home to a family situation that is similarly hierarchical, obstructive, and violative of their personhood. The same arrangements obtain for women whose place of work is the household. As a consequence, they may experience similar losses of voice, self-presence, and autonomy. These women are not likely to be especially receptive to the feelings and losses their partners experience at work, having suffered similar pain from the arrangements these partners have imposed at home. Such women may understand the nature of these losses, but they may have difficulty helping their partners become "emotionally restored" when they are the imposers of the structural violence at home. In addition, men rarely cast themselves in the role of "emotional restorer" for their partners, even when they do not impose structural violence on them.

In contrast to men and women who work outside the home, women whose place of work is exclusively the household may have their economic and psychological well-being and their life choices defined and restricted by the family wage earner and his career. As she receives no extrinsic rewards for her work, her partner may severely restrict her choices, movement, and interaction with others. He may expect that she see the world through his eyes; that she see her future and the futures of the children through his eyes and his "success"; and that she live vicariously through him. He may impose family routines that restrict her development as a person. If her work in child care or home management is not intrinsically rewarding or if he does not provide intrinsic rewards (e.g., continuous acts and expressed feelings of appreciation, reinforcement for her competency, greater degrees of autonomy and shared decision-making, expressions of support and acknowledgment of the difficulty of her work), then her pain and loss with these family arrangements will become more poignant, unsatisfying, and present in her consciousness.

She may then initiate an exploration of how her needs are not being met. At least initially, however, her consciousness is likely to mirror both prevailing dominant cultural themes and popular cultural themes specific to her (e.g., black women) (Peterson-Lewis, Turner, and Adams, 1988). She is likely to blame herself for her unsatisfying circumstances and for her limited personal achievement. She is likely to attribute his violence to external factors. She may even believe that her life circumstances cannot be altered (Gil, 1987:13; Miller, 1982; Matza, 1964, 1969).

She may retain this ideological framework even when she is battered, in part because her social reality is isolated. Her positive sense of self and life purpose are focused within the home. The interactional or material reality of other sources of personal worth may be absent. She may be totally dependent on him for emotional support and continuity. She may initially accept his reality, attributions, or explanations for the violence (Benedek, 1989:8) and feel responsible for his decisions to batter her.

Some authors seem to blame battered women for accepting the batterer's version of events and for blaming themselves. Others see this attributive behavior as constituting rationalizations that entrap these women in victimization. Still others imply that such attributions allow these women to remain in the relationships (Okun, 1988; Ferraro and Johnson, 1983; Strube, 1988). These common attributions may, however, principally result from the physical pain received in the battering episode, from the spiritual self-loss occurring in these processes, and from the initial stages of grief. Examining one's behavior, attempting to take responsibility for this behavior, and trying to place one's feelings and experiences into context with those of others are a normal initial grief reaction to a loss that is not yet accepted (Kübler-Ross, 1975; Turner and Shapiro, 1986; Adams, 1989).

In an attempt to make sense of his violence, the battered woman may perceive herself as his only "safe" outlet for frustration and dissatisfaction with his life situation (Peterson-Lewis, Turner, and Adams, 1988:120). She may think that blaming him and calling the police will result in violence being directed toward him. Or she may fear that his violence against her will not be taken seriously by the police and, consequently, that she will be further victimized (Peterson-Lewis, Turner, and Adams, 1988:120).

Many battered women fear the negative self-meaning attached to seeking professional help. Their initial framework of external attributions and perhaps self-blame, rather than self-exploration, may be reinforced if they do seek professional help (Flitcraft and Stark, 1978). A battered woman may hold onto this interpretive framework even if she is severely and repeatedly battered and regardless of whether she actively supports, does not resist, or attempts to institute different coping or survival arrangements in the family. Her framework may remain intact even if she temporarily "freezes out" the batterer or severs the relationship permanently. To alter this framework, she must begin to transcend the social arrangements and ideological structures of violence (Turner and Shapiro, 1986).

Like the men who feel the devastating effects of developmentally obstructive work contexts and yet do not undertake interpersonal violence in that context because it is unsafe to do so, women who work at home in structurally violent circumstances do not generally initiate nonsafe interpersonal violence in the home. They do not act out against their "boss," against the person who is the primary source of their material well-being, emotional support, continuity, and positive sense of self.

Given these structural conditions and dynamics, it is not surprising to discover the prevalence and specific patterns of family violence and battering that exist in our society. Men in positions of hierarchical power within the family who acquiesce to the same power at work are likely to attempt recovering their lost real selves and their power-based selves in safe violence within the family. Women who are subjected to patriarchal divisions of labor, nondemocratic decision-making governance in family life and/or wage work context, and loss of voice and real self are likely to express interpersonal violence against safe members of the family. Although there are women who direct this violence against their partners and some who "resolve" their captivity and survival by killing their husbands, most select safer members of the family—young children. Yet because many battered women feel that interpersonal violence toward their children is unacceptable and unsafe, and the resultant suffering would further erode their self-concepts, they only allow themselves to inflict pain on themselves. The position of women in the structures of safe violence leads them to believe that they are the only safe outlet for their own violence.

The Reality of "Nonsafe Violence"

Battering is a socially isolating series of experiences for the victim. As her body displays the wounds, as her consciousness is permeated with pain, headache, bowel disorder, muscle trauma, disorientation, dread, and depression (pain that cannot be confirmed through medical technology), she tries to transform or escape the battering relationship. Or she tries to mediate her constant pain through self-deconstructive behaviors that reinforce her initial grief, loss, and isolation and perhaps also her continuing susceptibility to his inflictions of pain (Flitcraft and Stark, 1978:82–83).

Although comprehensive community education, intervention, advocacy, support, and shelter programs have recently been developed through the efforts of the women's shelter movement,[2] medical definers frequently address only the symptoms, the sequelae, of this pain. They frequently prescribe "painkillers" or "tranquilizers" and refer battered women to other professionals for psychiatric counseling. Whatever the intended effect of these therapies, the actual consequence has often been to contribute to the diminishment of a battered woman's ability to alter her initial framework, to escape the cycle of violence and her partner's decisions to batter her, and to break out of the field of negative interaction.

The underlying premises and the structure of this model of treatment communicate to the battered woman that she should accept responsibility for his violence. Her feelings that perhaps she is at fault are intensified, while the socially pervasive attitude of blaming the victim, especially when the victim is a woman, is reinforced (Williams-White, 1989:51). Flitcraft and Stark explain:

> The process of medical labelling stimulates a host of self-destructive behaviors that now begin to appear alongside both the apparent nervous symptoms and the physical results of the battering. On the one side, the doctor is driven to the limits of medical perception by the persistence of the battered woman and by the failure of his/her cure. S/he now considers the possibility that something is

wrong with the woman as a whole person, not simply with part of her body. On the other side, her/his attempt at an individual (rather than a symptomatic) diagnosis coincides with the appearance of problems that can be detached from battering and are made to appear independent. Alcoholism, drug abuse, and mental illness are now constructed as isolated events that happen to the woman as a person, not simply to her body. If battering isolates the woman from her peers, the treatment for these allegedly independent problems further isolates her and discourages her from sharing her problems, i.e., problems created for her by a battering male, with others. ...

The woman begins to develop "symptoms" associated with battering but also separable from it, both in time and space. These symptoms are partially the result of a prior attempt by medicine to stereotype the female patient with psychiatric labels. The transformation of medical ideology into an actual set of individual medical symptoms such as alcoholism or drug abuse permits precisely what the battered woman has demanded from the outset, the formulation of psycho-social diagnoses and referrals. But since the medical symptoms appear to characterize only the problems the woman faces as an individual, they can be treated apart from the family context. The symptoms can be temporarily relieved (e.g., going through detox programs) without threatening the family. Once the emergence of an independent set of medical symptoms permits medicine to develop a psychological diagnosis, the doctor, social worker, or psychiatrist can acknowledge that "the family is in crisis." Initially we might have predicted that the battering and its associated problems would cease only if the family dissolved. Now, however, battering appears amidst a complex of associated psychopathological problems and not necessarily as the most serious. Indeed battering may even appear to result from these problems: the woman is beaten because she drinks or, more broadly, because drinking and violence go together in the culture from which she comes.

The woman's autonomy has been by now fundamentally compromised. The problem is now "the family in crisis," not her beating. Or, worse, the battered woman is defined as the family's problem.

Beatings continue and injuries escalate. But by now even the woman may believe her injuries result from the broad psychological pathology associated with alcoholism, drug addiction, mental illness, and hypochondriasis. The family is now the classic "multi-problem" family: suicide attempts, miscarriages, child abuse, alcoholism—among these problems, battering is barely visible. The violent family has now been stabilized, at least temporarily. Medicine's purposive failure is the patriarchy's success. (1978:82–83)

The underlying premises and structure of this treatment model collaborate with those of battering patterns to continue placing the battered woman in a power position that disallows her needs. In these "therapeutic" relationships she is not in a position to evaluate what form of assistance she desires (Williams-White, 1989:51). Rather, she is in a position like that within the battering relationship—she is being controlled by others. She is neither safe nor empowered. She is not enabled to recognize what works best for her and to learn not to depend on either the batterer or the therapist to control her decisions and her life (Schechter, 1982; Williams-White, 1989:52).·

Structural Battering

This chapter has emphasized that many men who work in structurally violent organizational contexts imitatively organize and impose decision-making processes and labor arrangements within the family that render them inflictors, rather than receivers, of structural violence. It is within hierarchical family arrangements—reflective of the hierarchies experienced at work—that men who batter express their hurt and loss by inflicting pain on their intimate partners.

This violence is both interpersonal and structural. It is perhaps expressive of the batterer's own susceptibility to violence or even his own double bind acceptance-rejection of hierarchy and control. But it is also expressive of and instrumental in establishing and maintaining his hierarchical positioning in the structurally violent social arrangements of his family. If he is subjected to others' control at work, if he is punished for being late for work, for not doing what he is told or not doing it correctly, for making errors in judgment, or for talking back to those who exercise power over him, he may recreate similar policies, procedures, and punishments at home.

Men who batter commonly come home to inspect the domestic work, to make sure it has been done and to their liking, to see how the children have been disciplined, to have their orders and wishes filled, and perhaps to demand and expect sexual access as part of their partners' domestic labor (Allen et al., 1989:86). He may discipline and punish to inflict pain and to display his power and position in the family order. He may physically punish both the children and his partner. He may raise the attributes of power through making emotional outbursts or withdrawing, through withholding emotional support or himself, through telling them to get out of his way, to do it his way or shut up, or to speak only when he asks.

Men who batter are emotively and cognitively situated in structural contexts that require the acceptance of a cultural contradiction: The structural violence to which they are subjected (e.g., at work) punishes them *and* rewards them. The structural violence to which they are subjected is culturally praised, accepted, and infrequently questioned. In contrast, the structural violence they imitatively create or reactively inflict at home in retaliation for their loss and pain may be similarly designed to reward them and may receive some lingering praise within popular male culture. But it is increasingly being questioned, challenged, and denounced as unacceptable by many men and women. Violence becomes increasingly unacceptable when it passes from structural violence (institutionally channeling and delimiting the development of family members through patriarchy and divisions of labor based on gender) to interpersonal violence (personally limiting the development of these same family members through physical, sexual, spiritual, or emotional violence). When violence passes from "the ordinary structural violence" of hierarchical family arrangements to such forms of violence as neglect for the physical needs of children, coerced sex acts, or the physical confinement of the partner (forms of violence that fuse with interpersonal, rather than structural, violence), they are without significant cultural support.

Most researchers have perceived, defined, and addressed battering as a form of interpersonal violence or as a form of interpersonal violence rooted in a context of structural violence. They have not focused on the structurally violent or institutional form of battering. Again, most discussions of battering as a social phenomenon have defined battering as an act or series of actions composing a pattern of behavior that inflicts pain and suffering on an intimate partner. Rarely have these discussions identified the hierarchical or nonparticipatory power arrangements themselves as constituting a system of battering. If this were the defined reality, we would have to explore each division of labor and decision-making arrangement within the family that systematically violates the development of any individual member of the family, designating it a form of structural battering.

A structural definition of battering must be explored if we wish to analyze social arrangements that embody violence, loss, and pain. While designating these arrangements battering, we must also look at the interpersonal violence patterns that frequently accompany these structures. It is clear that battering as an interpersonal form of violence most frequently takes place in the framework of patriarchal/hierarchical family social arrangements.

Structural and interpersonal forms of battering often fuse, forming an integrated and reinforcing pattern of violence. Analytically, however, it is important to differentiate these forms. *Structural battering* is a generally accepted pattern of interaction in which loss and pain are inflicted on an individual through refusal of access and denial of choice to participate in specific developmental opportunities or spheres. *Interpersonal battering* is an increasingly questioned and intermittent pattern of interaction in which one intimate inflicts pain and loss through direct physical, verbal, or emotional acts that deconstruct the partner's presence, participation, voice, self-respect, and sense of self and that consequently obstruct her development and the unfolding of her potential.

3

The Interpersonal Dynamics
of Battering

The interpersonal dynamics of battering are best explored as a process (Denzin, 1984, 1984a; Stets, 1988; Ferraro, 1988; Giles-Sims, 1983; Mayer and Johnson, 1988). This process is experienced by couples who withstand repetitive battering episodes, by those who sever their relationship after an initial violent episode (Russell, 1982:392), by those whose experiences are minimally violent, and by those whose violence is so severe that the battered survivor may suffer "battered woman syndrome."

Because of the brevity of the relationship or the lesser emotional commitment or investment of self-identity, couples that experience battering during courtship live through an emotional process not nearly as extensive as that experienced by couples whose real violence becomes a stabilized pattern over many years (Mayer and Johnson, 1988). Because of the diversity of experience, the dynamics of battering can be most fruitfully explored when they become an enduring, yet destabilizing, feature of the interaction of partners who have "been together" for some time (Denzin, 1984, 1984a; Stets, 1988; Ferraro, 1988; Giles-Sims, 1983; Walker, 1979). For these couples, battering becomes conscious through a progressive realization rather than as a result of an isolated event with an undisputed meaning (Mayer and Johnson, 1988:197). They also experience leaving the relationship and severing ties as a process (Giles-Sims, 1983).

For couples undergoing repeated battering, violent episodes do not seem to have an exact point at which they begin and end; instead, they form a continuing, integral part of the relationship (Dobash and Dobash, 1984:272). In these instances, periods of violent interaction fade into periods of tense interaction scarred by impending violence (Walker, 1979, 1979a; Stets, 1988; Coates and Leong, 1988; Dutton and Painter, 1981). The duration of these periods varies tremendously from, quite commonly, several weeks to two or three months. There are, of course, couples that are involved in these episodes almost daily and those who go a year or two between them. These differences, along with variances in the severity of physical and emotional injury and dissimilarities in patterns of battering, indicate that battering is a complex phenomenon about which it is difficult to generalize and toward which considerable effort to differentiate must be directed.

Among couples whose battering becomes an enduring pattern, relatively peaceful interludes are eventually broken by psychological, sexual, or physical violence. For the partner who is battered, this violence gives rise to feelings of betrayal (Mayer and Johnson, 1988), shock, fear, anger, bitterness, distress, dependency, and dread (Zehr, 1990; Russell, 1982). It may also result in physical injuries, the most typical of which are bruises and cuts from being repeatedly slapped or punched in the mouth, face, or body or from being repeatedly kicked or kneed (Dobash and Dobash, 1984:274).

At the conclusion of these initial episodes, the battering partner typically offers explanations, apologies, and promises and communicates that he considers the violence and the disputed issue to be over; "everything should go back to normal." Initial relational reinforcements (e.g., apologies, discussions, promises) are often accompanied by showers of attention, affection, and gifts, which the battered partner often perceives as attempts to win her back or as indications that she is still loved (Walker, 1979a; Stets, 1988:102, 127; Coates and Leong, 1988).[1] However, these initial relational supports do not ordinarily become an element of subsequent episodes, indicating that battering processes are dynamic and change over time (Dobash and Dobash, 1984:281).

A cycle of violent battering episodes often continues in spite of the considerable effort most couples make to end it (Denzin, 1984a:190). When violence erupts again and again, each partner tries to make sense of the situation and the batterer's actions (though this effort may not be communicated). The battered partner attempts to comprehend her pain and involvement (if any) in the interaction that led to the battering. Unhappily, these efforts frequently lead to attributions of responsibility, explanations, and denials that result in individual and collective bad faith—a fiction that acts to secure a relatively permanent place for violence in the couple's interaction (Denzin, 1984; Stets, 1988).

Initiating and Discontinuing
Battering Processes

Battering is, as has been stated, fixed within a framework of superordinate and subordinate relationships that mirrors the structural contradictions and ideological tensions of the larger social order. Battering is thus situated within the timetables, rituals, and routines of arrangements for earning and spending money, preparing meals, sleeping, expressing intimacy and sexuality, and taking care of the household and children—in short, within the family's division of labor and decision-making arrangements (Denzin, 1984; Ferraro, 1988). When disagreements about or challenges to the accepted or assumed understandings that underlie these arrangements arise, violence can erupt to clarify or reassert the reality and authenticity of these arrangements. Family arrangements and practices are, then, the arena for a clash of moods derived from extrafamily experiences or hierarchical family arrangements themselves. They are the arena wherein conflicting conceptions of self and personal need satisfaction requirements are contested—and the acceptability of obstructions to self-development are disputed.

Responding to Loss

According to Norman Denzin (1984:488–489), the interpersonal violence exhibited in battering is an attempt to regain, through the use of emotional and physical force, something that has been lost. What has been lost can be directly traced to the self of the person inflicting the violence—the self and feelings of the batterer are at the core of the violent behavior. If violence is a function of how physiological arousal is shaped by learned ways of interpreting experience and justifying behavior (Glaser, 1986:27), we must articulate what is lost and the contextual cues that precede, arouse, and set violence into motion; that is, the antecedents that set off the feelings from which violent actions follow.

Intimate relationships contain an implicit expectation that each partner will support and nurture the other's sense of self. Often, however, the needs of one partner impinge on those of the other. Tension develops in the course of mediating accommodation, acquiescence, or resistance to the other's expectations. According to Kathleen Ferraro:

> Both partners are aware, at least subliminally, that allegiance to the other's self
> is strained and unnatural. The commitment of each partner is under scrutiny.
> The meanings of actions and words are open to negotiation and are potential

symbols of allegiance or rejection. The conscious intent of the other is not important in the development of perceptions of threat. The individual perceives the other as threatening based on his or her own needs and ideas. When these are unarticulated, subterranean expectations, reactions to threat are particularly unpredictable and uncontrollable. (1988:129)

The violent partner's perception of threat to self is tied to the feelings, meanings, and actions that he regards as critical for self-continuity and survival. Anything that an intimate does or says—even her presence in the face of loss suffered in another interactional realm—that violates his expectations of allegiance and support may be interpreted as a threat (Ferraro, 1988:128).

Most of us are not aware of the totality of feelings and meanings that constitute our sense of self. Moreover, many meanings that are most important in this regard (especially for those of us who are not particularly introspective) remain undefined until they surface when we feel threatened. Many men who batter, at least initially, do not recognize the centrality of dominance and control to their sense of self; yet they become agitated and aggressive when these elements of self are threatened.

Because meaning is culturally and situationally specific, a wide array of actions by others (or even moods present in a setting) may be perceived by a person as threatening, even when there is no intent to threaten. Regardless of their "objective validity," the perceptions of a batterer may be that his partner is attacking him. His violent response can be understood as an effort to subdue or prevent the threat to self he perceives she represents. Even if the response is not just, deserved, provoked, intended, or in any way legitimate, it is at least understandable from the batterer's frame of reference (Ferraro, 1988:129).

A close examination of the underlying themes and contextual cues that precede battering episodes reveals that they have to do with the issue of control (Adams, 1989, 1990; Stets, 1988:70, 97; Ptacek, 1988a; Ferraro, 1988)— to control, to be in control, not wanting to be controlled (Allen et al., 1989:86). The partner who batters may perceive that his partner is challenging his power, decisions, or authority over her (Dobash and Dobash, 1984). He may perceive that she is attempting to control him or his sense of self or that he is not in control of the relationship (e.g., controlling the degree of intimacy). Alternatively, he may perceive that he is becoming too dependent on her—losing control of his sense of independence (Ellis, 1989:244).

Many men who batter monitor their partners' thoughts and daily activities to maintain relational control. As long as the battered partner can be convinced that she is responsible for his violence, that he undertakes violence to teach or discipline her (because he loves her or needs to be assured that she will never leave him), then he can successfully control the definition of their relationship. The following two excerpts illustrate how many men who batter attempt to impose their definition of reality and prevent their partners from thinking critically about themselves as persons with separate identities— standing back from their daily existence and clearly seeing what is happening in their lives:

> SARA: My husband used to constantly attack anything or anyone I liked. No matter what opinion I had, he either said it was dumb or that I didn't really understand what I was talking about. I got so I hardly ever opened up my mouth when people were around if he was there.

> CINDY: I can't remember ever coming home that he didn't question me about where I was or what happened—not the kind of questions that meant he was interested, but the kind where I felt I had to answer and report to him. (Pence, 1987:15)

For many men, control is central to their (masculine) identity. Yet in many life spheres real and symbolic support for this identity is structurally denied. As a result, these men may perceive control issues in the family as especially consequential. This does not explain, however, why some men perceive threats to self in their intimate relationships and respond with physical or psychological battering patterns while others do not. Nor does it explain why some men perceive their partners as "disloyal" and "disobedient" regardless of what they do while others do not. Those who are supported by peers in their male-dominant, woman-controlling, and violence-accepting behaviors; those who are economically dependent and believe in male rule within the household; those who place a high value on "autonomy control" (Stets and Straus, 1989); and those who activate their hierarchical rule to increase their "fate control" over their partners and themselves are especially likely to react with violence to perceived threats to their self-concept and autonomy—their control (Ellis, 1989:244).

The conflicts that precede and embody battering actions specifically have to do with control of the battered partner's routines (how she performs her domestic work), family finances (how she spends the money), and child care practices (how she disciplines the children). With similar frequency these themes involve loyalty, possessiveness, and jealousy issues—attempts to control whom she sees (especially her relatives and friends), where she goes, what she does, and how she relates with him. In the later stages of battering, these themes are supplemented by his perception of her threats or real attempts to leave him (Dobash and Dobash, 1984:273; Coates and Leong, 1988:192; Ferraro, 1988).

Many men who batter describe their partners' attempts at independence as a loss of control and attempt to persuade or coerce their partners into adopting their definition of the relationship (Dutton and Browning, 1988a:165, 1988a; Ferraro, 1988). They do not wish to be controlled. They do not want others to make decisions (Allen et al., 1989:85–87). At the same time, however, many of these men feel unwilling to assume responsibility for the quality of their intimate relationships or their families' lives. Consequently, many episodes of battering coincide with sudden transitions in both responsibility and intimacy such as pregnancy, marriage, or the birth of the first child.

The death of a close relative or friend, sudden unemployment, or new, acute financial problems may also undermine confidence in the meanings that constitute the self. When the self is under attack from external sources (e.g., work or loss of work), an intimate is expected to show an extraordinary degree of allegiance. In these circumstances the batterer's partner comes under close scrutiny. He may interpret her slightest deviation from total support and allegiance as an additional threat to self (Ferraro, 1988).

In times of acute need, when control and self are in jeopardy, the batterer may require loyalty as proof of acceptance. In a context of domination and control, loyalty is vital to security. Like political despots, men who batter demand unquestioning allegiance. They severely punish expressions of uncertainty and independence of thought and action (Ferraro, 1988:131). They view any ostensible indication of disloyalty as a vicious attack. They may perceive a refusal to talk, spend time, or be intimate on demand, or even a simple phone call from a friend, as an act of disloyalty (Pence, 1988a:18). Their suspicions of disloyalty give rise to increasing demands for demonstrations of commitment. They monitor such demonstrations closely, which become a consuming focal concern. Ferraro elaborates:

> In a situation in which loyalty is uncertain, friendship and closeness with others becomes a threat. The more involved a spouse becomes with others, the more they give evidence of rejection. Therefore, friendships with outsiders or other family members become a point of contention. ... Time spent with others is viewed as a statement of preference for them over the husband. He will become sullen and irritable about her involvement with others. She, in turn, be-

comes exasperated by his possessiveness and begins to withdraw. He interprets this as further rejection and becomes more concerned about her loyalty and becomes more possessive. Eventually, her loyalty to him is actually undermined. His sense of threat is expanded and he may become violent. ...

[Even children and] other family members, especially the wife's relatives, may ... be perceived as threats. ... Both partners, especially in youthful marriages, must move away from commitment to their families of origin to their families of procreation. Individuals demonstrate loyalty to their partners by making decisions without the interference of in-laws, by not spending all their free time with relatives, and by promoting the interests of their partners while in the presence of parents. When a husband feels that his wife is more strongly attached to her own family than to him, his sense of loyalty is threatened. He will become jealous of time she spends with her family, and act in ways that · alienate him from them. The allegiance of her family undermines his ability to control her.

Friends of the same age pose the greatest problems for a man unsure of his wife's loyalty. This group represents rivals for companionship and sexual involvement. Involvement with them is purely a matter of free choice, rather than family obligation. Time spent with friends is an expression of interest, and that interest may be threatening to a man needing constant reassurance of his wife's loyalty. ... Fear of a wife's promiscuity may be so strong that husbands fantasize lovers and develop paranoid perceptions of their wife's intentions. This leads to excessively controlling behavior. (1988:132–133)

In many instances the need to control and the need for partner loyalty appear to be related to deeper interpersonal feelings and difficulties with social inclusion and intimacy. Many men who batter develop only a few close friendships and are very cautious and conscious of the degree to which they emotionally commit themselves. They often fear that they will become too close or too emotionally dependent on their partners (Allen et al., 1989:85–87).

For many couples, control over the degree of intimacy is a key issue (Dutton and Browning, 1988, 1988a). A perceived inability to regulate intimacy and keep it within the parameters defined by the "controlling partner" may lead to violence. However, many men who get angry at a real or feared loss of control over intimacy verbally express these fears to their partners and dissipate their anger. Others diffuse these fears through conversations with friends or through self-abasement. But those men who have learned to convert their feelings of fear into feelings of anger and to connect expressions of anger with feelings of agency, male expressiveness, or self-determination may react with violence.

From the perspective of men who batter, intimacy issues revolve around an increase in a partner's perceived or expressed need (or desire) for affection, attention, and emotional support. Just as frequently, however, these issues revolve around a perception of her need or desire for greater independence or freedom of expression in spheres he does not control or from which he is absent. As mentioned earlier, intimacy issues may also result from role rearrangements when, for example, the birth of a child redirects a partner's attention to the child and away from him, simultaneously increasing an expectation for him to take greater responsibility in and for the relationship. Feelings of jealousy and attempts to control a partner's interactions with others are commonly mentioned precipitant cues for battering.

Donald Dutton and James Browning (1988, 1988a) indicate that intimate partners continuously negotiate and renegotiate a zone of emotional closeness (or distance) within which they feel comfortable. Invasions (coming too close) and evasions (remaining too distant) of this jointly constructed "intimacy comfort zone" may initiate anxiety, resentment, and guilt. These, in turn, may cause the batterer to feel threatened by a deep dependency on his partner (Renzetti, 1988; Pillemer, 1985) or by loss of relational control. The end result may be battering. The partner who batters may experience invasions as "engulfments" and evasions as "abandonments."

A fear of engulfment may develop from (1) his perception that his partner is moving too close to him through her desire for greater closeness, attention, and affection; (2) his increasing need for greater emotional distance while her needs for intimacy remain unchanged; and/or (3) shifts or role transitions (e.g., marriage, pregnancy, fatherhood) that may increase his feelings of expected responsibility and either increase or decrease his parameters of comfortable intimacy (Dutton and Browning, 1988, 1988a). A fear of abandonment may be precipitated by (1) his perception that she is moving or wishes to move emotionally further away from him; (2) his belief that she is investing too much energy outside their relationship or becoming too involved with others; and/or (3) his need for greater intimacy (which he is perhaps unable to communicate or she sees as an invasion) in the face of her unchanged comfort zone, which he once saw as an optimal but now perceives as too great a distance (Dutton and Browning, 1988, 1988a; Mayer and Johnson, 1988:194).

Once the batterer reacts with violence to his perceived loss of control of intimacy, of her behavior or feelings, or of his desired sense of self, he may not attempt to control it, or he may consciously regulate the degree of pain and injury he inflicts. This process, from feeling loss and perceiving the acceptability of using violence to carrying out the violence and expressing postepisode feelings, relies on a great many factors. These include the batterer's past experiences with violence, his views regarding the acceptability of using violence, and his attributions for the violence. They also include his perceptions of her feelings and behavior (Stets, 1988:73) and of her attributions, definitions, and reactions to the violence. As a result, there are many times when he may hold back his violence.

Responding to Control

There is considerable debate about whether battering is instrumental—directed to control the "victim's" actions—or impulsive—primarily carried out to injure the partner perceived as having caused a loss (Denzin, 1984, 1984a; Berkowitz, 1983; Ptacek, 1985; Stets, 1988). Jan Stets (1988:103) argues that the first instance of violence by a partner is carried out impulsively to hurt and strike back. But over time and through learning, battering episodes become more instrumental. But whether the violence is instrumental or impulsive, it unveils the attributes of pain that are quickly transferred to attributes of the batterer's power.

Although violence may have affiliation, conformity, and expressive components (Ehrlich, 1990) and be either impulsive or instrumental in intent, it is clearly situated in power and control dynamics. If initial battering is impulsive, unexplainable ("It just happened"; "I lost my temper"), and out of control, later violence, though perhaps sporadically impulsive, is perceived by most men who batter as deliberate—carried out for the purpose of maintaining power and control (Stets, 1988:104). Three different modes that regularly appear in the dynamics of this process can be identified (Stets, 1988:105): (1) feeling threatened by a perceived challenge to his self-asserted entitlement to control; (2) feeling he is losing his power to control self (Gondolf, 1985a) or her and using violence to regain this control; and (3) feeling that he has regained control through her submission.

Many men who decide to batter do not wish to "give in" or "give ground." For them, letting a partner do things her own way means losing power or submitting to her control. Believing that he has a right to tell her what to do, he may demand that she behave in a particular way, for example, that she stop whatever she is doing and give him her full attention. She, however, may not accede to this demand, asserting that she is an equal and that he does not have the right to tell her what to do. Although a partner who is battered may agree that in some instances she meant to challenge his right to control her, usually she did not intend to challenge this right, although he interpreted her behavior in this way. Therefore, most often violence may erupt, not because of anything that the battered partner does, but because of what the batterer perceives her to be doing (Stets, 1988:106) or because of what he perceives is happening to him.

Some men who batter state that they feel out of control when a situation is not going their way. They feel threatened and fear that they will no longer be able to control the situation. They explain that though they ordinarily have control over how they act and feel, they do not feel they have control over their partners' feelings and actions. One way to get back in control is to use violence, and many battering partners learn that violence can help them regain this control.

Stets's interviews suggest that one of the reasons men who batter choose violent, rather than nonviolent, forms of conflict resolution is because the negative consequences they experience for behaving violently are minimal. Although some batterers, especially in the time frame of the initial episodes, feel guilt and remorse for their behavior, they are often able to quickly relieve themselves of these feelings. This process is hastened if their partners forgive them or in any way take the blame for the violent episode or if the batterers feel successful in regaining their perceived loss. Subsequent to these experiences, many batterers find it easier to batter.

Carolie Coates and Deborah Leong (1988:191) suggest that inhibitions lessen over time, especially when there are few negative consequences for the batterer. Many batterers discover that they will not be officially punished for their violence because the police will probably not be called or, in the case of arrest, criminal justice decision-makers will not generally take battering seriously. Furthermore, batterers know reasonably well that, if their partners strike back, they will not be physically hurt to the degree that they have or can hurt these partners.

As we have seen, batterers customarily view their actions as safe violence (Sonkin and Durphy, 1982). The following interview excerpts indicate how they regard battering as effective violence because it controls a situation and acts as a safe outlet for frustration or anger resulting from loss:

MIKE: I couldn't beat anyone else up, so then when I got angry, I had to take it out on my family. ... She was the only type of person that I could beat up.

WENDY: I think that he's afraid to have a fight with a man for fear that he'll get beat up, but he knows he can beat up women and he's not going to get hurt. (Stets, 1988:108, 109)

Carrying out this effective and safe violence often results in successfully forcing a partner to submit to the batterer's control, at least temporarily. The following two interview excerpts illustrate the common observation that instrumental violence is one way to exert power. These excerpts also reveal the degree of power and control that some men who batter attempt to exercise.

> MIKE: [But why would you hit her if she was going to be all the emotional support that you would have?] Simply because she wasn't seeing things the way that I would. I wanted her to fall into a role model, but if she got out of that role model, that's not what I wanted. ... I guess the only way that I could get her back in line was to hit her ... [Why do you think the physical abuse came up then, later?] Well, like I said before, it was just a way to get her to conform to what I wanted.

> KAY: He's the type of person that I could not make a decision for myself. If I decided to cut my hair and went ahead and did it, I would get into a lot of trouble. He would really get angry. If I decided that it was okay for the child to spend the night with a friend, he didn't like it. I didn't ask him first. If I go to the grocery store and I take a little bit longer than what I should have, he didn't like it because I was supposed to be where he wanted me to be at the exact time. I wasn't supposed to do anything that I wasn't told to do. (Stets, 1988:9–10)

Giving Up Control

Some men who batter are able to step outside the dynamics of the battering relationship and process. Unfortunately, most simply learn how to control or manage yet another aspect of their lives—their emotions. Nonetheless, this learning requires an admission that they are often unable to control their emotions. Other men who batter are able to step outside these interpersonal dynamics and substitute different behavioral reactions. This necessitates that they change their views on the acceptability or appropriateness of using violence and that instead of thinking about themselves, they begin to think about what their violence is doing to their partners.[2] Still others are able to stop trying to control their partners and stop believing in control at all costs. Hence, they begin to address and alter the antecedent contextual cues that, at least within the family context, give rise to acts of violence (Adams, 1989). These efforts are represented in the following interview excerpts:

> MIKE: I expected her to play the mother that I never had. Someone that stayed home and took care of the kids, had dinner ready and kept the house clean. But in expecting that, I realize now that I, that what I had done is I took

her personality away from her. I wouldn't let her see friends. I wouldn't let her go do things that she needed to be doing. I didn't let her take time for herself. And I'm doing that exactly right now.

KAY: Well, he's excited. He's letting me do things that I didn't used to be able to do. He always complained that I wasn't a woman. But yet at the same time, he didn't want me to do any of the things women do. Like, [inaudible] buying me some cosmetics or getting my hair done or doing any of this stuff, and now he takes me to the city, to the French Connection for my birthday, and lets me buy some cologne, custom just made for me. And he gets a thrill out of seeing me happy now. He draws happiness from seeing me happy. So I think it's going to work, and I think he's going to be fine. (Stets 1988:116)

It is through such processes that men who batter begin to change their thoughts and feelings about others, about the nature of the hierarchical arrangements they have attempted to establish or felt they were entitled to impose, and about who they really are. It is through introspection, empathy, and changes in structure-of-self and structure-of-interaction arrangements that battering patterns and processes can be discontinued (Adams, 1989). Until these men make such changes, they, and their partners, will remain ensnared in the tight grip of violent and deconstructing self-definitional and interrelational processes.

The Deconstruction of Selves

According to Denzin (1984:489), the self-meanings that the partner who batters presents are increasingly given through violence, denials of violence, self-deception, bad faith, and deceit. The violence-pervaded self is carried over from and/or carried with him when he leaves for work or enters other spheres of interaction. The self of the batterer haunts him. It is always just ahead of him or just behind—lodged in violent action he has taken or is about to take. A circuit of violent selfness attaches the batterer and his partner, whom he now relates to as an object, to the world of violence. As he attempts to impose his will on her subjectivity, he initiates a process that begins to annihilate her consciousness and being in the world. If emotional outbursts are centrally about "the moral and personal destruction of the other as a person" (Denzin, 1984:503), a system of battering instituted again and again is an attempt, not merely to destroy, but to systematically deconstruct the other as a person. It is, in fact, an attempt to torture.

Some partners who batter utilize tactics that over time create psychological and emotional sequelae similar to those experienced by victims of torture (Russell, 1982:273–285; Romero, 1985). Yet it is not typical that men who batter women use the specific torture tactics that agents of state use: application of electricity via electrodes, cattle prods, or shock batons to torso, genitalia, or mouth; submersion of the head in water polluted with excreta, thereby causing near drowning; suspension from a rod by the hands and feet; beating of the soles of the feet with rods; placing of needles under the toenails or fingernails; or the forced extraction of teeth (Plachta, 1989). However, sexual torture—the insertion of foreign objects into the vagina or rectum, coerced sex acts with animals or the batterer (rape) (Russell, 1982); burning through the application of cigarettes; sleep deprivation; enforced social isolation; the deprivation of medical care; and beating, kicking, and striking with objects to torso, genitalia, or mouth are not terribly uncommon, nor are they illegal among married couples in many states. Depriving a partner of essential needs and relief (e.g., diverse human contact, mental rest, or sleep) can lead the battered partner to become paradoxically dependent on her torturer.

In state torture

> the only person who can provide these reliefs is the torturer, and in the induced abnormal environment where deprivation and stress are the norm and other social contacts are withdrawn, the victim becomes dependent on the torturer as the sole source of support. Occasional, unpredictable, brief respites, when among other things the torturer becomes a sympathetic listener, make the victim feel obligated toward him. (Russell, 1982:282–283)

According to Amnesty International (1973:25, 46), enforced dependency, created debility, and resulting depression and dread are very common features of many systems of torture—of many batterers' patterns. The combination of these three sequelae carefully contrived and nurtured prepares either a resistant prisoner or a resistant partner for total compliance.

Experiencing such coercive stresses seriously affects a person's customary ways of perceiving and reflecting on herself. It deconstructs the self and distorts and erodes the person's existential presence. Table 3.1 indicates how methods effective in obtaining the compliance of prisoners of war and victims of state torture are also effective in obtaining the compliance of a partner. Whereas prisoners of war and state torture victims are trapped by

TABLE 3.1   Methods of Torture: Their Desired Effects and Application Within Intimate Relationships

Method	Desired Effect	Application
Isolation	Deprives victim of all social support for resistance Develops an intense concern with self Makes victim dependent on interrogator	Social isolation is frequently a characteristic of the nuclear family. The social isolation of battered women is even more pronounced. The battering partner attempts to control her contact with the outside world, her potential sources of support for a different reality.
Monopolization of perception	Fixes attention on immediate predicament Fosters introspection Eliminates any stimuli competing with those controlled by captor Frustrates all action not consistent with compliance	The possessiveness that some battering men display toward battered partners regarding their relationships not only with other men but also with women, jobs, school, or any other interest they may have effects a monopolization of perception as well as isolation and dependence. The battering partner enforces his definitions of reality on her, getting her to question her own perceptions and judgments.
Induced debility and exhaustion	Weaken mental and physical ability to resist	Physical violence is clearly one common method of inducing debility, as is the imposition of forced or unwanted sex acts. Psychological tactics, such as cruel putdowns, especially in front of others, can be effective. The battering partner attacks her personhood, demeans and belittles her, and undermines her self-worth.
Threats	Cultivate anxiety and despair	The battering partner verbally threatens to injure or even kill his partner. Many battered partners are intimidated by the batterers' physical strength, even when these partners are not directly threatened physically.
Occasional indulgences	Provide positive motivation for compliance Hinder adjustment to deprivation	There are usually more than occasional indulgences in most violent relationships, but in some, indulgences are orchestrated to gain partner compliance. The battering partner selectively withholds and distributes positive reinforcers within the relationship.

(continues)

TABLE 3.1 (*continued*)

Method	Desired Effect	Application
Demonstrations of omnipotence	Suggest futility of resistance	Coercion clearly serves to convey "omnipotence"; partner rape and the imposition of other unwanted sex acts appear to serve this purpose.
Degradation	Makes resistance appear more damaging to self-esteem than capitulation	Many battered women comply with their partners because they perceive that resistance may be more costly to their self-esteem than capitulation. Consequently, some battered women submit or do not fight back when being raped or physically battered by their partners; others, fearing physical injury, remain silent when being publicly humiliated.
Enforcement of trivial demands	Develops habits of compliance	It is common for battered women to describe their partners' violence as being set off by the most trivial things (e.g., an undusted shelf, a meal not cared for, a dinner not being ready when he got home, even though there was no way of knowing when he would arrive). Tyrannical behavior helps develop the habit of compliance, anxiety, and focus on him.

Sources: Adapted from Amnesty International (1973:49); Russell (1982:284–285); and Tolman (1989:163).

barbed wire, locks, and guards, many partners, structurally imprisoned by all the gender, political-economic, and cultural arrangements that foster inequality and obstruct their development, are also trapped as a result of the battering (Russell, 1982:285). Although battered woman syndrome suggests a complex psychological response unique to battered women, some raped and battered wives have much in common psychologically with victims of torture and mind control (Boulette and Andersen, 1985). Indeed, for those subjected to the most severely deconstructing battering processes, the results are similar.

As the battering partner seizes his partner and inflicts emotional and physical pain on her, he finds that he has in his hands some*thing* (rather than some*one*) other than what he wanted to take, something other than what he lost. As he takes her bodily into his grip, as he renders her speechless with pain, her will, freedom, and presence elude his grasp, are out of reach of his control (Denzin, 1984). His intent, to regain what he has lost, escapes him. He is drawn into processes that are converting this relationship from the possibilities of mutual respect and mutual affection into something focused on fear and coercion and fraught with antagonism.

He may be aware that this violence is eroding "what they had between them" and that he may lose his partner's affection entirely. "But these [consequences] are somehow more abstract, less immediate, and less visible or important than the benefits that accrue from the use of violence" (Dobash and Dobash, 1984:280). He is drawn again and again into this cycle. His violent actions are doomed to failure, for his very actions destroy the intimacy of their relationship, her unquestioned feelings of affection for him, and the structure of her sense of self. He can never succeed in establishing his dominance and will over her, for as he attempts to do so, the pain he inflicts embodies her consciousness—her voice and presence fade and are not there to be controlled. In a manner similar in structure to torture, the partner who batters and the partner who is battered become bound together in the processes of deconstruction and a field of negative experience.

What may have been lost at work or in another setting is not recoverable at home. The loss of his constructed sense of self or his considerable self-esteem, the loss of self-control or self-direction, or the loss of control over her at home is not recoverable through violent means. Her deconstruction, her pain, her loss of voice and being, her cries, her shattered world of physical and emotional safety, and even a confession provide only a temporary fiction of the batterer's power (Scarry, 1985, 1988). In the moment of violence the past, the present, and the future fuse. Her words, feelings, and thoughts are hurled back at her and converted to weapons.

Time is drawn out, as if in slow motion, and held still. Everything happens at once (Denzin, 1984a:197). Pain and dread make her unable to hear his rantings or differentiate the pain of each blow or slap. Consciousness fades; pain embodies (Scarry, 1985, 1988). The pulsating numbness that follows the pain forces a loss of thought and self, a loss of the attentiveness he demands. The room whirls and fades. The kitchen chair now becomes a weapon. The living room sofa that ordinarily provides bodily comfort and relief aids in her capture and prevents her escape. The oven that ordinarily produces nurturance now burns her. The bedcovers that had at one time encased their intimate warmth and passion now smother her. The hands that had held her close and with which he had lovingly caressed her cheek, the hair above her ear, the nape of her neck, now strike her in these same places. His marks display, not passion, but wounds.

The world of domestic objects, her world of domestic reality, is deconstructed. Her world of emotional and physical experience, her world of intimate reality, is deconstructed. His body itself becomes a weapon not merely inflicting pain but also deconstructing her world, its meanings, and her sense of presence. Her swollen lips and mouth cause her to swallow her words. Her words, her voice, and her symbolic world inflict pain on her. Her body, which now displays the violence he has inflicted, becomes the agent of her pain—the weapon-wound that most directly inflicts her pain. Her physical and psychological reality, her world of self, becomes deconstructed.

In the times between battering episodes, the conversion of domestic objects into weaponry is never fully erased. She hesitatingly states her feelings and desires, for she knows that he may use them to hurt her. She hesitatingly acts, for these actions may become his justifications for violence. When she looks at her black eye, the scar from a fork driven into her hand; when she scrutinizes her mind, her feelings, her future, and that of the children; when she thinks of how they were in the past, she recognizes that her mind and body have become his weapons and her enemy. They have and continue to deconstruct her reality. She cannot easily escape herself; everything has become a weapon; the world is unsafe. She is alone in her pain; she is isolated.

When she enters the kitchen, when she sets the table, when she rests during her kitchen routines, when she changes the bedcovers, when he comes home from work, when he speaks to her, when he again holds her and strokes her hair, she faces the weapons, and she recalls the pain. In search of a new foundation, like makeup on her bruised cheek and blackened eye, she may get rid of the kitchen chair or the bedcovers; she may replace the silverware and all the other objects he converted from constructions and extensions of culture into weapons (Scarry, 1985, 1988). But it is much easier to remove these domestic marks than it is to reconstruct her self and her feelings for him.

Both the batterer and the survivor are tainted and scarred by these episodes of violence and their deconstructing processes. If she continues to acquiesce to the rituals and routines of his domination, her hollow motions of compliance will mask her resentment, fear, despair, self-confusion, and inauthentic presence. There is now a fiction of intimacy—a pretending of the intimacy that once enveloped them. They are now hostages of their deconstructed selves and relationship. They are now outsiders to each other. The potentiality of violence becomes the veil through which all thoughts and interactions, all leavings and returnings, are first screened (Denzin, 1984:490).

They have lost the sense of affection and "oneness" that characterizes intimate relations, even those situated within hierarchical and therefore structurally violent arrangements. They have each lost a positive relationship with self. And neither their relationship nor either of these selves can be restored to nonviolence or positive interaction unless there is a break in the cycle of violent interaction and in the hierarchical and gender arrangements (both within and external to the family) that serve as the immediate structural sources of this violence.

4

The Developmental Process and Organizational Structure of Battering: The Initial Stages

The negative symbolic interaction that characterizes battering relationships adheres to a regular developmental process and organizational structure. Like developmental processes in other family crisis circumstances (Farber, 1964), these interaction patterns move through several phases. They then either stabilize into a tumultuous, yet somewhat tolerated pattern of recurring violence or are abandoned (as when the battered partner freezes out the batterer). Only when battering completely ceases can the affection and intimacy of the relationship and the healthy selves of the intimates revive.

Real Violence

Denzin (1984:504–507) suggests that violent interactions in the family are constructed, not on the premise "This is violence," but on the question "Is this really violence or something else?" An episode of violence only contains the *potential* for introducing new processes into family life that are not in accord with the wishes or expectations of one or both partners. Consequently, we must explore how this violence is understood or defined and to what it refers. Identifying slaps, shoves, punches, and emotional outbursts in an encounter as battering overlooks the fact that any action or series of actions may be defined by "outsiders" as violent without the participants defining it as such, and vice versa (Denzin, 1984:506). It is therefore imperative to propose a distinction between real violence, the intention of which is clearly understood by both partners, and spurious, playful, accidental, and paradoxical acts of violence that are subject to different meanings and interpretations, though they may turn into real violence (Denzin, 1984a:185–189).

To discover the jointly and separately constructed meanings of different acts of violence, we must enter the complex, private, phenomenal world of each intimate (McCall et al., 1970; Allen et al., 1989). It is necessary to learn how different acts of violence are defined and whether they occur in isolated episodes or constitute a pattern of recurring interaction. Real violence, Denzin explains,

> is intentional, believed in, authentic, doubted neither by the person nor by his family associates. In real violence the person embodies a violent line of action that he cannot willfully drop or walk away from once he has entered into it. Real violence grips the aggressor. He cannot get out of it as he pleases. ... Real violence radiates through the bodies of both the violent person and the victim. It is "naked emotion" with nothing held back. Its effects may be seductively intoxicating. There is a "sweetness" to its "madness." It is felt deeply in the inner stream of consciousness. Its reality crowds out other attitudes and beliefs. It totally destroys alternative definitions of the situation. In real violence the inner, moral, authentic core of the victim is attacked. (1984a:187)

Real violence, or battering, is a characterization that both partners strongly resist. The partner who survives the violence is unwilling to use this characterization unless the physical or emotional injuries severely affect her personal functioning (Sedlak, 1988a:54; Bograd, 1988; Peterson-Lewis, Turner, and Adams, 1988:113). The deeper the deconstruction, the greater the frequency and duration of the violence, the clearer her perception that her partner intended to physically harm her, the more she perceives his behavior as not understandable and her experience as not "normal," and the stronger she perceives their relationship as "not very close," the more likely she will be to define his violence as real violence or battering (Sedlak, 1988a:40; Peterson-Lewis, Turner, and Adams, 1988:116).

Real violence triggers distortive changes (considered undesirable by at least one of the partners) in the selves and in the affective feelings, values, and roles within the partnership (Farber, 1964:402). It cannot be controlled by merely erasing its effects and continuing life as before. Yet real violence also initiates processes that counteract these disruptive consequences and feelings.

The stages through which battering processes may proceed can be presented as follows:

1. Making attempts to respond to real violence within existing arrangements and affective feelings
2. Distorting affective relations and arrangements as a basis for defining the problem
3. Revising relationships with extrafamily individuals and groups
4. Altering affective relations and social arrangements within the family
5. Freezing out the batterer

The first two stages are described in this chapter; the latter three, in Chapter 5.

Making Responses Within
Existing Arrangements and Feelings

As stated earlier, an episode of violence injects the potential for crisis, rather than an actual crisis, into family relationships and feelings. It presents the potential initiation of processes of battering and deconstruction. If both persons define the episode as not significantly troubling or disruptive, and if both believe that family routines need not be changed as a result of this episode, then there is no crisis and no beginning of the processes of battering. Only when one or both partners perceive this violence or successive violent outbursts as unacceptable and disruptive of their feelings, expectations, roles in the family, and/or sense of self will there be a crisis in the family and the beginning of the processes of battering. Only when one or both persons find these behaviors neither readily understandable nor acceptable can the process begin. Otherwise, there is an attempt to dismiss or minimize the significance of the episode; to discuss it so as to better understand how and why it occurred; and to repair and reassert mutual commitment and love.

For many women, real violence, especially the initial episode, is so discordant with their expectations and relational histories with their partners that they just cannot believe it happened. Preferring to deceive themselves and hoping to place this out-of-character experience in the past, many hastily return to their positive everyday routines. This response is typical if the survivor's core self and affective feelings have not been severely deconstructed and if her partner is remorseful, is attentive, desires forgiveness, or shows that he is trying hard to forget his behavior, which he admits has genuinely ruptured his sense of self.

When episodes of violence are widely intermittent, they are far outweighed in significance by the survivor's positive commitment and interaction with her battering partner and by her continuing love for him (Coates and Leong, 1988:193). Just as many of us tolerate considerable physical pain before seeking relief by calling a doctor, many battered women tolerate a wide range of physical and emotional harm before defining or acknowledging it as battering—something for which they must seek help (Ferraro and Johnson, 1983:329).

Real violence is, however, not a desired, accepted, or easily understood feature of the interaction a person expects to have with an intimate partner. When it does occur, violence catches "the victim" off guard because feelings of affection, intimacy, and safety work against even the suspicion that she is unsafe and might be violated by her partner (Denzin, 1984a:177). In fact, most of us give violence an attribute of "otherworldliness" (Denzin, 1984:496). That is, we all know it occurs, but we do not expect that it will happen to us. Specifically, we do not imagine that we will be battered by those we love, even if we were abused as children or experienced violence in a dating relationship. Consequently, an episode of real violence often initiates immediate feelings of shock, confusion, and disbelief. It produces a process of grieving for what is lost.

The Grieving Process

The grieving process (Turner and Shapiro, 1986) begins with feelings of betrayal (Mayer and Johnson, 1988), vulnerability, emotional nakedness, and disorientation—a deconstruction of the survivor's interpretive framework. Ordinary emotional interaction and display are ruptured. A sense of self-death or emptiness ("I have lost everything"; "I am nothing") may ensue. The survivor is frozen in place and mind, not knowing what to think or do. Real violence attacks her inner self. In his attempt to make real his sense of self, power, and superiority, the batterer sees her as an inauthentic object to be used (Denzin, 1984:499). He denies her subjectivity.

Her self may be partially or almost completely annihilated through violence, degradation, and humiliation. Her voice and feelings may become so completely embodied within her that she cannot even hear his ragings, accusations, and demands for acquiescence. Through his violence he attempts to discard her moral presence in the belief that she would be more worthy of being in his presence if she agreed to comply with his demands or entitlement to control her (Ptacek, 1988a:255–256). He transfers the attributes of her pain to signify his (fictional) power.

As his battering tactics rupture her definition of the relationship and her sense of vulnerability and safety, her world becomes frightening and bizarre. She may become trapped within her pain- and grief-dominated interpretive framework (Denzin, 1984:497). Her terror may lead her to think of herself as unknown and unsafe. She may see herself as her own torturer. She may suffer alone in silence—without showing anyone her physical marks or telling anyone of her emotional and spiritual scars. As time passes, however, she may, for her own survival, seek out listeners who can help her extricate herself from both the escalated field of violence and from her now destroyed relationship with herself.

While her reality is embodied in spiritual and physical pain, the batterer understands, justifies, or explains his violence as (1) instrumentally required by his hierarchical position within the family; (2) provoked by her ostensible challenge to his entitlements or perceived insensitivity to his need to control the situation, his sense of self, and/or her; or (3) impulsively brought on by external factors and therefore out of his control. He may feel that in a blind rage his emotions momentarily overwhelmed him and erased his consciousness. Or he may recognize that he consciously controlled both his violence and emotions while inflicting pain or moral condemnation (i.e., punishment) on her in his desire to make his power and control "real." After the initial violence-defined-as-battering experience, the batterer may feel bolstered, justified, or self-reconstructed. But as these episodes recur and as he recognizes their destructiveness, he may begin to feel shame, remorse, loneliness, inadequacy, dependency, and loss. Yet for many men who batter, this recognition and these feelings do not develop until their partners have emotionally left them or physically frozen them out of the relationship (Adams, 1989:83–86).

An ironic tragedy has occurred. In the process of losing her, he paradoxically lost himself. Although he intended to leave his mark on her, discipline her, or force her to meet his needs, these marks incriminated and trapped him in his violence (Denzin, 1984:502).

The Fiction of Normality

When real violence first erupts, the partners typically define it as an incident to be erased from their collective memory, or they jointly pretend that it did not take place. Or they see the episode as an isolated event attached to familiar, recurring disputes (e.g., how tasks are to be done, her failure to meet his expectations, her relationships with others).

Like the wife of an "alcoholic" or "mentally ill" husband, the woman who is battered tries to handle these recurring episodes through existing family arrangements and through her prior affective feelings (Farber, 1964; Turner and Shapiro, 1986). She attempts to make sense of these episodes through language specifically constructed for these situations. She and her partner are both moved to offer persuasive interpretations for their actions and the situation. They both wish to make the battering episode more understandable and acceptable to themselves and to those they believe either deserve or require an account (e.g., children, pre-sentence investigators, counselors, researchers) (Bograd, 1988:62; Peterson-Lewis, Turner, and Adams, 1988:116, 123; Loseke and Cahill, 1984). Both attempt to "explain" the (his) violence and the (his) problem in a way that does not threaten their feelings of love and intimacy (Ferraro and Johnson, 1983:327) or existing family arrangements.

When, however, these episodes increase in deconstructive severity and/or persist, a disruption of the affective ties can begin and a loss of affection can surface (Denzin, 1984:491). If the latter is great, the battered partner is less likely to dismiss the episode and the batterer's responsibility for it. She is more likely to begin attributing the responsibility to him or to circumstances beyond his control, rather than to focus on herself, her pain, and how she might have prevented the episode. Until this time, attributing violence and injustice to the batterer's intention is too threatening. For if he really meant to harm her and deconstruct her being, he will likely strike again.

No survivors want to believe this extremely disturbing possibility (Blackman, 1989:41). To deny or minimize this possibility and erase the effects of the violence, most survivors work very hard at creating a fiction of normality. Correspondingly, at least initially, many batterers' denials of or explanations for their violence are part of a complex effort to devise a similar fiction (Davis, 1961; Farber, 1964; Stets, 1988; Denzin, 1984, 1984a; Ptacek, 1988a, 1988b).

If a joint fiction of normality is to be effective, both partners must cooperate. They must both refuse to acknowledge the need to revise their existing interaction patterns or wished-for (or held on to) feelings for each other. Thus, the battered partner must often direct at herself as well as at him attributions that maintain this fiction. Furthermore, she must attentively restrict her interaction with others to hide her bruises, terror, depression, or dread.

Such a curtailment, however, becomes an extension of the processes of torture and pain already in motion. As stated earlier, a survivor has trouble enough displaying her marks to herself. Their presence when she looks in the mirror or the pain she feels when she lies down at night to sleep makes their denial—the fiction of their absence and of the absence of battering—difficult. To display these marks to herself is to become conscious of the fiction; these marks are not real. To display the marks to her best friend or mother is to expose the fiction that this is not happening to her. It is to lay herself bare to the thought (or his accusation) that she has been disloyal—a betrayer of him and herself. Revealing the marks means she must grapple with the reality of his battering, her altered feelings, and the twisted, converted belief that somehow she is the problem, even though she knows that he is the true betrayer of her trust and safety. For her, the fiction is particularly tenuous.

Distorting Affective Relations and Arrangements

Researchers of family crisis processes indicate that family members do not define potentially crisis-provoking circumstances as inciting a crisis until the initial relationship, social arrangements, or emotional feelings have already been affected (Farber, 1964:404). For a couple that has greatly romanticized parenthood, for example, the marked changes in division of labor, intimacy, and companionship, with the accompanying dissatisfaction over these changes, produce the "parenthood crisis." A couple that finally realizes the husband's drinking or nonemployment is not temporary, and that experiences a considerable realignment of the family's division of labor and interaction patterns, may agonize over feelings of shame, resentment, and a sense of failure as husband and wife.

A couple attempting to confront the mental illness of the husband regards itself as experiencing real difficulties only when his atypical behavior is identified as a permanent feature of the relationship. This identification may occur quickly or slowly. After attempting to accept an accumulation of his bizarre thoughts and actions, which she does not readily understand, the wife may finally reach a threshold point. His behavior forces her to reexamine and adjust her life expectations and to find some way to account for his behavior. Her interpretation may shift back and forth from seeing a problem to not seeing a problem. Substantial adaptation must occur if husband and wife are to remain "together."

In an attempt to accommodate her husband's behavior, she may mobilize strong defenses—denying its existence, attenuating its abnormality, normalizing his behavior—against defining his behavior as psychotic. Yet she neither fully comprehends these behaviors nor knows how to respond to them.

She is at a loss to help him. Eventually, her defenses collapse, and the fiction of normality becomes unacceptable. She sees him as having the problem. She can no longer cope with the effects of his behavior on her and perhaps on others in the family. She can no longer adapt and let the situation continue because of the hardships and the changes that she, and perhaps the children, have had to make. She can no longer cope without assistance (Farber, 1964:396–397). Exhausted and perhaps exasperated at not being able to handle the situation herself, she seeks assistance and/or freezes him out at least temporarily.

Interpretive Frameworks and Relational Distortions

For many couples that experience recurring episodes of battering, the arrangements and feelings, family routines, obligations, and companionship relations that were present before the battering began can no longer be maintained. These couples can no longer wave aside "the problem" and revert to their previous life. For the partner who is battered, feelings of terror, isolation, betrayal, and loss of self prevent this reversion. Many times, guilt or anger at the effects the violence is having on the children makes this response increasingly inappropriate. Moreover, as Lenore Walker (1979, 1988) has indicated, the battered partner may suffer cognitive distortions, including dissociation, memory loss, a traumatic reexperiencing when exposed to associated stimuli, and a hypersensitivity to episodes of violence that create an expectation of harm and a readiness to protect and defend herself. She may develop perceptual distortions and reorient the home environment to keep the violence at a minimum level. She may feel overwhelmed by the combination of physically assaultive behavior, threats, emotional abuse, and the destruction of property that occur in rapid succession.

When the patterns of battering become random and her responses become unpredictable of stopping or preventing serious harm, a battered partner may change how she thinks and behaves to remain as safe as possible from the next attack. Regardless of her attributions for the violence, a survivor almost always attempts to change her behavior (Frieze, 1979). These efforts, similar to her efforts to find a confidante or express her inclination to leave, manifest a desire to regain control over her life and safety (Blackman, 1989:52). Her pain and the hardships that have resulted from the battering are what she perceives as most salient in the situation. When there are children in the family, the survivor finally realizes that the violence is spilling over to them. She may feel that she has been neglecting the children because of her depression or incapacitation or that they are being psychologically scarred by the situation. Finally, she becomes convinced that she must remove herself and the children from this circumstance (Giles-Sims, 1983; Wilson et al., 1987; Wilson, Baglioni, and Downing, 1989; Stacey and Schupe, 1983).

By this time, the distorted relations and feelings are very apparent (Giles-Sims, 1983). Denzin elaborates:

> The inner world of the family is fraught with ambiguity, guilt, hesitation, insecurity, and tendencies toward flight. A wish to not have things as they are is interwoven with a haunting desire for normality. The hovering, lingering sense that things might be different enters into every family interaction as an unstated background expectancy. ... [Family members] lie and deceive themselves into believing that things are getting better. They try to act as if violence were not in the background—or foreground. (1984a:195)

Many factors affect the nature of these relational distortions. The degree of distortion appears to depend on the nature of the violence (e.g., the degree of deconstruction) and the extent to which personal functioning is obstructed. It also appears to hinge on the extent to which the battered partner sees the batterer as human or his violence as comprehensible—which may, in turn, depend on her attributions for the violence (Peterson-Lewis, Turner, and Adams, 1988). Some battered partners who have used violence while resisting may believe this resistance mitigates the batterers' responsibility while accentuating their own (Sedlak, 1988:45). Those victims who take on responsibility for the battering may differ in the nature and degree to which they undergo profound changes in personal values, sense of self, intimate relationship, and family arrangements.

Hostility, anger, depression, and fear increase the couple's disagreements and misunderstandings over the agency of the continued violence. At this stage, those who are battered and those who batter do not share similar understandings of this violence (Bograd, 1988:67). Their explanations are not synchronized. This is especially true for those couples deeply entrenched in a fully developed field of negative symbolic interaction and violence. Each partner holds different perceptions of what is salient in these episodes (Taylor and Fiske, 1978). What is most salient for her is her pain, its effects, and what she has lost. What is most salient for him is the complexity of his circumstance—the external and internal factors that lead to his violence. Initially, at least, he may not be able to insightfully grasp why he becomes violent.

Those who are battered are deeply moved by the power of their pain. They are virtually compelled to understand their experience and quickly create an interpretation to make sense of their pain and their partners' violence. Some interpretations are more tolerable than others. Some thoughts are all but unthinkable.

Exposure to real violence damages and distorts a survivor's vision, diminishing her ability to think clearly and to imagine life alternatives. Battering forces her to focus on herself, her pain, and what to do about it. A narrowed field of concern emerges: her own contributions to the violence, her own strategies to prevent and survive it, and her own thoughts of why it occurred or continues to occur.

Commonly, an unusual level of cognitive inconsistency develops. Many battered women divide their energies between understanding the violence (which is important for their physical safety) and not understanding the violence (which is important for their psychological safety) (Blackman, 1989:158). Each survivor tries to cope with the fundamental contradiction of being with a partner who both loves and hurts her. The batterer has become someone she loves and hates, adores and fears, desires and dreads. Efforts to make sense of such an essential inconsistency seem all but doomed to failure. And perhaps it is most simply the failure to achieve resolution or "sense" that defies logic (Blackman, 1989:176).

Battered women are typically quite active and resourceful in their efforts to avoid violence. Yet they are often unable to discover how to leave these situations or alter their partners' violence. This inability is fundamentally disconcerting, requiring them to live in a "conflicting world of appearance and reality" (Blackman, 1989:116–117). Many battered women experience a learned helplessness that leads them to believe they are unable to control what happens to them. As a result, many survivors become depressed and convinced that any attempt to leave would be futile, if not provocative of additional violence. This sense of impotence is further exacerbated by the fact that, out of fear of reprisal or a sense of shame and lost self, most survivors endure these relationships in isolation. This dynamic is illustrated in the following interview excerpt:

> PAULA: As long as I went along with him it was all right. His mother made us go to his sister's for Thanksgiving. I objected. He knocked me around and put his fist through the wall. I went so he wouldn't hit me any more. ... I'd keep low. I didn't want to do anything and I didn't want to go anywhere. I didn't want to visit anybody. (Giles-Sims, 1983:130–131)

As the pattern of violence is repeated, this aspect of the resulting psychological change becomes more pronounced. And it is this psychological condition that appears to keep many women from leaving early on, though it may occur along with economic dependency or hardship, the need to care for young children, or the genuine absence of a safe place to go (Blackman, 1989:192–193). Whereas we might imagine that a case for intolerable injustice would be built in a linear, cumulative way, stacking one deconstructing episode of battering on another, for the person battered this building process seems to be accompanied by an equally strong dismantling process. It is as if knowledge is at once acquired and forgotten. Ideas that do not go together logically seemingly go together psychologically (Blackman, 1989:157, 162–163).

Initially, at least (yet after the violence has been defined as battering), battered women tend to attribute the violence to a partner's suffering (1) from a *transient* psychological state that temporarily reduces his capacity for self-control (e.g., feeling insecure or having some emotional problem) or (2) from a *transient* physical state that results from his use of alcohol or drugs or from external stress such as a temporary crisis at work or the loss of work. As a consequence, the survivor does not consider the battering partner responsible for his violence. Commonly, she tells him this. Yet just as often she tells him that she does not deserve to be battered. Embodied in her pain and grief, she realizes that discovering any "true" attribution for the violence is a difficult and complex process. She hopes she will not have to engage this process and does so only grudgingly.

The Framework of the Partner Who Batters

Meanwhile, the battering partner often attempts to place responsibility for his violence on his partner. He alternately explains his violence by telling her

1. That he lost his temper because she did not meet his expectations
2. That he felt she had challenged his control of the situation or his right to control her and that he wanted to show her who was boss
3. That he thought she was emotionally or physically aggressive or had psychologically attacked him
4. That he was out of control because of alcohol or drug use
5. That he did not know why the episode occurred

Yet the battering partner is just as likely to tell her that she deserved the battering; that he was trying to accomplish a beneficial aim such as getting her to stop talking, to listen to him, or to end the fight (Bograd, 1988:69); or that he either had not intended to hurt her or had consciously stopped himself from injuring her more severely.

At this stage in the battering process, the batterer waivers between feelings that his assertions of male privilege and dominance are proper (e.g., that his violence is motivated by a desire to silence her insubordination, to punish her for her failure to be a good cook, to be loyal to him, to be sexually available and responsive, or to be deferential [Ptacek, 1988a:255, 1988b]) and feelings that reflect misgivings, face-saving efforts, accusations, and excuses for not taking responsibility for his physical violence. At this time he tends to be nonintrospective or selectively introspective. What is most salient for him are the factors of his situation over which he has no control and the circumstance of his violence. He does not attempt to place himself in her situation. He responds to her worries, concerns, statements in defense of her self, accusations, or anger by making counteraccusations, yelling, demeaning her concerns, assaulting her personhood, and intending to devalue her (Adams, 1989:71; Coates and Leong, 1988:194). Frequently men who batter women are unable to recall their partners' actual words, actions, or specific complaints. Rather than attempt to understand their partners' concerns, batterers often characterize their partners' words and actions in a mocking, trivializing, or otherwise denigrating manner (Adams, 1989:71).

As many of these men report few close friendships, their lack of alternative outlets for intimacy may lead them to place demanding and unrealistic expectations on partners to be their sole emotional caregiver or emotional restorer. This places an enormous burden on these women to be responsible for their partners' every, often unexpressed, need (Adams, 1989:73; Adams and McCormick, 1982). Correspondingly, as presented earlier in some detail, many of these men report that they suffer chronic fears of abandonment and often feel "narcissistic injury" when partners fail to take care of them (Adams, 1989:65). At the same time, however, they often deny this dependency to maintain a fiction or illusion about their own autonomy (Adams, 1989:76; Dutton and Browning, 1988a:168, 1988). In part, this would seem to account for the attempts many batterers make to manage their self-esteem at their partners' expense (e.g., by criticizing them, trivializing their concerns, limiting their access to others, or not trusting them).

Many batterers at this stage in the battering process, and continuing until they are actually frozen out and begin to grieve the loss of their partners, do not see these partners as separate and viable persons—nor do they wish their partners to be. Rather, batterers see their partners as extensions of themselves (Adams, 1989:81). A batterer's deconstructing behavior serves to make his partner speak his words, echo his values and attitudes, and make her into his imagined image of her.

However, men who batter are not generally violent "monsters"; their violence emerges in specific contexts. Because men who batter are only episodically violent, many survivors perceive them as complex persons who most often display positive qualities. These men are often fun to be with, exciting, charming, and attentive. Typically they are emotionally committed and as affectionate as they can be without raising a fear of emotional dependency (Allen et al., 1989; Walker, 1979; Loseke and Cahill, 1984:305). In interaction outside the family, they are rarely perceived as controlling and demeaning. In fact, they often project a friendly, warm, and outgoing image. Many are respected and admired in their communities and at work.

For many batterers, though not all, controlling behavior and interpersonal violence tend to be restricted to their partners or other family members. This often makes it hard for persons outside the family to believe a survivor's account of what is happening in the home and difficult for her to understand why he has isolated her as the target for his violence—why he sometimes treats her so differently from others. These facts make intelligible a survivor's thoughts that perhaps, like he says, something is wrong with her.

These realities explain why, when battering processes are in full swing, both partners begin to curtail almost all outside contacts. As they become encased in the battering, her caregiving and emotional restoring may allow him to maintain a relatively high degree of personal functioning and competence with others (Adams, 1989:80). At the same time, these same qualities may increase his dependency on her, his consequent resentment of "being controlled by her," and his need to reassert control over their relationship. Such feelings may occur even if he acknowledges to himself that his control is more on the self-surface than hers. Perceived dependency (Pillemer, 1985), then, may lead him not only to momentarily destroy her (Denzin, 1984, 1984a), but also to control her actions through a pattern of battering that attacks her core (beneath her self-surface) by deconstructing her real and different, authentic presence in his world, her domestic world, and her soul.

The Framework of the Battered Partner

At first, when the episodes begin or are infrequent, the battered partner may experience confusion, disorientation, a deconstruction of her feeling that he loves her. She may feel a double bind: If he loves her, as he continues to tell

her after each battering episode, then why does he batter her? If he would
say that he no longer loves her, his violence would be more disturbing but
more understandable.

At first, the messages following his violence may serve to bind her to the
relationship. She wants to believe that the violence will not occur again. Believing that she can change the situation herself (Denzin, 1984:507) and feeling motivated, as she is the one most harmed by the violence, she often takes
the responsibility on herself to change. To hang on to her hope, her love for
him, and her sense of future, however romanticized, she must tell herself
(perhaps concurring with his interpretive framework) that the violence is either unintended or accidental. Perhaps it is her fault and therefore deserved.
Perhaps it is an emotional out-of-control outburst having nothing to do with
his feelings for her.

Because she wishes to convince herself, or truly believes, that he still loves
her, she may elect to perceive herself as having some influence over his future behavior. She may prefer to consider his behavior as somehow related to
what she has done or said, rather than to attribute it to some unknown or uncontrollable, and more terrifying, source (Langer, 1982). In this way she may
be able to frame his behavior as a reaction *to* her, rather than as an action
against her. Thus, she holds on to her love for him; she tells herself she is not
married to a brute or to someone uncontrollably disturbed; she retains her
belief that he loves her.

In accord with her grieving, she may wonder if she could have prevented
the violent episode. For example, she may wonder if she was, or if it was reasonable for him to think that she was, domineering or nonsupportive of him
(Peterson-Lewis, Turner, and Adams, 1988:123–124). Perhaps she could
have been or could be more conciliatory and nurturant. Perhaps she could
have been less assertive and less participative in the conflict and violence
process (Ferraro and Johnson, 1983:329). And yet all these ponderings may
make her more vulnerable to future victimization.

Given her desire for attachment, her pain and emptiness, and her new
world filled with his meanings and reality, she must try to fool herself. She
must lie to herself and say that what occurred did not "really happen to her"
or to the "real her." The "real man" she loves did not do this to her! She must
fall into a pattern of bad faith (similar to his) to sustain a fiction about the two
of them and their relationship (Denzin, 1984:492).

Such denials and the fear of change place all the family members in a collective state of bad faith. They deceive themselves into believing that the violence is not real, does not exist, and will not occur again (a contradiction of

the belief that the violence did not occur). By fooling themselves (or trying to) or by acting as if they accept what they do not believe, they disarm in advance all arguments that might reveal they are deeply embedded in a violent situation that requires action on somebody's part. Yet their bad faith does not succeed in making them believe what they wish to believe, and it is precisely this situation that traps them all (Denzin, 1984:507). As long as the battered partner is emotionally committed and deeply involved in trying to help him, and as long as she maintains a positive image of him and is committed to maintaining the relationship, she is likely to resist the supposition that his violence is permanent or internal to his real self.

Battering Becomes a Permanent Feature

Battering processes eventually lead to a "critical incident," a significant emotional break in her feelings for him (Shields and Hanneke, 1983:516), a choice point (Giles-Sims, 1983). If at first there was a tendency to submit, to become confused, to waiver, and to blame herself, she now begins to attribute the battering episodes to him (Shields and Hanneke, 1983:523; Frieze, 1979). Increasingly she comes to question the validity of all her attributions and his as well. If early on she contended that she had "made him" feel attacked or that she had challenged him, this no longer explains his violence. If initially she thought that his violence resulted from her failure to meet his hierarchical expectations, that he had a right to physically punish her, or that her own violence mitigated his, this explanation no longer holds up. Painfully, she realizes that she can neither stop the violence herself nor help him and that she needs help. Grudgingly she acknowledges that the violent episodes are arbitrary. They are not related to any specific family routines or arrangements or to her noncompliance with these routines and arrangements.

Finally, she is forced by the severe and perhaps even life-threatening consequences of his violence to acknowledge that it is no longer temporary; she can no longer attribute his violence to either transitory external or internal circumstances. She may agree with him that to some extent his violence has to do with his childhood experiences or his emotional problems. She may accept that some of his violence is situational, that it is, for example, due to circumstances at work. But she realizes that he is not confused, that he does indeed mean to hurt her by choosing to batter her, and that she is not to blame. She now concludes that he batters her to control her feelings and perceptions, her friends and children, her work, and their relationship. And she does not deserve to be battered!

5

The Developmental Process and Organizational Structure of Battering: The Later Stages

One of the most notable ways family life is altered to cope with recurring patterns of battering is for family members to disengage from participation in extrafamily relationships. Those most significantly affected tend to withdraw from the community and to screen and limit their contacts to specific persons and groups (Farber, 1964:423).

Revising Extrafamily Relationships

When battering occurs on a regular basis, older children may withdraw from school activities to get home to protect their mom. Younger children may no longer bring schoolmates home. Yet the person who feels the greatest distortion from the situation, the battered partner, is the person most likely to fully disengage herself from contacts outside the family. She experiences the isolating attributes of pain. She carries the physical marks and psychological bruises of his violence. Her senses of trust and safety have been violated. She is the one who does not know what she should do, whom she should tell, or what she should say.

As the days pass following each violent episode, his agency fades. Her pain, marks, and need to survive confusingly transfer the problem to her. Her body and mind become the agents of her pain. Her blackened eye "causes" her pain. She fears others will notice her emptiness, confusion, depression, and dread. She becomes preoccupied with what she can do to change the situation and feels she must disengage and reorganize her activities. His presence—what he would like, what he will do, when he will be home, whether he will approve of her activities—becomes her focus. She feels responsible for what is happening to the children and to her and for decreasing the visibility of the violence.

Typically, her initial selective disengagement maintains the fiction of normality and may unwittingly support both the process of her deconstruction and the continuation of his battering. This withdrawal is from people she perceives as a potential threat to the family, people who might be "hostile" to what is going on or to her response. She continues to interact only with those select few who support her and her definition of the situation.

The focus of her interaction outside the family is battering. Will the people she might interact with confirm or challenge her definition of the situation? Will they agree or disagree with her attributions for the violence? Do they encourage her to get out or to remain in the relationship? Do they think she should try to change her situation, or do they believe it is her duty to acquiesce to this interpersonal or structural violence?

A minister, counselor, lawyer, friend, or family member may attempt to convince her that her partner is not responsible for his actions or that his violence is episodically triggered by extraordinary circumstances and will cease when these circumstances change. Some may subtly suggest that his violence may be her fault and that she should try to work things out or become a better and more forgiving partner (Peterson-Lewis, Turner, and Adams, 1988:112). Others remind her that she took an oath to love, honor, and obey and that in accord with this sacrament she should pray for him and serve him as he serves God (Ferraro and Johnson, 1983:330). They advise her not to reject him, to carry her cross and nurture him in his time of need—to "stand by her man."

Another person, however, may challenge her to sort out her feelings and consider that right now her partner is willfully violent, out of control, and dangerous. If she believes she or the children are in real danger, she may be encouraged to consider freezing him out temporarily or helping him by supporting his decision to freeze himself out (Denzin, 1984a:190).

These contacts and relationships are often pivotal in helping a survivor define the reality of her situation and the children's future. Many times they are crucial to her choices for rearranging what happens in the family. Such choices, especially if her partner considers them contextual cues for battering, are critical for her survival.

Altering Family Arrangements

The continuation of family life in crisis is sustained through a substantial reconfiguration of family arrangements and feelings. As the family becomes socially isolated, the "violence problem" of the battering partner may or may not be identified as the problem. But the survivor's physical marks and pain force her to choose whether to make the violence visible to others. If she defines the batterer's violence as the problem, she may attempt, or be coerced into agreeing, to decrease its visibility.

Unable to control the violence, the depth of its deconstruction, its hardships, and required "adaptive" affective and social-organizational changes, both partners may experience increased grief, resentment, anger, and loss. Violence is now a permanent part of the family, and, at least within the family, attempts at hiding it are relinquished.

Revised Routines and Feelings

The batterer's role within the family's routines is now revised as others accommodate his violence and presence. Patterns of avoidance are set in motion and routinized. The home may become an empty meeting place devoid of warmth, intimacy, and safety. In his attempts at normalizing his battering, he seeks out each family member. There is no place to hide from either his emotional outbursts or his instrumental violence. As in torture, the times between episodes become problematic. Waiting for him to come home can be interminable. As Denzin remarks:

> Minutes stretch into hours. Time both races forward and seems to stop. On the one side, as long as [he] is away from home, the greater the fear that something has happened to him grows, as well as the anxiety that surrounds the waiting for his return. The fear that violence will occur when he does return home increases the likelihood that his arrival will be met with anger, confusion, and hesitation. This in turn, increases the likelihood that ... [he will choose to batter]. (1984a:197)

His partner and children may mistrust or ignore him. Overwhelmed by the atmosphere of violence, she may become less able to perform her routines. Her interaction with him may so consume her that she is unable to care for the children. When he arrives home, she may focus all her attention on him.

Contrarily, she may begin to assume a greater role in making family decisions, become the family manager, and focus her activities and emotions around the children because she can no longer depend on her partner or because he has begun to spend less time at home. Unfortunately, no matter what changes occur, they may increase the tension in the family (Denzin, 1984a:193) and provide a contextual cue for further real violence.

When real violence approaches, she may position herself as a protector of the children, or she may place them between herself and her partner. The children may shift their allegiance primarily to their mother. Older children may attempt to act as mediators between the battering parent and the younger children, or they may take it on themselves to receive the violence intended for their mother, younger sisters, or brothers. They may begin reading the moods of both parents and attempting to allay impending violence. They may try to soothe the violent emotions of their father and unwittingly stimulate more violence if he interprets their actions as attempts to control, manipulate, or take power away from him (Denzin, 1984a:193). Meanwhile, younger children often become passive victims, unable to defend themselves, or isolates, set outside the circles of family interaction.

In all, a whole new constellation of identities and routines, each drawn from the atmosphere of violence that surrounds the "family of violence," emerges. The age and gender structure, decision-making arrangements, and divisions of labor in the family undergo significant revision. No one escapes this violence. It disrupts everyone's sense of self and each and every family routine and ritual. His absence may become desired, his presence dreaded.

Sex-Act Violence

In addition to the increase in misunderstandings, disputed attributions, and spurious and empty communication, sexual jealousy and "sexual violence" may take their place within his diverse pattern of battering. As he becomes increasingly jealous and possessive of what he has already lost, he may not want her to go anywhere, to speak with anyone. This restriction of access reflects his assumed right to her as interactive and exclusive sexual property and his fears of her disloyalty and his consequent loss of self. Similar to her embodying, constricting experience of pain as a result of his physical violence, he now attempts to seize her movement and voice. Isolation, like the physical violence it hides or supplements, is an attempt to seize and consume her body, her subjectivity, her being.

His physical violence is often accompanied by accusations of infidelity, by the gathering of intelligence about her and about events that he knows are fictional. This physical violence, which leaves her with pain and loss of voice, combined with the imposed isolation leads to her annihilation. When the physical violence becomes marital rape or some other form of sex-act violence, his conflation of desire and injury, his transformation of himself into a weapon, destroys her desire for him. The loathing, humiliation, and rage she feels in response may begin to dissipate her confusion about his intentions, his justifications, and her rationalizations for her pain and suffering (Denzin, 1984:493).

Emotional Violence

When the violence takes an emotional, rather than a physical, form, the batterer inflicts his feelings, values, and moods on her. He takes her hostage and demands, as a condition of her temporary release, acquiescence to his moods and demands. He inflicts his emotions in a process of moral condemnation and punishment. He may place her in an emotional paradox, asking for love after he has morally degraded her or depleted her self-esteem. He may coldly attack her inner core and calculatingly deconstruct her ideas, feelings, and personhood.

He may claim to be, or actually be, out of control. While he inflicts his reign of terror on the household (Denzin, 1984:503), he may try to make her feel responsible for drunken outbursts, insane rantings, emotional withdrawal, or unwillingness to come home. Although he may claim that he is not responsible for his actions because he was out of control, he is accorded a position of control within the family, if only as a guise so that others may take greater control over him and their lives. Emotional captivity, emotional paradox, and emotional outbursts merge into a solitary field of experience. Violent, insane thoughts grip the entire family. Together and alone, family members live out the nightmare of overt and suppressed violence (Denzin, 1984:503).

Physical and emotional battering distorts the selves of the intimate partners. It distorts their feelings, timetables, and interactional arrangements. Now they no longer understand each other. Their minimal interaction is the result of habit, duty, or lack of perceived alternatives. Daily interaction becomes problematic and unpredictable. She never knows when he will act violently toward her or the children. The children may become violent toward one another as a reaction to or a mirroring of the violence they see and feel all around them. Normal reciprocal interaction becomes impossible.

The progressive escalation of violence and negativity binds all family members. If she meets his violence with violence, more negativity ensues. If she meets his violence with avoidance, passivity, acceptance, or passive-aggression, he may take her actions as reinforcing the acceptability of his violence. Unless she freezes him out, she remains bound within this negative, violent interactional field. Unless he freezes himself out and seeks help in breaking the chains of violence, he is bound to feelings and actions that render him unable to recapture any part of what has been lost.

Freezing Out the Batterer

The processes of battering may temporarily cease when the survivor seeks refuge at a shelter or with friends so that she has some reflective distance from the batterer and a chance to empower herself. Cessation may also occur when the battering partner is temporarily removed through arrest and court action or when he removes himself, though this is rare. Typically, after a brief period of separation, the partners get back together, and he resumes his pattern of battering. Even when she prohibits his return, when she refuses to return, and sometimes even after they are divorced, he continues his violence (Giles-Sims, 1983:138; Ellis, 1989).

When the batterer is frozen out, there is an acknowledgment, through a rearrangement of emotional feelings, role structure, and divisions of labor within the family, that his "domestic career" has been indefinitely suspended or ended (Farber, 1964:406). Because he is perceived as severely obstructing the development of all family members and as he has seriously disrupted everyone's routines and relations, the family must be reconstituted without him, at least temporarily.

With his departure, everyone's roles, especially the survivor's role, within the family expand. She has to take over many of the activities he previously performed or had neglected because of his battering. Her relationships outside the family are now altered, for she is not only a "single person" and perhaps a "single parent" but also "a battered wife" (Giles-Sims, 1983). Such new roles may involve her with new acquaintances at a shelter, at a social service agency, or in her private life. During this time, however, she is grieving deeply for the loss of her real and hoped-for relationship with him (Turner and Shapiro, 1986). This grief must be addressed while she carries on (Ferraro and Johnson, 1983:335).

Revisions and Decisions

Many couples do, however, survive without freezing out the battering partner permanently. Through unrealistically hopeful or utterly despairing pro-
jections for the future and through "creative and adaptive" (though perhaps
very destructive) rearrangements of self, affective commitments, and family
routines, some of these relationships survive for long periods of time. The
depth to which family members are developmentally paralyzed by his violence, the degree of pain and suffering attributed to his battering, the perceived personal incapacitation and tolerance of these effects, and the extent
to which definitions and resources outside the family are available and act as
a catalyst for change (Ferraro and Johnson, 1983:331) are major factors affecting a survivor's choice of alternative responses to battering.

Each survivor must decide whether to obtain temporary shelter, file for
divorce, seek the help of a women's counseling and support group, attempt
further violence-ending strategies, or encourage him to get help. Her attributions of agency for the violence are critical in these decisions. A survivor
who continues to hold on to feelings of responsibility for her partner's decisions to batter her is more likely to cling to the perception that his battering
is understandable. She is therefore more likely to include him in her future
intimate and family plans. Still believing, or praying, that she can change the
situation, she is likely to work very hard at not freezing him out.

A survivor who does not regard herself as responsible for his decisions to
batter her, yet who hangs on to her love for him, believes in his love for her,
and consequently feels responsible for his well-being and for their relationship may feel considerable guilt at thoughts of rejecting or abandoning him.
In spite of considerable pain and hardship, she may retain a deep love and
lifelong commitment to him. As a result, she may put forth an exhaustive effort to not freeze him out. She may see him as deeply troubled, alcoholic,
drug dependent, or incapable of surviving without her nurturant care and
protection. She may fill her emptiness and lost sense of self with this new
sense of personal identity and commitment as the savior, the rescuer—a
martyred version of caregiver. She may continue to attribute his battering to
afflictions that she believes are out of his control, not to his willful intent to
deconstruct her person. She may remain steadfast in her belief that he loves
and is committed to her (Ferraro and Johnson, 1983:328–329; Turner and
Shapiro, 1986).

A different survivor facing this situation may, however, realize that her
feelings of love and intimacy have been replaced with emptiness, loneliness,

and futility. She may remain in this relationship, at least temporarily, because she is caught up in a period of emotional flatness or dormancy. She may survive each day by going through the motions, while at the same time grieving relational death and perhaps hanging on to life through the vibrancy of the children. She may, in fact, not freeze out her partner for the sake of the children (Williams-White, 1989:50).

A survivor is more likely to freeze the batterer out under the following conditions (Farber, 1964:414–422):

1. When she can no longer tolerate the severe disruptions of affect and perceives her partner's behavior as a very real threat to her or the children's survival (Strube, 1988:98; Pagelow, 1981; Stacey and Shupe, 1983; Wilson et al., 1987)
2. When fear consumes all her thoughts and energies (Ferraro and Johnson, 1983:331, 334)
3. When the violence becomes public and she can no longer save face (Ferraro and Johnson, 1983:332)
4. When she defines his actions as expressions of disdain, contempt, or disrespect ("He no longer loves me, even if he says he does") or as a confirmation that he has become a mean or violent person whom she can no longer help
5. When she concedes that she is unable to find a set of rearranged feelings or social arrangements within the family to "manage" his battering and its effects

Disengaging, Uncoupling, and Recoupling Processes

Of all the personal strategies and help sources tried, battered women retrospectively perceive temporarily leaving their batterers as the most effective way of decreasing or ending the physical violence (Bowker, 1988:86). Leaving, like defining an experience as real violence, is a process (Giles-Sims, 1983). Temporarily freezing out the batterer and then resuming a life together is a survival strategy frequently tried and often repeated. Only after survivors have experienced a series of separations and rejoinings do many of them finally decide to leave—to permanently freeze out the batterers.

This should not surprise anyone. Lengthy periods of leaving and returning are characteristic of the uncoupling processes experienced by many couples that are separating or divorcing but that are not engaged in battering (Loseke and Cahill, 1984:304). Uncoupling or disengaging is typically quite difficult, takes considerable time, and is often accompanied by great personal turmoil and loss for both persons. For most couples, uncoupling brings on feelings of guilt and worry, concern and regret, bitterness and disappointment, depression and confusion—a wavering as to whether uncoupling is what they wish or even if it is what is best.

Although temporarily freezing out an intimate is very difficult, terminating the relationship is even more complex and disturbing. If the partners have been together for a considerable period of time, they have developed a "coupled history," a shared biography, and a bond of experience that, no matter the quality of the relationship, are part of each partner forever. Even if the partners are experiencing the trauma of battering, they, too, are experiencing much, much more. Relationships are complex and multidimensional. Unless the battering processes have developed so fully or the pain, fear, and grief have become so overriding a veil to all other relational experiences and personal qualities, most persons separate and return (Loseke and Cahill, 1984:304). A decision to separate permanently, though it may have become necessary, often brings on the feeling of yet another self-loss: a relational death and a death to part of one's self (Turner and Shapiro, 1986).

Being Frozen Out:
The Batterer's Framework and Experience

Sometimes the only way the battered partner can make it clear to the batterer how serious she is about his changing or seeking help is to freeze him out. This may be the only way she can step back and reflect (Pence, 1987) and step forward and become more competent at living separately from him (Okun, 1988:117) and healthfully "for herself."

During this process, the batterer may for the first time feel the real weight of what has been lost in the relationship. Whereas her grieving process began with the initial episodes of real violence, his may not begin until he feels the shock of her having left. Until that point, he had not been listening to her or trying to understand what his torturing and deconstructing meant for her. He had not been paying attention to her grieving.

Now that he is frozen out (or, in his view, "now that she has frozen him out and left"), all his self-depending, self-securing, and relational assumptions are called into question. Initially, his energy may be mobilized into coaxing or coercing her into taking him back. He may feel desperate. He may feel lost without her. He may feel emptied. He may resort to giving her gifts or threatening to take away the children to get her back. If and when she does not respond to these tactics, he may promise that *this time* his violence will stop. He may promise to acquiesce to whatever she wants. He may promise to seek counseling. But, as David Adams points out,

> unfortunately, many abusive men enter counseling wanting guarantees of marital reconciliation and promptly drop out when guarantees are not given. This type of angry and manipulative behavior constitutes initial grief reaction to a loss that isn't yet accepted. This initial denial is accompanied by anger and accusations directed at the wife for abandoning and "humiliating" the man, and bargaining for her return with promises of changes and/or counseling. If these ploys don't work, the man becomes depressed and feels unable to care for himself. In therapy, he is very dependent on the therapist for a "quick fix" or formula for creating the appearance of change. (1989:84)

Sadly, there are few men who enter counseling voluntarily; most enter via court order or as a condition of "getting her back" (Gondolf, 1985a). And many therapeutic interventions with men who batter (like those of the past that purported to support and aid battered women) perpetuate violence by not confronting the real issues of gender and power (Ptacek, 1988:151)—of male violence as an instrument of control. The perspectives of many clinicians wittingly or unwittingly validate the batterer's account that he is not responsible for his violence. They all too often obscure the batterer's motives and the benefits his violence may momentarily secure. They may not even address the complex issues of control, focusing instead, for example, on anger control training or skills development. They may not see that physical violence has links with other battering patterns and that his emotional outbursts are situated in a particular pattern of intimidation and social arrangements employed to achieve dominance and control over his partner (Ptacek, 1988:159, 1988b:152–154).

Indeed, programs that have focused exclusively on anger control or anger management, communication skills, or self-esteem have many times aided the batterer in becoming a more successful psychological batterer.[1] That is, they have increased the batterer's skills in a different pattern of battering—one in which emotional and spiritual deconstruction has been substituted for physical battering. Rarely have these programs addressed the hierarchical social arrangements within the family that constitute structural violence. Seldom have they looked at the deeper interpersonal difficulties some of these men have with issues such as intimacy, dependency, and inclusion (Allen et al., 1989). Adams concludes:

The abusive man must be held accountable for his controlling behaviors and attitudes toward women. ... Any approach that focuses exclusively on individual or psychologic change is doomed to failure, since sexist attitudes and behaviors on the individual level are socially sanctioned and reproduced. It is essential to make these connections between the psychologic and political and to understand the ways that political structures and hierarchies shape individual feelings, attitudes, and behaviors. [Note: These arrangements are located in the family divisions of labor and decision-making arrangements as well as in the organization of other institutions of the society including the organization of the state and economy.] The work to eradicate male violence toward women demands both social and individual change, confrontation and compassion. (1989:94)

Fortunately, there are some excellent programs for men who batter women.[2] These programs encourage men to give up the attributions for their violence that they have held on to for so long. From the shock, loss, pain, and grief over being frozen out, many batterers begin to enter what Adams (1989:83) calls the disequilibrium stage of awareness. But before they can genuinely become self-motivated to change, they must work through their grief. Moreover, before they can begin to examine their own behavior, they must accept that they have no entitlement to control and no "real" (deep existential) control over a partner's feelings or behavior.

In the disequilibrium stage of awareness the batterer's introspection is at first shaky and provisional, but slowly he recognizes that he must take responsibility for his own behavior and feelings (Adams, 1989:84). He may for the first time locate his feelings and perceptions of reality in the broader context of others' feelings and experiences. He may grudgingly start to recognize that his partner can exist apart from him and that he must accept her independence and autonomy. He may even acknowledge her as a multidimensional, different, and viable person separate from him (Adams, 1989:89). He may become more able to express his feelings of hurt, fear, inadequacy, and self-anger. He may reveal the exaggerated dependency he has on her, which he previously masked by his attempts to make her dependent on him or to control her behavior (Dutton and Browning, 1988a:168). This revelation is significant, for he used to disavow these feelings for self and transfer them to his partner. With his loss of control over her and his situation, he experiences an aching emptiness filled with confusion and feelings of hopelessness and despair (Adams, 1989:86; Fogarty, 1979).

With considerable effort, support, and challenge from other men who have battered their partners (Adams and McCormick, 1982; Gondolf, 1985, 1985b), a batterer can enter the decision stage of awareness (Adams, 1989:88). Listening to others' stories, sharing opinions, developing friendships, and hearing a recounting of others' relapses and successes are the program elements retrospectively perceived as most significant (Gondolf, 1988a:137). Entering the decision stage, a batterer realizes that change means no longer fully attributing his problems to external factors—those factors that were most salient to him and perhaps still are. He must decide to attribute his problems principally to his decisions and himself (Corenblum, 1988)—his inability to negotiate intimacy, differentiate his partner from himself, and let her be herself. He must make a commitment to work on himself, even if he knows (and is not convinced otherwise by the counselors) that his choices are made in a structural context and are not entirely of his making and that "working" only on himself is a fiction of individual responsibility and of therapy focused on individual change.

In the decision stage of awareness, a batterer comprehends that to retain relational control, he withholds both affection and nonmaterial rewards for his partner's pleasing behavior or good qualities. He may become conscious of his partner as a person who, like himself, needs to grow in her own self-chosen directions. He may finally realize how he obstructed her development and deconstructed her. He may for the first time recognize that his violence thwarted his own development and positive sense of self. He may become aware of how he devalues women, for example, by interrupting them when they speak. He may acknowledge that his and his partner's family routines and arrangements were sexist and violent. He may become acutely aware of how these same degenerative processes and arrangements operate in other institutions within the society.

Research indicates, however, that men who have successfully completed these programs and stopped battering their partners retrospectively state that they relied primarily on specific behavioral techniques and willful self-restraint to stop their violence, rather than on deep personal or family arrangement change. These responses may reflect a reluctance to admit that personal or relational arrangement change was required or desirable. They may also mirror the batterer program's truth that these men are, at the core, good persons who principally need to change their violent behavior. According to Edward Gondolf (1988a:142), successful batterer program participants most often cite taking a time-out when angry, self-talking about restraint, recalling the consequences of violence, and visualizing the reactions of other program participants as some of the best strategies for dealing with violence.

There is, however, little evidence to suggest that these limited techniques are more successful than others for stopping the violence. In fact, evidence does indicate that focusing solely on these techniques may obstruct men who batter from developing more substantial strategies that would at a minimum address what instigates the choice to batter. In any case, retrospective reflections of successful stopping techniques conform to willful masculine conceptions of self-reliance. Few respondents mention learning to share decision-making, changing an appraisal of women, or cultivating an awareness of sexism as a critical factor in helping them stop their violence (Gondolf, 1988a:139, 142).

Unfortunately, many men prematurely drop out of the sequenced processes of addressing grief and loss, personal growth, awareness, and change (Gondolf, 1985a, 1988a:137; DeMaris, 1989; Hamberger and Hastings, 1989; Saunders and Parker, 1989; Edleson and Syers, 1990). They return to both their partners and their familiar cycles of interpersonal violence. Many do not wish to believe that the next temporary freeze-out is only a matter of time or that it may be their last temporary absence. Additionally, some men become permanently frozen out of their partnerships while undergoing these awareness changes. Because continuing in the program will not "bring her back," they no longer see a reason to continue. Nevertheless, some who are or become permanently frozen out have progressed far enough in these sequenced processes to realize that even though their partners are not coming back, they do not want other relationships to turn out this way. Their grief and loss are just too severe.

Being Frozen Out:
The Survivor's Framework and Experience

Successive temporary freeze-outs may afford a battered woman an opportunity to build up her financial, educational, occupational, and emotional support. She may need these resources if she eventually decides to freeze him out permanently—though this is not a frequently stated intention. Her intention is stopping the violence, and her insistence that he get help does appear to influence him to try stopping his battering (Gondolf, 1988a:142; Giles-Sims, 1983). Those women who get the battering stopped are exceedingly persistent and successful in communicating their unwillingness to tolerate further battering (Bowker, 1983).

Successive temporary freeze-outs may place a survivor in an assistance context wherein friends or helping professionals (1) acknowledge the existence of the battering patterns; (2) help and encourage her to stop the battering by removing herself from the battering site, if only temporarily, and then attempt to help her strengthen her abilities and sense of personal power; and (3) help her clarify her mixed emotions and grieve the losses she is experiencing (Williams-White, 1989:51–52). She may then be able to confirm her own capabilities and strengths and regain her self-confidence. She may also have an opportunity to bond with other battered women, and realize that she is not alone. She may begin to revitalize herself and learn to better protect and act on her best interest and determine her future, regardless of whether this means returning to live with her partner (NiCarthy, 1986; Sedlak, 1988; Margolin, Sibner, and Gleberman, 1988).

That many women take a long time to progress entirely through the battering process suggests that powerful forces are urging them to return to their partners and sometimes to the grip of continuous battering (Okun 1988; Peterson-Lewis, Turner, and Adams, 1988; Ferraro and Johnson, 1983). That many take four to five years from the initial episode of real violence (Okun, 1988:118) to a temporary or permanent freeze-out suggests that these forces are perhaps as powerful as those that seize their partners in the decision to continue battering. As Denzin (1984, 1984a) suggests, both partners interact in a negative force field that is larger than either partner's sole action.

Battering processes and the affective and social arrangement changes that lead to a freeze-out are often made while the survivor is in a state of tremendous self-doubt, extreme social isolation, dissociation (Wilson, Baglioni, and Downing, 1989), anger, terror, inadequate information, and insufficient community support (Pfouts, 1978). She cannot assume that threatening to leave, attempting to break up, or finding (if she can) a separate shelter for herself and the children will be safe from his intrusion and further battering (Okun, 1988:108; Schwartz, 1988a).

Apart from internal reasons, many battered women are reluctant to temporarily freeze out their partners because of emotional and economic dependency on the relationship to meet the children's needs. Lewis Okun reports that

> study results clearly demonstrate the importance of economic considerations in the shelter residents' decisions whether or not to terminate their conjugal relationships. In general, the data show that the greater the woman's own inde-

pendent economic resources were relative to her mate's income, the greater
the likelihood was of cohabitation terminating (presumably at the woman's in-
stigation). Couples in which the battered woman was unambiguously the main
income producer were twice as likely to experience immediate breakups as the
rest of the shelter sample. (1988:116)

Other researchers indicate that working outside the home and having
children who are not infants provide the survivor with at least some measur-
able degree of independence and facilitate a greater willingness to leave a
battering partner (Wilson, Baglioni, and Downing, 1989). In addition to
some degree of economic independence, working outside the home indicates that the survivor is actively participating in a social setting different
from her home and is thus afforded an opportunity to develop social relationships and networks apart from her partner. This may not only validate a
woman's self-esteem but also increase the chance that she can make an emotional break if she desires one and enlist the aid of other formal and informal
sources of help (Wilson, Baglioni, and Downing, 1989).

The longer women who are less independent, less enmeshed in a supportive
social network of friends, and fearful for their own safety and that of the children are frequently afraid that they will not be able to "make it" on their
own—a belief often fueled by years of battering and developmental oppression (Ferraro and Johnson, 1983:330). Such a survivor may feel that if she
freezes him out temporarily, he will make the separation permanent, leaving
her unable to support herself and her reconstructed family. The thought of
being unbearably lonely frightens her. Her vulnerability and confusion over
what she really wants make her anxious. She worries that she will not be able
to find another partner, that there is something wrong with her, and that no
one will find her attractive. Yet intermittently she has generalized feelings of
anger and resentment toward men. She questions whether she even wishes
to relate with another man.

The longer the survivor was in the relationship before the onset of real violence or remains in the relationship after the battering begins, and the
greater the love and commitment she has given to the relationship, the
harder it is for her to accept that leaving is the best option for her (Strube,
1988:95), and the less likely she is to leave the relationship (Strube and
Barbour, 1983, 1984). These are difficult decisions. The circumstances are
terrifyingly complex.

Although some battered women decide quickly to leave their relationships, most others take considerable time to admit that there is a problem,

that they are victims of battering, and that they need help. Although many programs face impermanent funding, cooptation, institutional transformation, and other strains of tenability, there are many excellent, empathetic shelter programs, counseling services, and professionals who are committed to helping a survivor step back, introspect, and make the decision that she feels is in her best interest. Committed professionals accept the decisions that each battered woman makes for herself.

It is, however, disquieting that some battering "experts" define leaving a partner as the normatively expected, reasonable, and correct response to the experience of battering. By implication, they seem to suggest that staying in the relationship or returning after such an episode (or series of episodes) requires an explanation. At the very least, they are disappointed and often depressed by a survivor's decision to return to her partner, which they perceive as a rejection or betrayal of all their help. Furthermore, they interpret returning to the batterer as evidence that battered women are in need of even greater help because battering has robbed them of the ability to make "correct" decisions.

To these experts, battered women need to be saved. As a result, in some programs a survivor may lose control over her self-definition, interpretation of experience, and, in some cases, private affairs. In this sense, some battered women are battered twice, first by their partners and then by the experts who claim to know what is in these women's best interest and who act to deprive them of choice (Loseke and Cahill, 1984:306).

Getting Out and Restoring Self

Freedom from battering can begin only through an open confrontation with real violence and, at least temporarily, a movement out of the violent situation. It can occur from within only very rarely, for the forces that foster battering and require adaptation to survive are not tied solely to a single act or person; they are part of the larger interactional processes that encircle the entire family (Denzin, 1984, 1984a).

To restructure the relationship, both partners must recognize that neither person can change the situation while still in it. Moreover, even if the survivor temporarily leaves this relationship or permanently freezes out the battering partner, neither one can move to healthful relationships without restructuring the relationship to self.

6

Interventions with Men
Who Batter Women

Efforts to publicize the extent and severity of battering have resulted in a general recognition that battering, especially physically violent battering, is a serious social problem that requires significant legal, scientific, and ameliorative responses. Through the efforts of the battered women's movement, community organizing, and enabling legislation, the number of shelters for women and children has greatly increased. According to *The 1991 National Directory of Domestic Violence Programs*, there are more than 1,550 domestic violence programs offering a surprising array of services for battered women and their children (Osmundson, 1992:1). The number of programs responsive to the safety, empowerment, and quality-of-life needs of battered women has also expanded. At last, the legal system has begun to provide protection to battered women and to define a batterer's physical violence as a serious act that should be prosecuted.

In contrast, efforts to understand how to successfully intervene in the lives of men who batter women[1] and decrease the prevalence and incidence of battering and the acceptance of battering (and violence) in our society have not progressed as appreciably.[2] Nevertheless, an explosion of clinical and investigative interest in men who batter women developed in the 1980s. A wide range of punitive and therapeutic modes of intervention have emerged (e.g., jailing, mandated counseling, accountability education, supervised self-help groups, anger control treatment, and couples [family] therapy) (Gondolf, 1987:335; Jennings, 1987). Unfortunately, most of these interventions have been uncoordinated and limited in their success. Counseling programs have experienced both recruitment problems and high dropout and recidivism rates (Gondolf, 1987). Moreover, most interventions have narrowly focused on extinguishing physically violent battering patterns, thereby neglecting the long-term process of ending battering altogether.

Cultural and Social Structural Supports

Acceptance of batterers' use of physical violence and terrorist tactics has been and is a significant cultural support for the battering of women (Pence, 1985, 1989). The absence of collective condemnation or legal intervention communicates to those who have chosen (or might choose) to batter that there are no significant official objections to their patterns of battering or their claimed entitlement to dominate and control.

The absence of this negative collective response, however, is not by any measure the sole or even the most essential cultural support for violence against women or for women's inequality. Of far more significance is the strongly articulated belief that a man has the right to control or punish his partner for perceived hostile or harmful behavior. To confront battering, we must fully understand and challenge this belief, the legal system's response, and those cultural and social structural supports that underlie these behaviors.

Three additional cultural and social structural supports underpin the battering of women and the acceptance of this battering: (1) the belief that hierarchical social arrangements in general and hierarchical arrangements based on sex and gender specifically are natural and immutable; (2) the widespread use of linguistic structures, established in specific economic arrangements, that objectify women; and (3) gender socialization and social arrangements that place and keep women in a subordinate and disempowered position in our society.

Hierarchy Based on Sex and Gender

As stated earlier, men who batter women frequently believe not only that they should be able to control their partners but also that they should take on the role of disciplinarian or assume legitimate entitlement to her obedience and service. Historically, our culture has supported patriarchal family arrangements wherein the male assumes a superordinate position and takes the role of controller of the household.

The idea that all social arrangements should be hierarchical is reinforced by the overwhelmingly hierarchical social arrangements in our society. From the classroom to the workroom, from the big house to the statehouse, from the boardroom to the bedroom, hierarchy defines our expectations, behaviors, and relationships. Many parents do not even question their assumed natural hierarchical authority and claimed right to control "their" children. It is ironic that control and entitled obedience are recognized as at the root of child battering (child abuse), yet these same roots are denied their central place in woman battering. As hierarchies based on age and sex are so prevalent in our society's social arrangements, it is not surprising that men and parents expect obedience and acquiescence from subordinates in the family. Nevertheless, historical and cross-cultural research indicates that hierarchy based on sex, hierarchy based on age, and hierarchy itself are not universal, natural, or necessary (Levinson, 1988; Miller, 1976; Tifft, 1979; Tifft and Sullivan, 1980).

Objectification

To psychologically or physically batter a human being consciously recognized as an equal is difficult and unusual. Men who batter women frequently depersonalize their victims prior to and during an assault. This should surprise no one in our culture, where the language of objectification, and therefore of dehumanization, is affixed to persons who are perceived as different or as objects to be used, controlled, exploited, or killed. Homophobic fears are often expressed in the dehumanizing expressions "queer," "dyke," "fag." Misogynistic language derogates males who do not exhibit expected gender "characteristics" or superiority. For instance, men who are perceived as non-aggressive or who show concern for the feelings of their partners are called "wuss," "pussy," "woman," "pussy-whipped," "hen-pecked." Women who do not "know their place," who assert their presence, or who demonstrate their independence are called "bitch," "slut," "whore." Nonhuman, denigrating descriptions of women abound—"pig," "dog," "cow," "old crow," "dumb bunny," "horse face" (Cantor, 1983). Language that reflects the idea that women are not human or are simply body parts for sex-act use is very common—"chick," "bird," "fox," "piece of ass."

Language expresses our feelings of hatred, fear, objectification, and disgust for those who disagree with us, for the "enemy" who is not us—"feminist," "lesbian," "communist," "nigger," "jap," "terrorist," "vermin." In many of our social arrangements objectifying language is so commonplace we rarely recognize it—those who work are "personnel"; people are "the masses"; a newborn or a young child is referred to by the pronoun "it"; those who serve are called "boy," "son," "honey," "girl"; people are known by their roles, as if they have no personal identities—"the old man," "the wife," "the old lady." In regard to this latter use of language, Ellen Pence (1985:3) relates that "in seven consecutive court-mandated counseling sessions involving thirty-two male batterers, ninety-seven references were made to the men's victims. Only once was a victim referred to by her name."

Objectification is continually reinforced by those who use women's bodies to sell commodities; who trade in torture and violence against women and children, as in pornography (Pence, 1989:3); who view people as commodities to be acquired, traded, sold, or employed; who sell themselves or rent their time, body, or mind in the job market; who see people as "human resources," "economies of scale," "cost factors," "labor," or "oxen." In the extreme, objectification fuses into nonexistence or human nonpresence. U.S. military briefings during Operation Desert Storm illustrated this fusion. Persons in the Iraqi military were "attritted," "softened up," and "neutralized." Military positions were "pounded," subjected to "carpet bombing" or "saturation strikes." Persons who died but were not in the military were officially designated "collateral damage." In the language of this specific war, only tanks and aircraft were "killed" and counted—the number of "enemy" killed (especially those who were buried alive by earth movers) did not count and were not counted.

Because we live in a society dominated by economic arrangements, it is not surprising that individuals are thought of in terms of "use value" (the degree to which they can be used), rather than as ends (as sacred). An individual is primarily valued and receives benefits on the basis of what she or he produces (for what someone else defines as the value of a person's "work"), for her or his produce value. In terms of this primary cultural and structural dynamic, women in the home, women or men who care for young persons, children who are learning and not producing, those who are no longer producing or who are no longer allowed to produce (the retired, those not employed), those who are unable to work (e.g., persons mentally unable to work), and those who care for them have reduced, little, or no productive use value. In sum, in a culture that values people on the basis of their use, as in producing value that can be accumulated, when they cannot be used or when it is not economical to use them, or when they can be used but do not produce what can be accumulated, they are seen as *worth-less,* not worthy.

The disproportionate degree to which women are objectified and diminished reflects who defines what is of social value and who is allowed to participate in value-defining processes. The disproportionate degree to which women are dehumanized and dismissed is undoubtedly reflected in the prevalence of men who batter and women who are the victims/survivors of these men.

Disempowerment and Gender Socialization

I concur with Pence (1989:6) that the roots of battering are so deep that to eradicate the battering of women, we must eliminate the imbalance of power between men and women and redefine the nature of intimate relationships. Battered women are systematically subjected to the tactics of power exercise. A woman's childhood socialization rarely reflects an empowering environment free of gender diminishment, subordination, and submission. A woman is situated in a circumstance of dependency when she is unable to materially provide for herself and her children without the financial support of a man; when she is unable to find safe and nurturant childcare so she can work; when she is exploited and/or harassed in the workplace; when she must ask permission to attend school or work outside the household; when she fears the loss of her children, the loss of a father for the children, or the threat of retaliation if she tries to assert her needs, get help, or report being battered.

When a woman gradually accommodates these circumstances of dependency

1. She may develop a sense of "learned helplessness" or a fixation on the "batterer" as provider, protector, and rescuer.
2. She may become terrified of the world inside as well as outside the home.
3. She may find the outside world uninteresting.
4. She may in her seclusion and isolation be encouraged to compete with and distrust other women.
5. She may become conditioned to the rewards of "love" and "well-being" and the punishments of withdrawal of love and financial support or the threats of abandonment, rape, and battering. (Cantor, 1983)

Strategies of power exercised against women are carried out by individual batterers in a culturally reinforced environment. Battering is almost always accompanied by continual attacks on the victim's self-esteem, integrity, and self-concept. As revealed in survivors' accounts, many men who batter are successful over a long period of time in convincing those they batter that the physical violence and other forms of battering are brought on by the survivor's behavior, deficiencies, assertions of independence, complaints, expressions of unmet needs, or resistances to the processes of domination and control.

The batterer's perspective is frequently reinforced by his or the survivor's relatives, the clergy, the police, or the therapist who defines the victimization as the result of relational conflict or who believes the victim is suffering from an assortment of clinically defined defects, including "learned helplessness," "addiction" to the relationship, "loving too much," or "codependency" (Pence, 1985:6). The batterer's perspective is reinforced by all who believe that a woman should know her place, and that her place should be defined by men and specified by "her man."

The Nature of Battering

Analysis of the supports for battering clearly indicates that the scope of behaviors involved in the battering of women ranges far beyond the physical violence to which the legal system has now become more responsive. As presented earlier (in Figure 1.2), men who batter women utilize a vast range of violent, manipulative, coercive, and controlling behaviors to establish or attempt to establish dominance. Understanding the entire configuration of tactics the batterer uses to control the survivor should be as important to a judge, probation officer, prosecutor, or therapist (counselor or educator) as is knowledge of the specific criminal act that brought the batterer into the criminal justice decision-making process (Pence, 1985:24). Although we know batterers construct patterns of battering that involve quite distinctive tactics, processes, and interactions (Pence, 1985:24–25), at this time well-developed paradigms do not exist. For this reason, and many others, therapeutic intervention programs for men who batter women lack an adequate theoretical base.

To protect the survivor, end her victimization, and help her empower herself, the nature of battering must be more thoroughly understood. Likewise, we must discover how to help the batterer end his violence and achieve personal growth at a level deeper than ending a specific pattern of violence. Given the deeply entrenched patterns of interaction that characterize battering, highly unrealistic expectations for change have been placed on both men who batter and those who provide programs designed to help them end their violence (Jennings, 1990). Many programs expect not merely the cessation of physical violence but also change in the batterer's attitudes and values. Yet these programs only rarely address the cultural and social structural contexts within which batterers make their choice to batter.

Before discussing the interventions that define battering as a social problem—and therefore advocate changing the cultural and social arrangements that constitute structural violence and foster the interpersonal battering of women (Chapters 9, 10, 11)—I wish to assess those interventions that define battering as an intrapersonal or interpersonal relational problem and subsequently propose intrapersonal (Chapter 7) or interpersonal relational change (Chapter 8).

7

Intrapersonal
Intervention Programs

Only a small percentage of men who batter women concede that they have acted unacceptably. Even fewer acknowledge that they have a "violence problem." Consequently, most neither seek help on their own nor are mandated by a court to treatment (Hamberger and Hastings, 1986a). When researchers believed that the battering of women was an infrequent phenomenon, they tended to look for pathology in the batterer, the survivor, both partners, or the relationship. As a result, the focus of research findings on individual pathology reflected both the selective observation of hospitalized or incarcerated persons and the psychiatric perspective of the definers. This perspective led to a definition of battering as a manifestation of pathology, not as choice behavior (Margolin, Sibner, and Gleberman, 1988:94).

Choice Versus Character Deficiency

Men who battered women were consequently diagnosed as passive-aggressive, addiction prone, sadistic, pathologically jealous or passive, and dependent (Faulk, 1974; Shainess, 1977; Snell, Rosenwald, and Robey, 1964). Others were seen as suffering from neurological and biochemical disorders (Elliot, 1977; Schauss, 1982). This perspective fostered the beliefs that only men with pathological personality problems battered women and that these men were not responsible for their acts of violence because they were "ill."

Not surprisingly, clinicians also "discovered" that the hospitalized survivors of battering had pathological personality characteristics. Battered women were described as either aggressive, masochistic, and immature

(Scott, 1974; Shainess, 1977; Snell, Rosenwald, and Robey, 1964) or as anxious and depressed. This perspective fostered the assertion that battered women were responsible for their own victimization and that only women with specific pathological characteristics were battered.

With the "rediscovery" that battering is a relatively pervasive phenomenon, and the "discovery" that blaming-the-victim perspectives are themselves tactics to maintain male dominance, researchers now recognize that most men who batter choose, within a perceived set of choices, to batter. In light of these discoveries, clinicians generally view the symptoms that professionally treated battered women suffer and exhibit (e.g., depression, anxiety, substance abuse) as sequelae, rather than as concomitants or precursors, of battering. As pointed out earlier, the fact that many men who batter women are violent only toward partners and only in the "home" undermines the "pathological personality characteristic" and the "deficient impulse control" explanations for battering. It places responsibility for battering on those who choose to batter.

Although I indicated in Chapter 1 that men who batter women do not appear to differ from other men experiencing relational discord or from men in the United States in general, many batterers were exposed to violence as children, either as witnesses to interparental violence or as victims of parental abuse. Moreover, many of these men do have problems with alcohol, although there is little evidence that alcohol plays a direct role in specific battering episodes or patterns. Many of these men rigidly adhere to patriarchal gender and sex-role expectations. Furthermore, many men who batter women have been described as exhibiting low self-esteem, excessive dependency needs, and inordinate levels of insecurity, passivity, and jealousy. They appear to express greater approval of violence than do nonviolent men, and like many men involved in relationally discordant but nonviolent relationships, they are generally unassertive.[1]

It has also been suggested that men who batter women are inarticulate in acknowledging and expressing emotions other than anger—they are emotionally illiterate. Moreover, Hamberger and Hastings (1988:768) assert that "male spouse abusers seem to have more difficulty than non-abusers in modulating affective states and in feeling comfortable within intimate relationships with all their attendant conflicts and stresses." To paraphrase Gayla Margolin, Linda Sibner, and Lisa Gleberman (1988:95), men who batter women exhibit a learned inability to express feelings other than anger. Despite patriarchal and gender expectations, batterers are frequently unable to establish and maintain these features in interaction with their partners. This inability can lead to a diminished self-esteem and to angry reactions to perceived threats to the validity of these expectations. At home with their partners is the one domain where batterers believe they should dominate.

Acknowledging that the battering of women is a social problem with significant links to the practices of male entitlement and privilege claims, Hamberger and Hastings (1988) assert that in response to the increasing pressure to attempt to rehabilitate men who batter, it is appropriate to study the characteristics of these men. Through such research clients who need treatment can be identified and then matched with interventions suited to them. Hamberger and Hastings also point out that understanding the psychological characteristics and relational/cognitive processes of "batterers" does not in any way detract from the ultimate goals of battering research and intervention: the cessation of violence, the safety of the survivor, and changes in sexist cultural beliefs. Furthermore, attempting to understand the psychological workings of men who batter in no way condones, excuses, or should deflect responsibility for this violence.

Personality Styles and Treatment Modes

In their assessment of the clinical characteristics of male batterers, Hamberger and Hastings (1988:769) believe they have located evidence of a "deeply ingrained, highly treatment-resistant, and often perplexing set of behaviors." Their research confirms the judgments reached by many others that there is no stereotypical "abuser" personality. Nevertheless, some men who batter women appear to exhibit behavior and personality styles similar to persons with differing types of personality disorder. For these persons, modified treatment modes would be quite appropriate. Hamberger and Hastings elaborate:

> Elbow (1977) and Symonds (1978) have offered psychodynamic formulations of the personality styles of batterers, emphasizing their heterogeneity. These formulations can be examined against the unitary concept of personality disorder. According to Elbow's global description, the batterer is highly rigid and unaccepting of the partner's need for autonomy, has problems with intimacy, and projects internal conflicts onto the partner. Such rigidity in coping and perceiving, together with difficulties in supporting intimacy, are the hallmark of personality disorder. Elbow then describes four types of spouse abusers—categories that also show considerable overlap with certain categories of personality disorder—that can be compared with the three categories described by Symonds.

The first of Elbow's four categories is *the controller,* someone who is unable to reciprocally meet another's needs in a relationship. The controller exercises tight control over the partner's daily personal and social activities. When the partner asserts independence, the controller uses violence as a means of reestablishing control. In many ways the partner exists only to gratify the controller's needs and strivings.

When the partner does not meet the controller's needs, or thwarts or challenges them, the controller responds with hostility, vindictiveness, and violence. Conversely, when the partner is able to meet his needs, the controller becomes a "nice guy." Indeed, that may be the very dynamic that leads the casual observer to view batterers as "nice" people when the only level of involvement is superficial.

The description of the controller is clearly consistent with that of a patient with antisocial personality disorder. Symonds (1978) says that for the batterer, violence is ego-syntonic, or consistent with the batterer's view of himself and the world. For him, battery is just another acceptable way of dealing with people who obstruct the attainment of his goals.

The second type of batterer described by Elbow is *the incorporator,* an individual who requires a symbiotic relationship to feel complete as a person. As the partner struggles to become free of the symbiosis, the incorporator fears a loss of self and intensifies, to the point of violence, efforts to prevent the loss. The incorporator is similar to the controller in that he may totally dominate the partner's life. What differentiates the two is the controller's need to maintain control of external situations, and the incorporator's need to preserve the self. The incorporator does not experience existence apart from the relationship.

This personality description is similar to one offered by Symonds (1978) for a batterer he describes as "Dr. Jekyll and Mr. Hyde." For this batterer, constant internal dependency needs and aggressive conflicts occasionally result in explosions, particularly when they are disinhibited by alcohol. However, unlike the controller, for whom violence is ego-syntonic, the Jekyll-Hyde batterer usually expresses considerable guilt and remorse after a violent episode.

As can be seen from the description of the incorporator or Jekyll-Hyde type, in such a profile—consisting of identity disturbances, symbiotic relating, rapid unpredictable mood changes driven by lack of personal integration, and exacerbation by alcohol abuse—Elbow and Symonds have described many primary features of the borderline personality disorder.

Elbow labels her third type of batterer *the approval seeker.* This individual acts primarily to receive recognition and external validation as a good and worthy person. He can achieve intimacy only when so validated by a "perfect mirror." When his partner fails to reflect his "goodness," or actually reflects his negative features, he perceives rejection by her and responds with violence.

This batterer's need for constant validation, together with his retributive acts when validation is lacking, is consistent with the major dynamic of narcissistic personality disorder. Although the narcissist, like the patient with antisocial personality, does not tend to develop reciprocating relationships, he does subdue the controlling aspects so typical of antisocial personality in favor of more positive attempts to get the partner to validate him. For example, a patient with narcissistic personality may try to manipulate his partner to revere him by doing special favors for her or lavishing expensive gifts on her. His anger and violence erupt when she spurns his efforts or takes them for granted without any show of appreciation.

The final type of batterer Elbow describes is *the defender.* He is basically insecure and defends against that feeling by selecting a partner whom he perceives is weak, vulnerable, and dependent on his strength and ability to take care of her. If the partner attempts to support, defend, or nurture him, he is likely to become violent and attempt to subjugate her. Symonds describes a similar type of batterer, one who maintains a sense of adequacy by focusing on the partner's weaknesses and inadequacies.

This kind of batterer is more difficult to view in terms of a specific category of personality disorder. However, the externalization, the problems in tolerating differentiation, and the profound sense of personal inadequacy and insecurity are all consistent features of personality disorder and may represent overlapping categories of personality disorder. Indeed, it is not uncommon to observe features of more than one personality disorder in one person. (1988:765–766) (italics added)

In conclusion, Hamberger and Hastings present the following recommendations for intrapersonal interventions with men who batter women:

We do not propose that psychopathology is a necessary and sufficient cause of spouse abuse. However, the reports of identified batterers reviewed above argue strongly that psychopathology must be considered part of the picture for a majority of identified batterers and, as such, offers clear directions for treatment. Studies using established clinical psychometric instruments and in some instances, large sample sizes, are beginning to show clearly that batterers consistently produce scores commonly accepted as indicating pathology.

However, the concept of psychopathology applied in spouse abuse research must be altered from the more traditional medical model of mental illness. The psychopathology of abusers can best be viewed as that of a disordered personality—as a deeply ingrained, highly treatment-resistant, and often perplexing set of behaviors. ....

This review does have several implications for clinicians who treat [male batterers]. Although spousal violence is not limited to men with identifiable personality disorders, such individuals tend to be over-represented among the identified population. Hence treatment programs need to address the special concerns presented by patients with personality disorders. They include the provision of highly structured program guidelines with frequent reinforcements of rules, procedures, and sanctions.

To reinforce abusers' participation in treatment programs and their compliance with program rules, participants should be monitored by agencies with sanctioning power, such as the courts and probation and parole agencies.

The focus and goal of treatment should be clearly and realistically defined, consistent with the limits of a particular treatment program. The goal should be to stop violent, abusive behavior, including psychological battering and terror. Given the time-limited nature of many violence-abatement programs, it is not reasonable to expect that participants' basic personality processes will be significantly restructured. Indeed, it may be difficult to stop psychological battering with only short-term therapy. The batterer's spouse should be advised of this limitation of treatment so she can make an informed decision about whether to continue the relationship with the spouse.

Treatment of alcohol-abusing batterers presents special challenges. Such individuals show more severe psychopathology, have greater difficulty with program compliance, and are more likely to revert to violence than nonalcoholic batterers. Alcohol-abusing batterers should be referred to alcoholism treatment services as well as violence-abatement programs, and their compliance with such referrals should be monitored. If the abuser refuses to comply with the alcoholism treatment referral, at the very least the spouse should be informed of the batterer's continued high risk for repeated violence so she can plan for her safety.

In a recent study of behavioral typologies of batterers, Gondolf [1988] suggested that some batterers may be so dangerous to the victim, and so resistant to conventional outpatient intervention, that development of residential treatment programs for this group is indicated.

Developing appropriate treatment options based on the identified characteristics and needs of batterers is a realistic goal. But such a focus should not detract attention from the ultimate goal of the battered women's movement: ensuring the right of all women to live in comfort and safety as autonomous human beings.

This review offers no panacea for the treatment of male batterers. The increased knowledge and understanding of the intrapsychic aspects of spouse abusers will be important to the continued development of flexible, effective intervention programs. Clearly considerable clinical and theoretical work remains to be done in solving the problem of male-to-female spousal violence. (1988:769–770)

Although the intrapersonal level of explanation and intervention has until recently been the major approach to battering, Murray Straus (1977:195) points out that it is doubtful that more than a small fraction of the battering of women can be attributed to the intrapersonal pathology of the batterer. Conceding this, we should not infer that intrapersonal intervention with some specific men who batter cannot alter the dynamics of the interaction patterns that provide the context within which they choose to batter. It is in this endeavor that intrapersonal and interpersonal strategies of intervention appear to make a contribution.

8

Interpersonal
Intervention Programs

Interpersonal research has generated considerable insight into the dynamics and processes within which some persons resort to violence, whereas others, though perhaps profoundly unhappy or distressed, do not (Margolin, Sibner, and Gleberman, 1988:99). The violence-cycle, learning, and systems approaches have all provided intervention strategies designed to alter the interaction processes that support physically violent behavior and lead to a decision to batter.

Research indicates (as noted in Chapter 1) that battering relationships are often characterized by distorted and inarticulate expressive communication. Both partners are frequently cut off from interaction with friends, relatives, and community. Moreover, they often hold quite rigid expectations regarding loyalty, secrecy, privacy, and control. Because these features fit into the sense of self-insecurity each partner feels, they may together create a "traumatic" intertwining or "dependent bonding" (Giles-Sims, 1983; Cohen, 1984; Ferraro and Johnson, 1983; Dutton and Painter, 1981; Walker, 1979, 1984).

However, relational characteristics do not provide an adequate understanding of the intricate processes of partner interaction that foster the decision to batter. These dynamics and those of the battering processes themselves contain cognitive, affective, behavioral, and interpersonal dimensions. An interrelational description of how partners interact to develop and maintain a battering component of their relationship does not, however, imply that they are equally responsible for the violence or the mode of battering. To recognize that both persons are involved in the dynamics of battering neither blames the survivor nor isolates the batterer from the context in which he has made his choice. Intervention in the cycle of battering may suggest the need for changes on the part of both persons, but responsibility for the violence and the choice to end it and change the power dynamics of the relationship must be taken by the person who acts violently.

In 1982, Barbara Star (1982:76) concluded that we knew very little about men who batter women and even less about how to prevent further battering. In her extensive, nationwide search, she was able to locate only forty programs and services specifically for men who batter women. At that time, most of these services and programs were with self-referred men. Since then, programs for batterers have become increasingly mandated by the courts, and the number of such programs has greatly expanded. By the mid-1980s, Maureen Pirog-Good and Jan Stets-Kealey (1985) reported that there were ninety programs specifically for men who batter women; Jeffrey Edleson (1985:487) estimated that there were more than two hundred programs "to help men who batter" (Feazell, Mayers, and Deschner, 1984; Roberts, 1982). Such services and programs were then, and are now, organized and offered by a wide variety of agencies—multiservice agencies, mental health centers, men's collectives, shelter-based services, and so on (Edleson, Miller, and Stone, 1983; Ganley, 1981; Sonkin and Durphy, 1982; Pirog-Good and Stets-Kealey, 1985).

Because of the newness of these programs, research that assesses the comparative effectiveness of different types of intervention programs and attempts to provide data-based guidelines matching client selection and program content has only just begun (Jennings, 1987; Bagarozzi and Giddings, 1983; Hamberger and Hastings, 1989; Saunders and Parker, 1989; Tolman and Bennett, 1989; Edleson and Syers, 1990). Consequently, there is considerable diversity among the modalities available, the programs offered, and the assumptions and theories underlying these modalities and programs. (For a brief history, see Jennings, 1987.)

Therapeutic Modalities and Orientations

Some interventions offer a family or couples therapy modality (Cook and Frantz-Cook, 1984; Taylor, 1984; Margolin, 1979). Others provide individual or group counseling (Purdy and Nickle, 1981; Star, 1983). Within the group counseling modality some treatment programs are behaviorally oriented (Deschner, 1984; Saunders, 1982) or cognitive/behavioral. Others have adopted a self-help, support group orientation (Goffman, 1984; Jennings,

1987; Gondolf, 1987a). Still others have introduced a consciousness-raising (Adams and McCormick, 1982; Garnet and Moss, 1982) or theme-directed support group approach (Gondolf, 1987a).

Recent programs combine several of these orientations and employ a structured sequence of psychoeducational group sessions (Stordeur and Stille, 1989) designed to teach skills (e.g., assertiveness, anger management, communication skills, and relaxation) that control or "disenable" violent behavior (Jennings, 1987). These programs are based on the premise that battering is learned and triggered in the context of a deficit of alternative conflict resolution skills in a social environment that implicitly approves of men controlling women. Anger control and anger management skills supplemented with stress management and communication skills training tend to be the core of such programs (Russell, 1988). To illustrate, Daniel Sonkin and Michael Durphy (1982) and Daniel Sonkin, Del Martin, and Lenore Walker (1985:90–93) offer an extensive, structured psychoeducational program embodying the following goals:

1. Decrease isolation and develop an interpersonal support system
2. Increase feelings of personal control and power
3. Increase feelings of self-esteem
4. Increase the batterer's responsibility for his violent behavior
5. Increase awareness of the dangerousness of violent behavior
6. Increase acceptance that violent behavior has real consequences
7. Increase awareness of violence in society in general
8. Develop communication skills
9. Develop assertiveness skills
10. Develop stress-reduction skills
11. Develop an ability to empathize with the partner
12. Increase understanding of the relationship between violence and sex-role behavior
13. Develop control over alcohol and/or drug use
14. Support individual therapy or couples therapy goals

According to Edward Gondolf and David Russell (1986:2), a gradual refinement of treatment orientations has occurred as well as an emerging consensus on both goals and content, especially among programs that exclusively offer group counseling for men. After an assurance that the survivor and other family members are safe, the primary goal in this consensus is that therapeutic intervention help these men change their violent behavior

(Brisson, 1982; Edleson, 1984; Saunders, 1984). Most of these groups take a group discussion format and incorporate, with varying degrees of emphasis, anger control, communication skills, and sex-role resocialization (Purdy and Nickle, 1981).

Other programs, whether exclusively for men or for men and their partners, provide training in emotional awareness and expressiveness, problem-solving and communication skills, and anger and stress management. They also include an exploration of personal and relational biography, sex-role and gender conceptions, the building of a support system, and the adoption of behavior and interaction patterns that preclude battering (Saunders and Hanusa, 1986; Margolin, Sibner, and Gleberman, 1988). Such programs are based on the beliefs that battering is learned and chosen behavior and that it progressively develops into a self-perpetuating system of interaction. These programs also maintain that battering patterns and behaviors are intensified by self-dialogue and occur in response to specific, identifiable anger- or stress-provoking stimuli (Bolton and Bolton, 1987:269).

For these programs to be successful, it is necessary to know the nature of recurrent battering processes and be able to identify critical points in these dynamics. Alternative responses can then be introduced at these critical points via special techniques and new skills (e.g., emotion differentiation, anger control, problem-solving skills, different conceptions of the partner [Bolton and Bolton, 1987:259; Deschner, 1984:79; Edleson, 1984]).

In many programs, anger control has become pivotal, and a diversity of behavioral, cognitive, and affective intervention strategies have been developed to help these men control and dissipate their anger. Margolin, Sibner, and Gleberman explain:

> From a behavioral perspective, the objective is to impart skills, through assertiveness or relaxation training, that are incompatible with aggression (Saunders and Hanusa, 1986). From a cognitive perspective, the goal is to modify cognitions that accompany [battering]. In other words, the batterer is trained to monitor, evaluate, and then challenge his interpretations and assumptions about his partner (Bedrosian, 1982). He is also taught to use self-talk to lessen, rather than escalate, his angry feelings (Saunders, 1982). The affective perspective helps the men focus on pain, hurt, sadness, fear, and loneliness that often precede anger and may be mistaken for anger (Adams and McCormick, 1982). (1988:104)

Cognitive restructuring has become the most emphasized feature of these interventions (Bolton and Bolton, 1987:259–260).

Cognitive Restructuring

A variety of cognitive restructuring approaches have been initiated
1962; Meichenbaum, 1977; Beck, 1978). Those therapists who apply rational
emotive therapy believe that anger and aggression are the result of "irrational beliefs" (e.g., "I should never be frustrated or disappointed by my wife").
These clinicians believe that irrational beliefs and expectations lead to "irrational thoughts," which lead to "irrational actions." Many men who batter
women say to themselves (Bolton and Bolton, 1987:259): "I must have control"; "I cannot control my emotions"; "I feel out of control, and since it
could not be my fault, it must be her fault"; and "I am now so upset that I
can't help but hit her for upsetting me like this" (Edleson, 1984:238). Denying, blaming the victim, justifying the violence, and externalizing cognitions
or self-statements are anger-inducing activities and serve as antecedent cues
for battering behavior.

Albert Ellis (1976:309–313) suggests that counselors who use rational
emotive therapy with a couples therapy modality attempt to teach their clients the following procedures for dissipating anger:

1. Acknowledge your anger to yourself.
2. Assume full responsibility for making yourself angry. Do not blame
   your spouse for making you angry.
3. Accept yourself with your anger.
4. Stop making yourself anxious and depressed. Stop berating yourself for
   having these angry feelings.
5. Search for the nonverbalized expectations that you possess about your
   marriage, your mate, and how she should or must behave toward you.
6. Differentiate and discriminate your wishes concerning your spouse's
   behavior from your irrational commands and demands that she actually behave in accordance with your desires.
7. Dispute and debate your absolutistic demands about your spouse and
   her behavior until you are able to change the philosophic assumptions
   about how your spouse must behave toward you.
8. Employ behavioral and emotive means to dissipate, undermine, and
   eliminate your feelings of anger (e.g., act lovingly, rather than angrily,
   toward your spouse; be empathetic toward your spouse and attempt to
   understand her viewpoints and feelings; role-play or practice nonangry
   responses in situations that normally incite anger; administer self-re-
   wards when you respond in a nonangry manner toward your spouse;

use thought-stopping and relaxation to take yourself out of the anger-arousing situation).

Many researchers recommend that counselors do not use a verbally confrontive rational emotive approach with individuals whose perceived inability to verbally defend themselves is a major reason for their anger and their choice to use physical violence. These researchers also express great concern about the difficulties and contraindications of using this type of therapy within couples therapy. For example, Dennis Bagarozzi and C. Winter Giddings conclude:

> In our clinical practice, we have come across a number of marriages where inarticulate husbands who lacked resources valued by their verbally facile or more educated wives resorted to violence in their attempts to regain control of the relationship as well as to recapture their self-esteem which is damaged whenever a female is perceived to have gotten the upper hand. This was found to be true especially in the male-dominated rural cultures where violence often is an accepted way for men to settle interpersonal differences, resolve intrafamilial conflicts and maintain order. In such instances, the husband's use of force is sanctioned by the community and is reinforced by his male peer group who see such behavior as the husband's prerogative (Bagarozzi, 1982). In such cases, we found that questioning these husbands directly only served to heighten their anxiety and to engender additional defensiveness. This was especially true when the therapist was female, because the husband then found himself confronted with two women who possessed superior skills and verbal abilities. This condition only seemed to add to the husband's feelings of inferiority, powerlessness and low self-esteem. In order to prevent these men from prematurely and unilaterally terminating therapy, the therapist would attempt to form a positive, nonthreatening relationship with the husband by being warm, empathic, reflective and supportive and by not allowing the wife to be critical of him or to dominate the interviews verbally. Once the husband's trust had been secured and he no longer perceived the therapist to be coaligned with his spouse against him, a skills training approach to conflict management similar to the one suggested by Margolin (1979) was introduced. (1983:11–12)

Margolin's approach, like that of Bagarozzi and Giddings, is philosophically grounded in learning theory, research on social interaction, and behavioral therapy (Bagarozzi and Wodarski, 1977). In these approaches battering is presumed to have its genesis and maintenance in the following existential conditions and social-relational processes:

(a) continued exchanges between spouses which are perceived to be inequitable cause both spouses to become dissatisfied; (b) this dissatisfaction drives both spouses to reduce the felt inequity and to restore a more equitable balance of exchanges; (c) when the behavior change strategies employed by spouses are primarily coercive, a negatively escalating process of reciprocal coercion ensues; (d) communication breaks down, constructive problem solving decreases, and successful conflict management becomes less likely; and (e) the marriage becomes one in which a cycle of mutual avoidance, coercion, violence and conflict recur. This pattern may continue for years, especially if the abused spouse perceives the marriage to be a nonvoluntary relationship (Bagarozzi, 1983). (Bagarozzi and Giddings, 1983:9)

Within a couples therapy modality, Bagarozzi and Giddings recommend the following procedures for disrupting this escalating cycle of violence and creating different patterns of interaction:

1. Assess the marital interaction in order to identify those cues that contribute to angry exchanges and the escalation of conflict (e.g., the circumstances surrounding the anger, specific behaviors emitted by each spouse, reactions to those behaviors, and the manner in which the conflict was resolved). These data can be gathered through naturalistic observations, simulations and role plays of marital conflict, or through the use of a behavioral diary.
2. Establish ground rules that define physical aggression of any kind to be an unacceptable method for resolving marital disputes and differences. In order to enforce such ground rules, negative consequences for rule violation must be instituted (e.g., separation, divorce, legal action, etc.).
3. Develop a collaborative plan of action to interrupt the conflict pattern once it has been identified. This new behavior pattern should be devised and agreed upon by both spouses and should consist of the following two components: an immediate action plan to disengage from the conflict and an agreement to reunite after a specified period of time in order to resolve the problem.
4. Re-cue the victim so that he/she does not continue to emit specific behaviors that repeatedly provoke a violent response from his/her spouse.
5. Modify faulty cognitions, unrealistic expectations, and untested assumptions about relationship functioning which inhibit constructive problem-solving.
6. Teach spouses to develop functional communication skills, to increase pleasing interpersonal exchanges and to decrease the frequency of punishing and coercive interpersonal behavior change tactics. Formalize this change through the use of specifically outlined agreements. (1983:9)

In a different cognitive restructuring program, the batterer is asked to identify maladaptive thoughts and self-statements that occur prior to, during, and after the choice to batter. The therapist then helps him develop more appropriate thoughts and behaviors as well as mechanisms for self-reinforcement while thinking these more appropriate thoughts. The batterer then practices or rehearses these self-message processes (Bolton and Bolton, 1987:259). Jeanne Deschner (1984:69) indicates that changing the self-messages that operate in violent interactions should curtail not only the frequency but also the degree of rage and explosiveness. Based on the assumption that the batterer may have previously convinced himself that he could not control his feelings or his consequent behavior, this therapeutic strategy attempts to help him convince himself that he can contain his emotions, understand them, and control his behavior.

In yet another cognitive restructuring program, "stress inoculation" procedures are introduced to help the batterer better prepare for the situations in which he becomes violent. He is encouraged to mentally rehearse the contextual situation and find different self-talk. Assertiveness and relaxation skills are utilized to help him solve problems nonviolently. He keeps an anger log or journal, used to record the anger-provoking situation, the self-talk used, and the feelings aroused, which he reviews with the counselor. The anger log helps the batterer identify the irrational or false beliefs that he utilized to justify the actions he took in each specific conflict situation (Edleson, 1985:238; Bolton and Bolton, 1987:259).

Francis Purdy and Norm Nickle (1981) and Daniel Saunders (1984) provide illustrations of these intervention orientations within a group counseling modality for men who batter women. Purdy and Nickle view men who batter as victims of their own lack of communication skills, fears of intimacy, and dependencies. Purdy and Nickle perceive these attributes as developing from (and see these men as victimized by) a social order that trains men to be inattentive to their feelings, dependent on women, problem and action oriented as opposed to process oriented, and programmed to think quite rigidly (e.g., anything less than near perfect is failure). Purdy and Nickle present the following working assumptions for group counseling with men who batter:

> The abuser is solely responsible for his own violence and abuse. No matter how much stress there is in a relationship, the abuser is not provoked to use violence. He chooses violence as a means of coping with stress. The abused cannot cause or eliminate the abuser's violence. Once the abuser uses violence to cope

with stress, he will rarely stop using violence spontaneously. Violence is a behavior that is addictive and immediately effective, even if destructive in the long run.

Violence is learned behavior. It is learned by individuals through the culture. The dominant culture teaches that people who are in authority or are "right" can control or manipulate other people. For example: parents can "discipline" or hit a child for not thinking or behaving the "right" way; churches can dictate the "right" way to think and feel; schools can determine the "right" job for each person; advertising describes good behavior for each sex and race, etc. The more the family believes and practices the principles of this culture, the more likely the individual is to learn this behavior.

In counseling, the problems of the relationship cannot be the initial focus. It is too dangerous to discuss the problems of the family until all members are safe from being abused. Couple or family counseling with the abuser present should never happen until the violence has stopped and the abused is no longer afraid of the abuser. Any problems with communication cannot realistically be addressed while one is blatantly abusing power or force. To develop trust, equal communication, and the mutual support necessary for solving family problems, safety must first be achieved. Group counseling is much more effective than individual counseling. Groups lessen the shame, guilt, and isolation felt by each family member by demonstrating the commonalty of abuse. Because group members are at different stages in their efforts toward non-violent behaviors, individuals have more opportunity to teach and practice skills already learned or learn from positive role models.

Group leaders must be aware of their, his/her, own attitudes and experience with violence. The group leaders provide information and positive role models, and confront violent values and behaviors. The group leaders should be sensitive to the overt and subtle destructiveness of all violence. A male-female co-leader team appears to be the most effective method for modeling, teaching, and discussing non-violent communication skills and behaviors and the effects of socialization. (1981:112–113)

To these practitioners, group counseling involves first making certain that the survivor and the children are safe and have a detailed, practical plan of escape in case the batterer chooses to again become violent. Second, it involves breaking through the elaborate denial strategies that each man uses to relieve himself of the responsibility for his behavior and for changing himself. At this stage the batterer must learn that, even if he is not in control of others or the situation, he can always control his feelings and actions, and only he can do so. He needs to know what violence is, how he learned to be violent, and why he continues to use violence to control others (Purdy and

Nickle, 1981:115). Feelings of fear, hurt, insecurity, inadequacy, guilt, invisibility, and lack of control of a situation are common.

For men who have not been encouraged to identify and express these core feelings, anger is often the first and only feeling they express. To control anger, men are taught to establish a warning system (cues) to prevent the anger-aggression-battering cycle. They are taught to listen to their self-talk, to hear themselves beginning to convert their real feelings to anger and then their anger to aggression. They are taught positive self-talk to interpret and dissolve this transformation and escalation process. Relaxation strategies, self-care strategies, and means of unlearning abusive communication and sex-role myths are also helpful in breaking the battering cycle. Figure 8.1 shows the format Purdy and Nickle (1981:120) suggest for an anger-aggression log to help these men become aware of their interaction and expression patterns.

Saunders (1984) has described a similar program, Alternatives to Aggression (ATA), for helping men end their aggression toward their partners. ATA, a skills-oriented program with a group intervention modality, employs assertiveness training. This comprises learning skills, such as coping with criticism, assertively making requests and saying "no," empathizing with others, and expressing feelings as well as systematic desensitization, imagery, relaxation, and cognitive restructuring similar to that already described. The men in these groups also explore the social and personal roots of their battering, which sensitizes them to violence in general and male role prescriptions in particular.

These self-focused, context-specific, and concrete treatment programs address the issue of direct responsibility for the decision to batter. The use of contracts, theme discussions, and skills training gives the batterer techniques he can immediately practice to alter his behavior and control his anger. However, an exclusive or even a pivotal focus on anger control has serious contraindicative effects. Programs that perceive the batterer as unable to adequately communicate his needs and/or understand and express his feelings must be sensitive to timing and to coordinating skills development with the termination-of-violence process. Whereas the specific programs just presented appear sensitive to this concern, others do not. Consequently, therapists must be alert to the appropriateness and timing of skills training (Hamberger and Hastings, 1988b).

The seriousness of this issue is pointed out by Barbara Hart in her discussion of battering interventions with women who batter their partners in lesbian relationships:

Description of the situation when I became angry	Negative self-talk	Recalling the situation, I am aware of these feelings	Myths that I am aware of that support my converting feelings	Positive self-talk
				(This becomes material for the 3″ × 5″ cards.)[a]

FIGURE 8.1   Anger-Aggression Log

[a]To help examine the myths he has incorporated into his everyday thinking, the batterer fills out a 3″ × 5″ card for each anger situation. The set of cards helps him recognize the nature of the situations to which he responds with anger and the patterns of self-talk, feelings, and myths that lead to violence. Once these patterns are recognized, alternative self-talk and responses to these situations can be developed.

Source: Purdy and Nickle (1981:120). Copyright © 1981 by The Haworth Press. Reprinted by permission of The Haworth Press, Inc., 10 Alice St., Binghamton, NY 13904.

Battered lesbians report that batterers often appear to be looking for something about which to become angry to provide rationalization for battering. They also find that the batterer many times becomes angry only after she assaults to control and assault does not produce the desired compliance.

Whether anger is present or not, it does not eliminate the batterer's capacity to choose violence as a tactic of control. That choice is fully hers.

Battered lesbians are often told by partners who have sought help from therapists not informed about battering that she batters because she is not able adequately to communicate her needs and feelings and is unable to express herself adequately. She somehow short circuits and becomes violent, with violence being a reflection of frustration, not a tactic of control.

Underlying this claim is a misconception that better communication would produce a better understanding of needs and feelings which would, in turn, result in the partner working harder to accommodate the batterer and violence being thereby thwarted. This assumes that the batterer is a person whose needs are not well understood and that the battered lesbian has a responsibility to go the additional distance to respond positively to the batterer's needs.

Both assumptions are often false. Many batterers are excellent communicators. Batterers who have worked in therapy to increase their communication skills, without first achieving the termination of violence or threats of violence, become more skillful, sophisticated controllers of their partners—better terrorists. (1986:24)

Couples Therapy

Serious reflection must be given to the selection of a couples therapy modality, regardless of the substantive orientation of the intervention program. The couples therapy modality has come under attack for many reasons (Margolin, Sibner, and Gleberman, 1988:104–106; Sedlak, 1988a; Bograd, 1984; Edleson, 1985:487; Neidig, 1984; Pence et al., 1984). Many practitioners and critics consider it antiwomen and supportive of patriarchy (Walker, 1979; Martin, 1981; Straus, 1977). When the survivor receives no information about alternative programs for the batterer or herself, couples therapy may reinforce a no-options cultural support for patriarchy.

Couples therapy has also been called inappropriate and dangerous. Fearing reprisal, a survivor may be reluctant to report the full extent of her abuse, fear, terror, and desire to leave the relationship. Couples therapy requires a trust and an openness that a battered woman cannot and should not engage in as this may endanger her safety (Sedlak, 1988a). For many, the structure of couples therapy implies that the survivor is co-responsible for the violence, which allows the batterer to deny his full responsibility for the choice to batter (Bograd, 1984).

In spite of these objections, many practitioners support couples therapy or family counseling under certain conditions (Taylor, 1984). According to Jeffrey Edleson (1985:485), couples therapy may be helpful when it is chosen by both partners and when the safety of the survivor has been assured. Such an assurance is commonly held to exist when the batterer has ceased to use violence and threats of it.

If, however, the batterer has not completed a program to end his violence, couples therapy may be counterproductive. For this reason most therapists recommend that the batterer enter and complete a program specifically designed for men who batter before couples therapy is considered for addressing relational and conflict resolution issues (Edleson, 1985:485; Pence, 1985; Margolin, Sibner, and Gleberman, 1988:105). Alan Rosenbaum and Daniel O'Leary (1986) suggest that the clinician conduct an extensive evaluation to determine if couples therapy is an appropriate modality for a specific couple. Minimally, the following questions must be explored: Is the victim safe? Is the victim fully aware of alternative programs and services for both herself and the batterer? Is the remediation of the relationship a viable and realistic goal? Does the batterer accept that he alone is responsible for his battering behavior?

Once such a determination indicates the viability of couples therapy, Margolin, Sibner, and Gleberman suggest the following approach:

The first step in couples therapy is to establish the ground rule that abusiveness is unacceptable under any circumstances. Further, to give this meaning, there must be consequences that, once established, will be carried through (Margolin, 1979). On the husband's part, this means accepting the notion that he is responsible for his behavior, regardless of any provocation he receives, and that at any moment, he controls the choice not to be violent. On the wife's part, this means that she has made a commitment to herself to no longer tolerate violence and that she has worked out the details to know that, if need be, she can leave her husband and/or use legal channels. ...

As with the treatments for the batterer alone, the primary objective in conjoint therapy is to stop the abuse. Here, however, the goals might be stated somewhat more broadly to include all types of abuse and to improve conflict strategies in general.

Further, the unique factor that couples therapy can contribute to these goals is the opportunity to identify and change repeating interactional cycles associated with abuse. Both partners can help to identify cues in themselves and one another that violence on the part of the husband may be forthcoming. That is, the husband can learn to monitor the emotions and anger-arousing cognitions that accompany his abuse. He can also learn to identify behaviors exhibited by the wife that trigger his anger, and experiment with alternative responses to those cues. Similarly, the wife can learn to monitor subtle nonverbal and cognitive cues in herself and her partner that signal the escalation of conflict. If caught early enough, these cues can be used to trigger coping responses (e.g., rapid departure from the situation) rather than terrorized, self-blaming, or combative reactions. Once these patterns are identified, their disruption may require learning to take temporary time-outs from the relationship, self-talk to guide oneself through a coping response or to combat an irrational cognition, and using muscle relaxation or imagery techniques to reduce overall arousal (Bedrosian, 1982; Deschner, 1984).

Although disrupting anger and violence-producing interactions is the initial focus, conjoint therapists contend that by lessening the overall number of conflict areas and by improving the overall tone of the relationship, there will be less cause for conflict and violence. Strategies typically employed to accomplish these goals involve behavioral skills, such as training in problem-solving techniques, receptive listening, and assertion training to express relationship desires as well as to accept refusals from the partner (Deschner, 1984). These also involve strategies to enhance intimacy, to bolster diffuse spouse subsystem boundaries (e.g., scheduling one-to-one enjoyable time, building a shared support system) (Bedrosian, 1982). (1988:105–106)

Anger Control Therapy

The couples therapy modality and programs that focus extensively or solely on communication skills are not the only interventions to come under critical scrutiny. The earlier review of intervention programs exclusively for men reveals that most utilize a group discussion modality and incorporate a varying emphasis on stress reduction, communication skills and emotive development, anger control management, and sex-role resocialization (Gondolf and Hanneken, 1987; Edleson, 1984; Saunders, 1984; Purdy and Nickle, 1981; Dutton and McGregor, 1991). A significant number of these programs focus centrally on anger control (Deschner, 1984; Sonkin, Martin, and Walker, 1985; Neidig, Friedman, and Collins, 1985), even though this approach may be not only inappropriate for many batterers but also counterproductive to the cessation of battering (Gondolf and Russell, 1986:2; Tolman and Saunders, 1988).

Anger control intervention may not be appropriate because battering is not necessarily anger driven or anger "out of control" (Schechter, 1982; Gondolf and Hanneken, 1987). The core issue for many men who batter is more centrally the partner—one tactic of a socially accepted and practiced "need" to control women (Gondolf and Russell, 1986:3). From most accounts, battering women is a pattern of direct and indirect controlling and degrading behaviors (Pence, 1985, 1989; Edleson, Eisikovits, and Guttman, 1985). It is not merely a series of impulsive, angry incidents but is often a premeditated system of deconstructing control. When a batterer stops his physical violence, his battering may not end. In fact, his psychological battering and isolating behavior may escalate and be as emotionally devastating as was the physical battering. Gondolf and Russell report in their program evaluation research that

the less successful men more frequently cited anger control techniques as their means of reducing [battering], even though anger control was a very small part of the program. The more successful men, however, were more likely to cite empathy, a redefinition of their manhood, and more cooperative decision-making as the means of ending their [battering]. ... [Those men] who had been nonviolent for at least 10 months revealed a process of change that went well beyond the scope of anger control. ... The less successful [men often avoided] the change process by reverting to anger control techniques. Most of their wives and partners, in fact, reported that while in some cases the physical [battering] was lessening, the psychological [battering] intensified. (1986:3)

Furthermore, intervention programs that centrally focus on anger control may prolong the batterer's denial of responsibility for the battering (Gondolf, 1988b). While such denial is particularly acute (Bernard and Bernard, 1984), many use anger as an excuse or rationalization for their behavior (Ptacek, 1988a), much as they blame alcohol, stress, or their partner. Interventions that focus primarily on controlling anger or only superficially on extinguishing physical battering may thus enable these men to evade responsibility for their behavior and for self-change. According to Gondolf and Russell (1986:3), an anger control focus may feed a batterer's feelings of self-pity and self-deception, allowing him to dwell on his own emotional discomfort rather than on the severe pain he has inflicted on others. Even the mechanics of anger control intervention may lead some batterers to blame the victim and deny responsibility. For example, one anger control technique requires a batterer to identify a hierarchy of victim provocations, behaviors, and attitudes. This may allow him to see his partner as responsible for his decision to batter and to conclude that she needs to alter her behavior.

Anger control programs may also reinforce batterers' willfulness in ignoring their deeper feelings and understanding their behavior and its effects (Gondolf, 1987, 1987b). A program's sanctioning of anger control may lead some batterers to believe that the way to stop battering is to simply extend control to one more aspect of their lives—their emotions—even though they need to "let go" of much of their control (Gondolf and Russell, 1986:3).

Typically batterers enter treatment thinking about power vis-à-vis their partners in an adversarial fashion: Her gain is his loss, and vice versa. Programs must encourage these men to think about power in a different way— to recognize that violence used to maintain power imbalance is unhealthy and unproductive for everyone (Dutton and McGregor, 1991:139). Programs must also help these men see power in interdependent terms: Through battering, each man loses a *vital* partner; by accepting a partner's empowerment, he actually "gains." To accomplish this point-of-view shift, programs can make salient the personal losses the batterer sustains as a result of his violence (e.g., her emotional and sexual withdrawal, mistrust, and chronic anger toward him).

Batterers can also misinterpret anger control techniques as a quick fix. If so, these techniques can prevent more fundamental personal growth and subsequently endanger battered partners (Tolman and Saunders, 1988:18). According to Gondolf and Russell, many men approach anger control as

> an expedient way to profess being cured and lure their wives back. The vast majority of men who join batterer programs do so in response to their wives' leaving them, threatening to leave, or taking legal action. The men then tend to use the program the same way they use their violence—to manipulate and control their wives. After learning a few anger control techniques, many batterers will claim that they have the problem "under control" and lure their wives into returning.
>
> Also, batterers, especially in anger control treatment programs, enter a self-congratulatory phase in which they feel that they are really on top of things and deserve praise. Their wives or lovers, however, are hardly ready to reward them for the humane treatment which they inherently deserve, or to be trustful of men who have unpredictably abused them over a long period of time. A woman's failure to be as congratulatory as the man expects may lead to further abuse. (1986:3–4)

An anger control focus may cut short processes that lead to a cessation of battering (Jennings, 1987). A report that physical battering has ceased provides little information about whether the environment of terror has lessened. As mentioned earlier, batterers may replace physical abuse with the increased use of other controlling tactics (Pence, 1989:33). Just as important, social arrangements that are structurally violent may be left intact. Serious questions must be raised about whether these programs should use the ending of physical battering as a criterion of success (Hart, 1988; Pence, 1989). Richard Tolman and Daniel Saunders (1988) further note that anger control techniques may be most appropriate as part of an anger regulation strategy. Out of context, men who batter can misuse anger control techniques to objectify women, find force and violence acceptable, and claim a socially accepted entitlement to continue exercising control over their partners. The cessation of battering in all its forms requires change in the social organization of the family in accord with the arrangements suggested in Figure 1.1.

Anger control techniques may also be misused by those who see these intervention programs as an acceptable "quick-fix" solution to a deeply embedded social problem. Pathologizing, psychologizing, and batterer-blaming interventions deny any collective responsibility for battering or for the acceptance of domination, control, and violence.

Alternative Interventions

Numerous alternative intervention programs have been created to avoid the shortcomings of anger control while helping batterers end their violence. Gondolf and Russell describe two of these programs:

> One alternative is a "resocialization" program, such as *Raven* of St. Louis, in which anger control is subordinate to changing sex-role stereotypes that contribute to men's tendency to control women (Gondolf, 1985a). The second alternative is a theme-centered discussion program on battering that does not include anger control techniques, such as *Second Step* in Pittsburgh (Russell, 1984). Our clinical observations and informal follow-ups lead us to believe that the effectiveness of such alternatives equals that of anger control programs, if it does not surpass them (Gondolf, 1985). At least the demonstrated results of such alternatives warrant further consideration.
>
> In the first alternative, a *resocialization* program, anger is identified as another means men use to get their way. The so-called provocations of anger are seen as the batterer's own distortions derived from his sex-role expectations and objectifications of women. For instance, the batterer's tendency to label arousal as anger is related to the male sex-role stereotype that would have men suppress feelings. The inclination to act out anger in aggressive and violent behavior is reinforced by a patriarchal social structure that rewards coercive power and brute force. In this approach, the anger becomes secondary rather than primary. It is just one more kind of control based on a false sense of manhood.
>
> The thrust of this approach is to prompt men to undo sex-roles and take social action. This can be accomplished through such activities as hearing speakers from local shelters, viewing films on male sex-roles, participating in sexist language exercises, making macro-analysis diagrams, charting household duties and decision-making, and keeping logs of controlling behaviors. Social action can be promoted through a variety of activities: requiring service to the program, supporting community action organizations, speaking in public about the problem of wife abuse, organizing a follow-up men's group, and staffing a men's center.
>
> The second alternative, the *theme-centered approach*, explores unresolved masculine issues and projects positive images of personal growth, nurturance, intimacy, and nonviolence through discussion of the commonalities of abusive men. Each meeting begins with the group leaders stating a prescribed theme. These themes are worded as positive projections of some unresolved issue

around violence or abuse. Some of the themes are: "Shouldering My Responsibility," "Shifting the Focus of My Control," "Forming Friendships," "Balancing the Needs for Closeness and Distance," and "The Challenge of Change." The batterers reflect in silence on how the theme pertains to them, what they would like to contribute to the group with regard to the theme, and what they would like to receive from the group.

A discussion of the theme then develops following the group leader's example and the group guidelines, which include speaking for oneself, addressing conflicts among group members, and limiting generalizations. The group leaders also promote a balanced discussion of personal experiences, the group process, and the task of stopping abuse. These group dynamics appear to move the men toward long-term change more directly than anger control techniques do. In a sense, they remove the crutch of anger control and more squarely face the issues underlying wife abuse. *Second Step* also requires a responsibility plan to be used in lieu of the anger control "time-outs" common to most batterer programs. In the responsibility plan, each batterer outlines steps to build a safer environment for his family and acquaintances. Each man develops his plan drawing on other group members' advice and his wife's assessment (if she is willing to offer it).

This sort of planning process moves beyond the more mechanical "time out" technique in which the batterer signals his mate that he is approaching the point of becoming violent and leaves the premises for a designated period of time. While "time outs" may provide some measure of safety for the abused woman, the initiative remains with the batterer. A responsibility plan might assure a woman access to shelter services in such a situation or specify that a friend or relative spend the night in the house. Furthermore, some battered women see "time outs" as one more ploy to "shut them up." The man leaves as soon as she begins to speak out or challenge him, and often with no assurance when and in what condition he will return. (1986:4–5)

Jerry Jennings (1987) offers a persuasive argument on the advantages of unstructured, closely supervised, supportive self-help groups rather than structured cognitive/behavioral or anger control programs. In the former groups, men gradually develop new skills (e.g., anger management, emotive development, and self-reflection skills) but do so through a process of active, self-directed, spontaneous participation rather than through passive-receptive introduction. They refine these skills in a context that reinforces, rather than counters, their capacity for self-direction and insight.

Within these groups, men benefit from listening and observing how others solve problems. With mutual peer support, they can develop tolerance for other points of view and learn how to negotiate, apologize, and accommodate. The open exchange of feelings and experiences allows these men to cultivate empathy, obtain assistance and understanding, share themselves, and discuss their problems. Most important, the group counteracts these men's social isolation and their dependence on their partners. It allows them to create new dimensions of maleness or personhood. The unstructured support group is ideal for the active practice of self-help skills, which is crucial if these men are going to transfer these new attitudes and social skills to the home environment (Gondolf, 1987a, 1987b; Gondolf and Hanneken, 1987; Jennings, 1987:208).

Psychologizing Battering

Anger control interventions and, to some extent, even alternative approaches may wind up allowing people in the community to think that the battering of women is being addressed. Rather than confronting the economic, cultural, social structural, and political factors that perpetuate the problem, these interventions may serve to frame it as an issue of psychologically deficient men who cannot control their anger or who need to be resocialized or taught different skills. Interpersonal intervention programs organized to change the batterer allow the rest of us to escape the need to confront ourselves, the cultural underpinnings that perpetuate the domination of women, and the social conditions within which men choose to batter women. Psychologizing the problem fails to foster equality and to provide adequate "rescue and protection" services for women.[1] Anger control and other interventions that do not address the cultural and social structural dimensions of violence against women ignore the facts that (1) battering has been a historical practice linking marriage and property laws throughout the course of Western "civilization" (Pence et al., 1984:477); (2) in this century in the United States, wife battering was a legitimate way for a husband to assert his legal and presumed moral authority over his wife; (3) battering is a social problem; (4) before its recent redefinition as an individual pathology, battering was considered as part of a systematic use of violence against women to maintain male privilege and status; and (5) psychologizing a social problem is, in part, a political maneuver to maintain these specific social and cultural structures, to solidify their perceived naturalness and universality, and to leave them unquestioned and unaltered, even if this results in a steady stream of men who batter women and women who are battered.

9

Community-coordinated Interventions and Change in the Criminal Justice System

I turn now to an assessment of the more comprehensive, community-coordinated interventions that have been developed in Minnesota, Colorado, California, Wisconsin, and Washington.[1] Initiated by the battered women's movement, these programs have the long-range goal of eliminating violence against women.

Their primary strategy is to establish and maintain shelters and programs of empowerment for women and children and act as advocates for these women. Tactically, these interventions include (1) "rescuing" women from environments of terror and physical violence and offering them a separate and safe place for self-definition and life-direction choices (Pence et al., 1984:479); (2) asserting the rights of individual women; and (3) promoting legislative, social service, and criminal justice policy changes that might better address the needs of battered women.

A correlative strategy holds men accountable for their use of violence by pressuring decision-makers in the legal system to respond to the battering of women as crimes rather than as domestic conflicts. In these ways, community-coordinated intervention programs have acted to systematically alter the official public response toward battering (Edleson, 1991:206) and counteract legal support of battering (Pence, 1989; Pence and Shepard, 1988).

The place of therapy or counseling programs for men who batter women is a subject of ongoing debate within the battered women's movement and community-coordinated intervention programs. Those who believe in the necessity of these programs support intervention modalities and programs only if (1) women's safety is the primary concern, (2) batterers are held solely responsible for their use of physical violence and other battering tactics, and (3) intervention focuses primarily on ending batterers' violence and does not protect them from legal sanctions for their crimes (Pence et al., 1984:480).

The Duluth Domestic Abuse Intervention Project

Activating the full force of the criminal justice system to respond to the battering of women is central to many community-coordinated programs. Experience in Duluth, Minnesota, has shown that law enforcement and criminal justice system intervention can undermine some of the cultural supports for physical battering.[2] By changing the traditional legal response to battering and developing policies and procedures that impede the facilitators of battering, the Duluth program helps survivors procure better protection from continued acts of violence and enables the community to begin developing a more general strategy for decreasing all forms of violent behavior. According to Ellen Pence:

> The decision by a community to enforce assault laws and civil protection orders in domestic abuse cases has extensive impact on the law enforcement and criminal justice systems of that community. Effective intervention requires two fundamental changes in current police and court practices. First, without imposing sanctions or actions on victims, the system must whenever possible shift the onus of imposing sanctions on assailants from the victim to the community. Second, a consistent response to assailants must be secured through coordination and interagency policy development. The actions and messages of the police, prosecutors, sentencing judges, probation officers, and mental health providers should individually and collectively impress upon the assailant the knowledge that his continued use of violence will result in increasingly harsh penalties. (1989:8)

Limiting the survivor's responsibility for evoking and imposing legal sanctions on the batterer decreases the batterer's ability to manipulate decision-makers and avoid the legal consequences of his violence. Specific practices that facilitate this policy concept include increasing the use of police-initiated probable cause arrests, not requiring the survivor to sign a complaint, mandating educational programs for assailants that focus on the use of coercive and violent behaviors rather than couples therapy or marriage counseling, and following up on police calls to provide identified survivors with safe housing and legal advocacy (Pence, 1989:10). The Duluth Domestic Abuse Intervention Project (DAIP) attempts to coordinate the criminal justice and other agencies to end battering by (Pence, 1989:21)

1. Protecting the victim by bringing the assailant into the criminal justice system, thereby reducing the "screening out" of cases
2. Protecting the victim by imposing and enforcing legal sanctions that will deter further acts of violence
3. Protecting the victim by providing safe housing, education, and legal advocacy
4. Protecting the victim by coordinating interagency information flow and monitoring procedures and policies

Bringing In the Assailant

Pence asserts that the DAIP's experience shows that specific policy and procedural changes in the criminal justice system can increase the likelihood of successful prosecution and increase the number of assailants coming into the court system:

> Arrest on probable cause, advocacy follow-up on nonarrest police calls, cooperation between prosecution and victim advocates, a strong educational support system for victims during the court process, and immediate court intervention to protect the victim from continued acts of violence are all steps the criminal justice system can take to reduce case attrition and increase the probability of legal sanctions being imposed on assailants. (1989:26)

Imposing Legal Sanctions

Formulated to reinforce the message that battering is unacceptable and will be sanctioned, the DAIP has helped create appropriate court sanctions and assessments for men who batter. As part of the legal sanction response, counseling and education classes are frequently mandated. Education classes and counseling groups offer the potential for increasing the safety of survivors and the opportunity for batterers to change their behavior and their adherence to attitudes that support battering.

Court-mandated education classes and group counseling programs are, however, recognized as individual responses to a social problem. They are also viewed as a potential drain on the scarce resources of the community, as the battering problem in many communities is of great magnitude (Pence, 1989:42). Consequently, the DAIP has attempted to confine costs by using existing agencies and low-cost education. To keep the focus on batterers' change and on their need to stop their controlling behavior, survivors are encouraged to report and monitor acts and threats of battering and to attend a women's educational group program (Pence, 1987). Batterers are first screened for program appropriateness and then court-mandated to attend two DAIP-conducted orientation sessions. They are then assigned either to twelve to sixteen weeks in a counseling group followed by eight to twelve weeks in an educational program or twenty-four weeks in an educational program. Pence (1989:26–44) has succinctly described these educational and counseling programs.

The DAIP Educational Program

The DAIP educational program assumes that the belief system underlying battering behavior is learned in our culture and, for many, in their families of origin. Even though much of the literature on battering has examined the personality attributes of batterers, it is far more important for the safety of survivors, for decision-makers in the criminal justice process, and for the "empowerment" of batterers to understand their patterns of abuse. The DAIP program is a departure from many of the previously discussed interventions because it challenges batterers' perceptions that they have the right to control their partners.

Educational classes center on the eight themes shown in Figure 1.2. Alternatives to these behaviors and tactics are presented with the intent of establishing egalitarian, nonviolent arrangements and relationships (Figure 1.1). Class sessions help these men recognize that their acts of battering are intentional (not uncontrolled responses to stress or anger) and have evolved into a whole system of interrelated behaviors directed at their partners to achieve and maintain power. Focusing on control and power continually sharpens and raises the issue of batterer responsibility.

The educational curriculum is also designed to provide participants with information and practical tools to facilitate a change in their attitudes and use of physical violence and other controlling behaviors. Specifically, the program is organized to assist them to (Pence, 1989:40–41)

1. Identify goals to reach a nonviolent lifestyle
2. Identify what behaviors constitute battering and what each participant's pattern of battering has been
3. Explore the intents of battering behaviors and the belief system that supports them

4. Understand the connection between painful feelings and beliefs about men's and women's roles
5. Identify the function and extent of member's minimizing, denying, or blaming
6. Explore fully the impact of physical, psychological, and spiritual battering on partners, children, and group members
7. Learn new behaviors by using role-plays to practice time-outs, positive self-talk, negotiation with partners, letting go of the need to win/control, and honest communication

The DAIP Counseling Program

In counseling groups, the use of weekly logs helps participants explore their reactions to situations in which they used violence or believed that their anger was out of control. Expected to be responsible for keeping their anger level to a point where violence will not occur, they are taught how to use time-outs and positive self-talk, how to talk their anger down, and how to express their underlying feelings. Finally, they are encouraged to give up the need to control that is often at the root of their anger.

The following objectives are common to the counseling groups:

1. Increase his responsibility for his battering behavior
2. Develop alternatives to battering (time-outs, empathy, problem solving, tension-reducing exercises, etc.)
3. Increase control of anger
4. Decrease isolation and develop personal support systems
5. Decrease dependency on the relationship
6. Increase his understanding of the family and social facilitators of wife battering
7. Increase identification and expression of all feelings

Advocating for Safety

Shelters provide a supportive, safe environment and the time and information women need to make choices about their situations. These shelters also provide a wide range of advocacy services, including legal advocacy for women both in and out of the shelter (Pence, 1989:44–48). Advocates teach women how to use the courts, gather evidence needed for trials, and work with prosecutors. Moreover, advocates organize groups for women whose partners are currently in court-mandated men's groups. They explain the men's educational and counseling curriculum and help survivors evaluate their options. Advocates also organize neighborhood-based informational classes and educational groups.

Stressing the importance of consistently holding batterers accountable for their actions, these educational groups focus on helping women understand the many different forms of battering. As women begin to name and explore the violent ways they have been controlled and the impact those controls have had on them, their relationships, and their children, batterers are less able to use their partners as shields from the courts (Pence, 1989:47; see Pence, 1987, for a description of this program). Self-help peer groups enable survivors to counter the effects of battering and to empower themselves, and women's action groups provide them with an opportunity to work on social issues that either directly or indirectly contribute to violence against women.

Coordinating Policy

The DAIP coordinates information and monitors each participating agency's compliance with the agreed-on policies and procedures. As batterers frequently deny responsibility for their behavior, minimize the violence they commit, intend to maintain control over their partners, and blame their victims for the violence, it is necessary from the moment of arrest or the service of a protection order that batterers receive a consistent message that regardless of their circumstances, they cannot batter their partners and that a tightly coordinated information exchange system has been instituted among persons in the criminal justice system to stop this violence (Pence, 1989:49).

Changes in the Criminal Justice Process

With the exception of community-based empowerment education programs, community advocate programs for women associated with shelters, and women's social action groups, the major focus of community-coordinated interventions has been on changing the official criminal justice response. The experience in Duluth and elsewhere has demonstrated that changing official policies and procedures can weaken this formerly significant societal reinforcement for the acceptance of battering. Such changes can support and provide safety for survivors and make it easier for women to work toward transforming the culture that violates "every part of their being and spirit" (Pence and Shepard, 1988:296). An altered official response can also encourage other members of the community to counter the core cultural and social structural supports for battering and help "create a more sane society" (Pence and Shepard, 1988:296). Disappointingly, many communities have not begun to adopt the excellent, ground-breaking changes developed in Duluth.

However, as a result of increased media attention on violence against women and the publication of key recommendations (the report of the Attorney General's Task Force on Family Violence [1984] and Goolkasian's *Confronting Domestic Violence* [1986]), decision-makers within the criminal justice system have started to show a clearer social responsibility for taking action against domestic violence (e.g., assault, battery, weapon use, kidnapping, unlawful imprisonment). Legislation in many states and policy development in many communities have forced police agencies to define guidelines for arrest practices (e.g., allowing warrantless arrests, shifting responsibility away from the victim in criminal proceedings). Legislation and policy have also

1. Mandated data collection and reporting
2. Required domestic violence training programs
3. Provided victim assistance and protection (e.g., pretrial release restrictions)
4. Authorized the use of civil protection orders
5. Issued flexible sentencing guidelines—for both first and repeat offenders—intended to give the messages that this violence will not be tolerated, that offenders will be held accountable for their violence, and that the needs of survivors and other family members will be met (Goolkasian, 1986a:2–5)

As in the Duluth program, police participation in many community intervention programs involves making probable cause arrests whenever possible. In some programs, at the time of arrest the police notify local support or advocate groups (e.g., battered women's shelter programs, batterer's counseling programs, victim-witness support programs), which contact the survivor (and/or batterer) to provide support, discuss alternatives, and make resources available. Some support or advocate programs follow up all calls to police involving domestic violence, regardless of whether an arrest was made.

Domestic violence is now much more frequently defined as criminal activity; men who batter their partners are much more likely to be arrested. At least ten states have passed "mandatory" arrest legislation (Law Enforcement Training Project, 1989). A survey of urban police departments serving cities with populations of one hundred thousand or more indicates that in June 1986, 46 percent preferred to arrest the batterer in cases of minor domestic assault. This percentage had risen from 10 percent in 1984 and 31 percent in 1985. In addition, there has been a decrease in the percentage of these police departments that do not provide policy guidelines on how to handle domestic violence (1984–1985, 50 percent; 1986, 35 percent) (Cohn, 1987:22).

Research supporting the practice of "arrest preference" police policy came from the Minneapolis Experiment (Sherman and Berk, 1985). Minneapolis police responded to misdemeanor domestic assaults with one of three randomly assigned interventions: arrest and overnight incarceration of the batterer, separation of the persons by ordering the batterer to leave the premises for eight hours, and advice that occasionally involved informal mediation. Initially both official police records and victim reports indicated that arrest and overnight incarceration were associated with fewer subsequent reported incidents of battering. Further analysis indicates, however, that there was a rapid decay in this association and that there were no real differences across the three interventions at the end of a six-month follow-up period. Andrea Sedlak (1988a:347) has suggested the following interpretation: Police actions at the time of a violent incident may be effective in interrupting a pattern of battering, but without additional intervention, violence quickly returns to its usual pattern within the relationship. This interpretation implies that community-coordinated intervention programs that systematically coordinate police, judicial, social service, educational, and preventive responses at the community level may have a greater long-term impact on both the prevalence and incidence of battering in the community (Steinman, 1988; Steinman, ed., 1991; Hirschel and Hutchinson, 1991; Ferguson, 1987; Goolkasian, 1986; Pence, 1983; Burris and Jaffe, 1983; Dutton, 1988b; Edleson and Syers, 1990).

Attempts to take the spirit of community-coordinated program developments beyond the criminal justice system have begun, but they are, unfortunately, few and limited. Moreover, arrest preference policy is not the practice of the majority of police departments. As a result, many men who batter experience few official, negative consequences for their violence, and many survivors come to the chilling conclusion that violence against them is not taken seriously and that there is little reason to report battering to the police.

These messages are infrequently contradicted by the decision-makers who follow the police in the criminal justice process (Sedlak, 1988a:345).

The Limits of Criminalization

Community-coordinated interventions embody exceptional vision in their programs for the empowerment of women and the reorientation of men. These programs rest on the supposition that battering is only one set of tactics men employ to control women. Such interventions address essential cultural and social structural supports for battering within interpersonal, family, and symbolic societal contexts (Gondolf, 1985, 1987b, 1988; Edleson and Syers, 1990). The best programmatic attempts to change the interpersonal context of battering focus on gender conceptions, sex-role expectations, conceptions of manhood and self that support battering, power relations, and "family" social organization change.

However, when the acceptance of violence, domination, hierarchy, and control is not vociferously countered in interpersonal level programs, some batterers receive support for merely controlling their emotions, anger, and/ or physically violent behavior and begin to control their partners through more "officially acceptable" tactics (e.g., withholding of finances, verbal manipulation, diminishing of their partners' role and participation in decision-making) (Gondolf, 1985:317). Worse, some become more self-assured and positive about themselves when they choose to batter.

To decrease battering, the legitimacy of controlling others and using violence must be addressed beyond the intrapersonal, interpersonal, and symbolic levels. Battering is about control and the exercise of power. Yet to control and to exercise power are highly valued, deeply embodied activities in our society. Our culture sanctions controlling nature, resources, employees, women, children, and emotions. To control—that is, to dominate and assert superiority—is central to most men's sense of manhood.

In this milieu, it is no wonder that the women's movement and the women's shelter movement have championed attempts to change power arrangements and to increase the degrees of freedom available to women to choose their own life directions. If women are to be taken seriously, violence against women must be taken seriously.

In this light, many people have supported the view that men who batter women in the home, like those who assault and batter persons on the street, should face legal arrest, prosecution, and incarceration or court-ordered intervention (Armstrong, 1983). Criminalization may indeed symbolize that violence against women is as serious as violence against men and may undercut an acceptance of this violence. But by itself, the criminalization of battering is not likely to decrease violence against women (regardless of the intrapersonal or interpersonal intervention strategies ordered, and regardless of criminalization's potential to form a foundation from which other more necessary and fundamental violence-addressing changes may occur). Criminalizing other behaviors without changing core societal supports has failed to decrease their rates. Even the perception, existence, and imposition of harsh punishments for homicide have not diminished (and, in the instance of execution, have contributed to) homicide rates. Beyond criminalization, we do not know what effects various community-coordinated interventions will have on the prevalence and incidence of battering in different communities (Hirschel and Hutchinson, 1991; Steinman, ed., 1991). In communities where the focus is confined solely to altering the legal response to battering, we should expect little, if any sustained impact on the prevalence and incidence of battering.

Criminalization, blaming the batterer, blaming the survivor, and blaming the relationship are approaches that many people find attractive alternatives to a serious attempt to change the economic, political, gender, and social-organizational conditions that perpetuate battering. Criminalizing the batterer does not change the social-organizational or cultural context within which battering takes place. Like any of the treatments of individual men, criminalization is not *sufficient* to change the problem of violence against women (Tolman and Saunders, 1988:18). It is an approach we must transcend.

Negating Power and Control

Criminalization of battering that is not supplemented by programs that directly pursue full equality for women is guilty of the same failings as after-the-fact, non-context-addressing, individualistic, pathologizing, structure-neglecting approaches. Whereas the couples therapy modality is objectionable because it may lead to victim blaming and cannot assure the end of battering, and anger control interventions are inadequate because they do not address the power/control issue, criminalization ultimately just replaces individual control with state control. If the logic of criminalization reinforces the acceptability of control and the exercise of power, then the logic of an approach to ending violence against women must negate power exercise. We must negate the entropic logic of escalated power exercise: Men exercise power over women; therefore, more powerful men must exercise power and control over these men to end the exercise of power. If, however, we accept an approach that negates power, the issue is, How do we move beyond the intrapersonal, interpersonal, and symbolic social control responses to battering to develop a proactive, before-the-battering approach? How do we transcend current interventions and change the core cultural and social structural supports for battering? How do we change these societal supports so that the prevalence and incidence of battering and power exercise are diminished? How do we organize a society wherein people develop strong self-esteem, confidence, and competence as well as a sense of autonomy and personhood that is not designed to diminish, objectify, or control other persons?

An approach to battering such as this would address the core contexts within which decisions to batter are imposed. Such a response implies fundamental change in our cultural and social arrangements; it implies a fundamentally egalitarian, nonhierarchical, participatory social life resiliently responsive to continuous change and both individual and collective empowerment. This orientation would envelop us in an energetic and creative, individual and collective effort to construct a multitude of environments that would foster the development of our full individual and collective potential.

10

Developing Our Full Individual and Collective Potential

To construct environments that might better foster our full individual and collective development, we must know what social structural and social psychological conditions directly nourish what Carl Rogers calls "the growth tendency"—our natural tendency toward becoming human. According to Rogers (Welch and Tate, 1985:20), our deepest human characteristics lead us toward development, differentiation, independence, and cooperation. Our impulses tend to harmonize into a complex and changing pattern of self-regulation. Our core essence is predisposed to preserve and enhance self and species and perhaps move toward further evolution.

Research by Rogers and others (Brammer and Shostrom, 1982) indicates that individual as well as collective growth is most fully nurtured when collective decision-making and economic arrangements are organized to meet people's needs. This growth is advanced in social psychological contexts where genuineness, congruence, acceptance, prizing, caring, understanding, self-regard, and positive regard for others exist (Meador and Rogers, 1984:162–164). When social arrangements encourage a basic trust in the ability of individuals to learn, think, and make choices for themselves, growth is sustained. In Rogers's view,

> if we are interested in having people around us who manifest qualities that can be trusted, our efforts would be better rewarded if we established a climate that allowed individuals to develop their individual nature and liberate their destinies. Such persons would not be disabled by an inadequate climate nor trapped by limited perceptions of their abilities and human capacities. (Welch and Tate, 1985:25)

Person and Community

As human beings, we are existentially indispensable and unexchangeable. Yet we are not separable from one another, from community. When actions are self-initiated and self-evaluated, they increase in meaningfulness and creativity. Yet self-actualization and individual freedom are inextricably connected to collective social arrangements that foster high levels of need satisfaction and human community. Victor Frankl explains:

> The more highly differentiated a man is, the less he resembles the norm—norm both in the sense of average and in the sense of ideal. At the price of normality or, as the case may be, ideality, he has bought his individuality. The significance of such individuality, the meaning of human personality, is, however, always related to community. For just as the uniqueness of the tessera is a value only in relation to the whole of the mosaic, so the uniqueness of the human personality finds its meaning entirely in its role in an integral whole. Thus, the meaning of the human person as a personality points beyond its own limits, toward community; in being directed toward community the meaning of the individual transcends itself.
>
> There is an emotional gregariousness of human beings; but beyond this, community has its task of quality. But an individual existence not only must have the community in order to become meaningful; vice versa, the community needs the individual existence in order for it itself to have meaning. Therein lies an essential distinction between community and the mere mass. Far from providing a frame of reference for the individual existence, the mass does not tolerate individuality. If the relationship of the individual to the community may be compared with that of a tessera to a whole mosaic, then the relationship of the individual to the mass may be equated with that of a standardized paving-stone to uniform gray pavement: every stone is cut to the same size and shape and may be replaced by any other; none has the qualitative importance for the whole. And the pavement itself is not really an integral whole, merely a magnitude. The uniform pavement also does not have the aesthetic value of a mosaic; it possesses only utilitarian value—just as the mass submerges the dignity and value of men and extracts only their utility.
>
> The meaning of individuality comes to fulfillment in the community. To this extent, then, the value of the individual is dependent upon the community. But if the community itself is to have meaning, it cannot dispense with the individuality of the individuals that make it up. In the mass, on the other hand, the single, unique existence is submerged, must be submerged because uniqueness would be a disrupting factor in any mass. The meaning of the community is constituted by individuality, and the meaning of individuality by community;

the "meaning" of the mass is disrupted by the individuality of the individuals composing it, and the meaning of individuality is submerged in the mass (while in the community it emerges). (1965:70–71)

Murray Bookchin further elaborates this interdependence:

If we are to explore human nature, we cannot ignore certain features about it that justify a belief in its cooperative and life-affirming tendencies. Human beings are more helpless and dependent at birth than most animals; their development to maturity requires more time than their nearest primate cousins. This protracted period of development which makes for the mental ability of humans to form a culture also fosters a deep sense of interdependence that promotes the formation and stability of community.

We are eminently social animals not because of instinct but rather because we must cooperate with each other to mature in a healthy fashion, not only to survive. This kind of cooperation, which involves a long period of parenting, indeed of touching and caressing, makes for a strong need to associate with others of our own kind. The worst punishment that can be inflicted on any normal human being is isolation, and the most serious emotional trauma the individual seems to suffer is separation. The love, care, aid, and goodwill that a group can furnish to an individual are perhaps the most important contributions it can make to an individual's ego development. Denied these supportive attentions, ego-formation, personal development, and individuality become warped. Speaking in ecological terms, the making of that "whole" we call a rounded, creative, and richly variegated human being crucially depends upon community support for which no amount of self-interest and egotism is a substitute. Indeed, without these supports, there would be no real self to distort— only a fragmented, wriggling, frail, and pathological thing that could only be called a self for want of another word to describe it.

The making of a human being, in short, is a collective process, a process in which both the community and the individual participate. It is also a process which, at its best, evokes by its own variety of stimuli the wealth of abilities and traits within the individual that achieve their full degree of differentiation. The extent to which these individual potentialities are realized, the unity of diversity they achieve, and the scope they acquire depend crucially upon the degree to which the community itself is participatory and richly differentiated in the stimuli, forms, and choices it creates that make for personal self-formation. Denied the opportunity to participate in a community, whether because it is incomprehensibly large or socially exclusive, the individual begins to feel disempowered and ineffectual, with the result that his or her self begins to shrivel. Divested of differentiated stimuli, opportunities, choices, and variegated groups that speak to his or her proclivities, the individual becomes a ho-

mogenized "thing," passive, obedient, and privatized, which makes for a sub-
missive personality and a manipulable constituent. (1986:34–36)

Human Nature and Being

Unfortunately, the conditions that Frankl and Bookchin believe necessary
for development of the growth tendency (e.g., participation, authenticity,
and cooperation) are only weakly supported by the social organization of our
society. The acute levels of distress and unmet needs many experience make
it necessary to conceptualize human nature as more complex and inclusive
than Rogers has. His conception adequately accommodates the truth that we
can transcend our biological and psychological conditions to create social
arrangements wherein we can act so as to neither stagnate nor prevent creativity and change; experience tension and anxiety in a healthy and stimulating way, and find meaningful and fulfilling lives, tasks, and loves. But this
concept insufficiently accommodates the truth that we suppress the growth
tendency, create structures of domination, construct concentration camps
and policies of apartheid, support low-intensity warfare and battering, and
organize social life so as not to meet most people's essential needs.

Human nature can more comprehensively be understood as dualistic—
composed of two sets of contrasting feelings (Kropotkin, 1924; Tifft and
Stevenson, 1985). In the first set (unity) are feelings that respond to our need
to feel of equal humanness and a certain oneness with others. These feelings
induce us to express empathy, commitment, and solidarity with others. They
encourage us to cooperate in efforts that require coordinated action and ensure safety and security (e.g., settling disputes, creating peace).

In the second set (diversity) are those feelings that respond to our need to
assert ourselves, our individual uniqueness, or our personhood. These feelings impel us to break the bonds that the collectivity (e.g., group, tribe, community, state) tends to require for inclusion as members. They stimulate expressions of personal creativity, risk taking, and talent development. While
impeding social stagnation, meaninglessness, group tyranny, and oppression,
they inspire both personal and social change. However, they can lead us to
conclude that our distinct individual and/or group characteristics make us
better than others. They can drive us to assertions of superiority, to the creation of social arrangements of domination and control, and to the use of
others for our individual or group ends.

A dualistic conception of human nature allows us to explore the positive
synthesis—that is, social arrangements that foster collective well-being while

concomitantly stimulating the creative and assertive energies and actions of individuals. Alternately, this conception permits us to examine those arrangements that foster the second set of feelings while retarding the development of the first. These arrangements pose a substantial barrier to personal and collective emergence, to the growth tendency. Human potential, the quality of social life, and the degree of personal dignity vary directly with conditions of oppression or liberation.

Assertions of domination and superiority have fragmented humankind into hierarchies, social classes, "races," nation-states, and genders. They have fostered patriarchy, nationalistic hatreds, imperialism, and a global philosophy that identifies social order with power and submission. Although developing relatively slowly in human history, these assertions have quickened in pace and have corroded the ties that once, to a greater extent, provided a sense of personal place and meaning. Within our cultural and social arrangements, domination has filled the existential vacuum (Frankl, 1965; Patterson, 1986:435) of lost community with nihilistic or antisocial developments such as "mass society" (Frankl, 1965; Mills, 1956), with its sprawling urban entities that are neither cities nor villages and its impersonal, manipulative elites, who view us collectively as "faceless masses of atomized beings"; global private power institutions (global corporations) that determine the material life and death of persons in even the most remote corners of our planet; and highly centralized nation-state institutions and military forces with unbridled coercive power that threaten not only the freedom of the individual but also the survival of species (Bookchin, 1986:53). George Albee explains:

> What stops the world's people from building a more just, more equitable world—a world in which preventable stress has been reduced for the majority of people—as is envisioned as a major goal by the World Health Organization? The forces that are barriers to a just world are some of the same forces that block significant efforts at reducing psychopathology in our own society: exploitation, imperialism, excessive concentration of economic power, nationalism, institutions that perpetuate powerlessness, hopelessness, poverty, discrimination, sexism, racism, and ageism. These forces control or influence the world's communication systems, especially mass media and educational systems, and they deliberately distribute rewards for conformity and for the support of injustice. (1986:894)

In part Albee is saying that the growth tendency and the satisfaction of a substantial degree of physical, psychological, and social needs are in conflict with the nature of current social structures. The level of human nourishment available to sustain persons in times of victimization, personal trouble, or psychic distress is inadequate, primarily because the level of nourishment "normally" available is deficient. The normal structural context systematically generates suffering, need deprivation, existential crisis, violence, battering, and death.

Sixty-five percent of the people on earth are subjected to structural arrangements and practices (e.g., the politics of food distribution and resource extraction, cash-crop conversion) that prevent them from meeting their essential, physical survival needs. The crisis of need among those of the "third world" results from their peripheral location within world geopolitical and economic arrangements. The crises among those of the "first and second worlds" result from their location within global corporate and nation-state arrangements. In this latter context, epidemiological research demonstrates a correlation of physical need deprivation, disease, stress, psychopathology, and victimization with one or more of the following structurally induced conditions: emotionally damaging infant and childhood experiences, poverty and degrading life experiences, powerlessness and low self-esteem, and loneliness, social isolation, and social marginality (Albee, 1986:891).

Facing conditions of oppression, isolation, and suffering, people are, however, neither necessarily nor characteristically passive (Frankl, 1965; Bookchin, 1986:59). Although many people believe that the degrees of political-economic injustice and need deprivation they currently experience are the natural state of human affairs, we know they are not correct (Albee, 1982; Kessler and Albee, 1975). Moreover, even in conditions of extreme domination, people are able to transcend fatalistic attitudes and the contexts that foster them, to construct structures of personhood, interpersonal relationship, and social arrangement that promote emergence and positive human transition.

Sources of Alienation, Victimization, and Distress

DOMINATION + MYSTIFICATION + ISOLATION → ALIENATION, VICTIMIZATION, AND DISTRESS

Structures of domination not only generate need deprivation and distress; they also intensify our natural anxieties concerning "freedom, responsibility, competence, isolation, meaninglessness, and death" (May and Yalom, 1984:367–370). They provide life experiences from which many of us learn neither to trust others nor to allow them to become emotionally close. From them we do not learn how to healthfully respond to the natural developmental transitions of life and relationship (Levinson, 1986). In fact, we often interpret one another's desperate attempts to preserve authentic elements of personality (e.g., autonomy, spontaneity, responsibility, and freedom to choose) as signs of pathology (Ford, 1966:364; Laing, 1965).[1]

Structures of domination fundamentally interfere with our thinking and problem-solving processes (Steiner, 1981:728). Within these structures, much of what we learn about solving problems and the realities of life is a result of systematic distortion ("lifelong lies") and denial of experience. Such structures alienate us from our capacity to love, appreciate, and cooperate with one another. We are even taught and frequently learn to feel estranged from our physical and emotive selves. Claude Steiner explains:

> Our intimate relationship with ourselves, that is, with all parts of our bodies, is interfered with by a number of alienating influences. We are told that our minds or spirits are separate from our body or flesh and that our body is, in some manner, the lesser of the two. We are told that those who use their minds are the ones who deserve power. We are encouraged to ignore our body's perceptions of dis-ease resulting from abuse, especially at the workplace, and to deal with them through powerful drugs that temporarily eradicate the symptoms of dysfunction. We are told that bodily pleasures are a dangerous evil. We learn to deny our bodily experiences that include our emotions, whether they be positive or negative. We eat adulterated food without nutritional value and are told to ignore its side effects. Eventually this systematic attack creates an alienation that puts our body's function and its experiences beyond our conscious control. Our bodies, which are the vessel, the matrix of our aliveness, become complete strangers to us and seem to turn on us through illness, addictions to harmful amounts and kinds of foods and drugs, and to unexplained and seemingly perverted needs over which we have no control. (1981:728)

Although we have a natural desire and capacity to enjoy productive activity, many of us feel a loss of productive autonomy and responsibility as a result of the way work is organized. Few of us are able to exhibit our creative talents and work at what we most enjoy. The pleasures of work (e.g., a sense of accomplishment, connectedness, and meaningfulness) are rarely realized, for we customarily do not decide what to produce; how much to produce; where, when, and how to produce; how the product is to be distributed; and for what use the product is suitable. Such conditions are contradictory to our existential indispensability and unexchangeability (Frankl, 1965:70–71) and injurious to our physical and mental health (Conrad, 1979; Case, 1980).

As stated earlier, domination is not merely justified in our society; it is taught and valued as a social ideal. Those who own and manage the means of production systematically control those whose labor they own (e.g., slavery), purchase, or rent. They assert their legitimacy, saying that everyone is free and has an equal opportunity to "succeed." Those who are not "successful" in meeting their individual needs (even physical needs) are adjudged as responsible for their own failures, crises, victimization, starvation, and even death. In an attempt to defend differential access to need satisfaction and privilege, "whites" routinely claim that "peoples of color" are inferior (e.g., less intelligent, creative, or talented). Children are routinely told that they are unknowledgeable human beings who should obey those who know best (i.e., "grown-ups"). Women are infrequently taken seriously. Rather, they are objectified and denied opportunities to develop their potentialities. Gays and lesbians are frequently perceived as morally inferior or as suffering from mental illness.

In sum, each specific system of domination requires a set of mystifications for a successful exercise of power. Many subjected to these mystifications adapt and survive by colluding with them and yet develop from this collusion feelings of estrangement, distress, and powerlessness. Steiner elaborates:

> Eventually the oppressed actually come to believe the lies used to justify their oppression. When a person has incorporated in his or her own consciousness the arguments that explain and make legitimate his or her oppression, then mystification and alienation are complete. People will no longer rebel against oppression, but instead will blame themselves for it, accept it, and assume that they are the source and reason for their own unhappiness. In addition, they will apply their internalized oppression to everyone around them and enforce other's oppression along with their own. ...
>
> Being separated from, and unable to communicate with, each other is essential to alienation. By ourselves, without the aid of others who are in similar circumstances, we are powerless to think through our problems or do anything about them. It is part of the American Dream that people should achieve and do what they must do as individuals in isolation. Only those achievements that we can claim entirely for ourselves are thought of as being worthy. As a consequence, we erect barriers of competition, secrecy, and shame between each other. When we are together we do not trust each other, we do not share our thoughts and feelings with each other, and we go at the tasks of our lives as separate individuals, each one with separate projects, living quarters, transportation, and nuclear families. The cult of individualism is an important source of our isolation and alienation. (1981:730)

In the grip of these existential conditions, we are faced with a choice (Steiner, 1981:730): Either reinforce the mystification of oppression and alienation by looking for the sources of victimization and distress within the victim, the assailant/dominator, or the interaction patterns of these individuals, or demystify the essential sources of estrangement and distress, that is, all the institutions of domination and oppression (e.g., "racism," ageism, sexism).

Empowerment and Social Transformation

CONTACT + AWARENESS + ACTION → EMPOWERMENT AND SOCIAL TRANS-
FORMATION

To reclaim and enhance our human potential, each element of the process that generates alienation, victimization, and distress must be counteracted. Empowerment can be fostered by *contact* to counter feelings of isolation, *awareness* to contravene mystification, and *action* to negate domination and oppression.

Nonsupportive social structures guarantee that most of us respond to oppressive life circumstances, victimizations, or transitions with demoralization, helplessness, guilt, depression, terror, disorientation, rage, or despair (Meridith, 1987; Robinson, 1982). Distress (as defined by each individual's subjective understanding) can also arise when a person cannot reconcile desires with what she or he is able to do or receive (Small, 1966:301). Nevertheless, some individuals are not distressed by these circumstances because they believe they have no agency in the matter. Such a view reflects a consciousness diminished by a belief in fate or determinism or by an "education for unfreedom." The distressed person at least consciously grapples with perceived existential freedom (Small, 1966:301).

Assuredly some experiences of suffering are inseparable from the rhythms of life associated with loss, bereavement, vulnerability, transition, aging, and death.[2] Unexpected events, loneliness, life transitions, personal responsibilities, isolation, and role conflicts are seemingly natural to the human condition regardless of the nature of differing values and structural arrangements. Other experiences, such as rape and battering, are, however, pivotally derived from the nature of specific ideas and dehumanizing arrangements (Leonard, 1975:51). In these circumstances, distress is not generated from the human condition or located in the personal qualities of those victimized. Feelings of rage, despair, and loss are not symptoms of psychopathology; rather, they are valid responses to extremely oppressive behaviors or arrangements (Miller, 1982:14).

Although each person creates his or her personal response, he or she is not responsible for these victimizations. To attach such responsibility is to blame, for example, an African American or a female job applicant for responding to discriminatory hiring practices with anger, reproach, or hopelessness. Correspondingly, it is to chide the survivor of battering or rape for responding with distress, depression, rage, or loss of self. Interventions that help these persons accommodate more healthfully to domination simply adjust them to circumstances that block their self-actualization. Michael Lerner explains:

> It is today generally understood that many of the bad feelings that women and blacks had about themselves in past decades were an inappropriate internalization of an external reality—inner reactions to prejudice. So suppose, as a therapist, you began seeing many black, or women, clients who told you that they were unhappy because they were not succeeding in the economic marketplace. Suppose further that they explained their failures in terms of their own personal inadequacies. Wouldn't it make sense that you introduce new elements into the discussion that were not thought of by your clients—social categories like sexism and racism? Indeed, wouldn't the most effective form of therapy be the creation of a civil rights movement or a women's movement?
>
> In this context, any therapist who continued to interpret the problems primarily in individual terms might actually be working counter to the real health needs of the people involved. And, to the extent that therapists reinforce this individual interpretation of a social problem, we would say that ... [they] ... may very well be helping to more firmly entrench the very set of problems that were a root cause of the pain from which their clients had come seeking relief. (1987:42)

As stated earlier in the book, many groups have been formed to assist women who have survived battering to understand their feelings and behavior in terms of their oppression (Pence, 1987, 1989). As a consequence, many survivors develop a deepened awareness of both the sociocultural reality that shapes their lives and their capacity to transform it (Pence, 1985; Bailey and Brake, 1975:9–11). They learn how class structures, gender stratification, and racism shape their thoughts and feelings about themselves and others. As a result of this changed consciousness, many increase their self-dignity and decrease their feelings of self-blame and sole responsibility for creating their present realities. They begin to channel their energies into altering their life circumstances and helping create strategies for changing the conditions for women in our society.

Feminist therapy, which is based on group support, consciousness raising, advocacy, and cultural and social structural transformation, has provided a basis for many survivor programs. Marylou Butler (1985:33–37) presents the following guidelines for feminist practice:

1. Reject the medical model of psychiatry, which locates the source of human conflict within individuals—that is, in a vacuum, with no relationship to the social organization of the society within which we live. Gender, class, and racial stratification are the key sources of the conflicts, low self-esteem, and powerlessness reported by many women who seek therapy.
2. Clients should be helped to understand the sources of their oppression through careful sex-role analysis and to conceptualize alternatives through a consideration of feminism.
3. Women should be supported in an exploration of their inner resources and capacity for nurturance and self-healing. Therapists should encourage the process of individual goal setting and support those client goals that transcend traditional sex-role stereotyping. They should encourage the exploration of various lifestyles and sexual orientations and support the acquisition of skills for self-directed and interdependent living.
4. Sex-role analysis and differential-power analysis can help women differentiate between internal and external sources of distress. This cognitive restructuring enables women to avoid engaging in a process of self-blame and helps them restructure their beliefs about themselves, about women as a group, and about their life situations. In this view, for example, depression and lack of assertiveness can be the result of the powerlessness of the female sex role rather than inherent personal deficits; rape is a tool of male domination of women rather than a result of female seductiveness; on-the-job difficulties may be a function of sexual harassment and discrimination rather than personal inadequacy; lesbianism is a choice to make a commitment to and love another woman rather than an expression of unresolved dislike for men.
5. The power relationship inherent in any therapeutic relationship should be demystified to foster a sense of commonality of experience among women.

6. An all-women's group therapy model can enable women to validate each other's strengths, develop mutual support systems, break down their isolation from each other, and help each other perceive various possibilities for growth. This experience can provide a resocialization experience for women in which they shift from identification with a male-defined social system to a female-oriented one, where they learn to love each other and themselves. The group experience helps women further their own individuation and complete unfinished developmental tasks in the areas of interdependence, assertiveness, and autonomy.

Similar guidelines have been recommended by those practicing radical therapy. Radical therapists create problem-solving groups to increase awareness of oppression, support personal growth, equalize power in interpersonal interaction, and encourage social action against domination. Patricia Parsons illustrates:

> Successful psychological adjustment to a capitalist patriarchal society requires that we internalize our oppression. We turn our anger and fear in on ourselves and those close to us instead of directing them toward the societal sources of our oppression. We become alienated from ourselves and each other, and we feel powerless to change our situation.
>
> We are taught to swallow our feelings, to hide them from ourselves and each other. Not surprisingly, we are not taught to pay attention to our emotions, to trust them, to express them clearly, to say what we want from each other and from society. If we were, we would have within us the seeds of rebellion. It is a suitable task for radical therapy to sow the seeds of rebellion by helping people to discover and reclaim their unexperienced emotions, to develop emotional literacy, and to explain the relationship between our crippled emotional selves and the nature of our society.
>
> Beginning with the understanding that emotional and interpersonal problems are linked to the conditions of society leads proponents of RT to therapy modes based on groups rather than individuals. ... Through communication in these groups, women [are] able to overcome their isolation from one another and to establish strong bonds based on their common oppression. RT problem-solving groups are grounded in the belief that sharing our common experiences and emotions will increase our awareness of the oppressive conditions that discourage us from intimate emotional contact with each other, and of the forces that prevent us from acting to change these conditions.
>
> Radical therapy ultimately leads to and must include collective action to change society. Unless and until we change the social and economic conditions which oppress us, RT contends, we will not be free of our psychological oppres-

sion. Concomitantly, we cannot successfully overcome the external conditions that oppress us without addressing our internalization of that oppression. RT can provide the tools to combat that internalized oppression through the development of cognitive and emotional awareness of oppression, mutual support, and individual empowerment. (1982:17–18)

Inherent in problem-solving, support, and consciousness-raising groups is a belief in the capacity of people to understand their situation and find ways to change it (Statham, 1978:4). All these group experiences provide an opportunity for members to speak about "the unspoken" and regain, or achieve for the first time, a sense of human dignity. Group processes help members become aware of the cultural myths that support the retention of specific relations (e.g., patriarchy, elitism, racism) and of individual conditioning. Developing a critical consciousness about the nature of gender, political, and economic relations enables members to assert their humanity and confront dehumanizing arrangements (Leonard, 1975:60; Wilson, 1980:41).

According to Steiner (1981), Contact, Awareness, and Action can reverse the processes that lead to distress and alter the arrangements that initiate these processes. In regard to Contact, radical therapists assert that to combat isolation, people must experience the power of working together and supporting each other through cooperation. In radical therapy groups, group members do not lie to one another by omission or commission; they do not keep hidden any of what is felt. No one fails to ask for all of what he or she wants; no one is to give or do more than what he or she sees as fair, and no one should do anything he or she does not want to do. As a consequence, group members respond and relate with one another as equals in a spontaneous, intimate, or aware manner. Such Contact facilitates Awareness and is supportive of Action.

Steiner continues:

Awareness: The expansion of consciousness, especially one's understanding of the manner in which oppressive influences operate to diminish our power, is the essence of Awareness. Consciousness-raising is the accumulation of information about the world and how it functions, and it is an important continuing task in expanding one's power in the world. Awareness of the function of class oppression, racism, sexism, ageism, heterosexism, coupleism, and so on is an essential aspect of consciousness-raising.

Constructive criticism is a vital consciousness-raising technique. In the constructive criticism process, people will offer information to those who want to hear it concerning their behavior and how it affects others. In addition, a person may offer suggestions of how another person's behavior may be changed and corrected for the benefit of all. Constructive criticism is greatly aided by self-criticism and assumes willingness in all who participate to accept and learn from other people's critical analyses.

Action: Action is the process whereby our awareness of things that need to be changed is put into effect. Contact alone, or Contact and Awareness, can lead to strong, increased, subjective feelings of power. However, objective power in the world is different from subjective feelings of power and cannot result from Awareness or Contact alone. Awareness and Contact must be translated into some form of Action that changes the actual conditions in a person's life. Action implies risk, and when a person takes risks, he or she may need protection from the fears and actual dangers that can result from that action. Potent protection in the form of actual alliances for physical or moral support are needed in effective Action and are an essential aspect of Contact. Action, Awareness, and Contact together are the elements that make it possible for people to reclaim their birthright and become powerful in the world. (1981:731–732)

Like many of us, feminist and radical therapy practitioners feel that we have a moral obligation to diminish the social and existential conditions that produce needless suffering. We have an obligation to alter the social conditions that foster child abuse, rape, battering, malnourishment, genocide, imperialism, and war. As responsible persons we must act so that there are many fewer persons to counsel regarding their choices to batter as well as many fewer persons to counsel as a result of this battering. Living in nonnourishing conditions, we will continue to stifle the growth tendency unless we initiate preventive, society-altering actions.

11

The Primary Prevention of Battering: A Structural Approach

The primary prevention of battering requires a recognition that battering is fundamentally a social problem with roots in a clearly delineated set of social arrangements that mirror and generate specific cultural values and beliefs. Battering reflects the degree to which societal arrangements foster or hinder the spontaneous unfolding of human potential (Gil 1977, 1979b, 1986, 1989). A significantly higher degree of individual and collective potential could be realized in cultural and social contexts where

1. Meeting people's needs is the primary concern of social activity
2. Stratification and hierarchy, when they develop, are situational and temporary
3. Intrafamilial and social equality are pursued
4. Intrafamilial and societal divisions of labor are symbiotic, self-directed, and cooperative
5. Personal and interpersonal stability exists simultaneously with constant change
6. All persons are accepted as similarly human, yet are prized for their uniqueness
7. The dignity of each person is recognized[1]

Structural Dynamics

In Chapters 1 and 2, I briefly outlined the structural dynamics of battering. Social-organizational conditions that obstruct human development constitute *structural violence*. It is only in the context of structural violence that the dynamic processes of interpersonal violence (Chapters 3–5) can be understood, for within structurally violent circumstances many individuals experience violence and create or learn the motivations and explanations for their actions.

As stated earlier, in many spheres of social life we receive benefits for controlling others. The extent to which we direct events, acquire and manage resources, and control the behavior and actions of others is often the basis of our personal or collective power and of our self-esteem. Those who intervene in the lives of others as agents of the state, decision-makers for global corporations, institutional policymakers, therapists, directors of programs for those who batter, and batterers accept this root of battering and the violence that stems from it (Pence, 1988a).

Social arrangements that are structurally violent inflict pain and set in motion other practices that enforce, restore, and regenerate these arrangements (Gil 1989:40). State torture, death squads, disappearances, assassinations, penal sanctions, coercive therapy, and battering all constitute *repressive violence*. These practices suppress the opportunity to develop (through discussion, speech, assembly, or organizing) need-meeting, and thus pain-reducing, social arrangements and are ancillary to structural violence.

At the same time, however, structural violence generates actions aimed at fundamentally changing these social arrangements. *Resistance* to violent social arrangements is ordinarily nonviolent, an attempt to negate the power maneuvers of those who benefit from such arrangements. Resistance, which aims to relieve the pain and suffering produced by structural violence (Scarry, 1985), is often expressed in music, theater, poetry, and social criticism. People are inspired to speak out against violent arrangements, organize religious study groups, or form consciousness-raising, educational, or empowerment groups. Nonviolent resistance against both repressive and structural violence has led to the creation of houses of refuge (shelters) for those who have been battered, to camps for political refugees, to demonstrations in city plazas, to organizing efforts in workplaces, and to the formulation of strategies of self-defense in many homes. Some resistance to structural and repressive violence, however, becomes violent—*resistance violence*.

Together, nonviolent and violent resistance form a set of actions meant to express an imagined social life without structurally violent arrangements and their consequent pain and suffering. Resisters act, if not for themselves, then for others so that they need not suffer in unnecessary and preventable ways.

These actions are taken so that children may experience family life without being abused or without witnessing abuse, so that as adults they may find work expressive of their dignity and talents, so that they may participate in decisions that affect their lives, so that they may, indeed, have a future. Actions that further the primary prevention of battering are actions of resistance to structural violence.

The structural violence of our society, the ideological system that justifies it, and the repressive violence that maintains and restores it also tend to set in motion reactive and reflective-imitative interpersonal violence. These acts of violence are *not* aimed at changing violent structural arrangements; rather, they are aimed at others who are caught within the destructive grasp of these arrangements. Violent crimes between strangers and intimates; the addictions of our compulsive, yet escapist culture; and many of our mental ills no longer seem senseless and irrational when we recognize them as reactive or reflective-imitative interpersonal violence enacted in response to violent societal practices and conditions. In fact, when we do so, the inner logic of these actions is revealed (Gil, 1989).

To illustrate, many of us find work to be organized in a manner that arrests the development of our talents, restricts our choices, excludes our participation and voice, and attacks our dignity and positive sense of self (see Chapter 2). Daily immersion in this structurally violent context may lead some to harm others (*reactive violence*) in an attempt to recover what has been lost (e.g., dignity, positive regard). Alternatively, some inflict pain in a mirrored replication of patterns of structural violence—*reflective-imitative violence*. Structurally violent arrangements and interpersonally violent acts thereby become reinforcing component parts of a cycle of pain infliction (see Table 11.1).

Unfortunately, most criminological and social deviance research focuses exclusively on the reactive and reflective-imitative interpersonal violence of structurally violated individuals and groups and thus disregards the structural violence that thwarts the developmental needs of these individuals. As a consequence, the dynamics of violence in our society are obscured. Segregated and fragmented studies of "moments in the cycle of violence" tend to serve those who "benefit" from the social arrangements of structural and repressive violence and deny, by implication, the "causal" dynamics of societal violence (Gil, 1986; Reiman, 1984). The few who benefit from the hierarchies and stratifications, those whose needs (and greeds) are met through these arrangements, do not have to take responsibility for their mode of violence, structural violence. The necessity of fundamental social structural

TABLE 11.1 Components of the Cycle of Violence

Type	Definition	Example
Structural violence	Structural arrangements in any sphere of life (work, family, political economy) that obstruct the development of human potential and therefore inflict pain	Hierarchical decision-making arrangements Divisions of labor based on sex Production and distribution arrangements that are not directed to meet core needs
Repressive violence	Specific practices and arrangements that enforce and restore structurally violent arrangements	Torture Death squads Disappearances Penal sanctions Coercive therapy Battering
Resistance	Actions directed to resist, negate, and change power maneuvers that others attempt to exercise through structural and repressive violence	Organization against these arrangements Nonviolent resistance DAIP Survivor resistance Creation of alternative arrangements
Resistance violence	Actions directed to resist and change structural and repressive violence arrangements that are themselves violent	Workplace violence Violence in the home Guerrilla maneuvers Terrorist movements Revolutionary violence

(continues)

TABLE 11.1 (continued)

Type	Definition	Example
Reactive violence	Actions that are not aimed at changing structurally violent social arrangements but rather are aimed at persons in the grasp of these arrangements	Violent acts between strangers
Reflective-imitative violence		Violent acts between intimates Battering Addictions Mental illness

Note: Battering is a complex process (involving actions, meanings, and arrangements) composed of the infliction of pain, the obstruction of the process of human development, and the annihilation of a partner's voice and presence. Battering takes many forms and can occur at different levels of social organization. Reactive interpersonal violence and resistance violence may constitute battering. So may reflective-imitative violence as it is an attempt to create arrangements within the intimate relationship that constitute structural violence within the family. When such arrangements are relatively established, they constitute structural violence. Interpersonal violence utilized to maintain and restore battering structures constitutes repressive violence. Such violence may also be defined as battering.

change toward nonviolent, egalitarian institutions is dismissed, while structurally violated individuals and groups are blamed and scapegoated (Gil, 1989:4). Nonetheless, reactive or reflective-imitative interpersonal violence is only one component in the cycle of pain infliction.

Both structural violence and reactive or reflective-imitative violence invoke attitudes that reinforce structural violence. They very often directly initiate collective actions (e.g., penal sanctions) that explicitly justify the infliction of pain. When the survivors of structural violence are held responsible by the state for their "counter-violence" (Gil, 1989), practices and interventions (e.g., penal sanction, coerced treatment) that constitute repressive violence increase. The cycle of violence is then magnified and restored.

The preceding theoretical analysis indicates that some arrangements through which pain and diminishment of human potential are inflicted are socially approved and accepted, while others are not. Nevertheless, each mode of pain infliction reinforces the cultural acceptability of inflicting pain on others and creates language to justify, explain, normalize, or make sense of this infliction. Whenever interpersonal violence and subjection to structural violence are "normal" aspects of social life, socialization sources (e.g., U.S. foreign policy, criminal justice and penal policy, formal educational organizations, reading materials, television and radio programming, and other sources of popular culture) customarily serve as witting or unwitting agents of this violence. Through these sources, children are taught sex inequality and the language of justification for it (Gil, 1977). They are also exposed to "violent tendencies and capacities" through individually competitive and violent games and sports, individually rewarding and punishing cognitive learning experiences, and the family's everyday structural and emotional milieu. Most critically, these tendencies and capacities, and the language for justifying them, are taught and learned through the division of labor, decision-making arrangements, emotional climate, and child socialization practices within the family. It is especially, though not exclusively, these arrangements that must change if we are to break the cycle of violence and prevent battering. Although battering tactics are widely institutionalized in other societal arrangements, family arrangements are the only ones that many individuals can perceive as capable of change, for they are constructed most directly by our consciousness and action. Most people ordinarily perceive changes in other spheres of social life as beyond individual constructive efforts. This analysis also indicates that the cycle of structural violence, resistance, reactive and reflective-imitative violence, resistance violence, repressive violence, and structural violence will continue as long as the cycle's primary root—social arrangements (the conventional workings of everyday life) that systematically obstruct human development—is neither acknowledged nor transcended within and among societies.

Primary Prevention Strategies

One task of this concluding chapter is to suggest specific actions and trans-formational processes (Tifft, 1979; Sullivan, 1980; Zehr, 1990; Pepinsky, 1991, 1991a; Pepinsky and Quinney, 1991) that might break this cycle of vio-lence. As stated clearly by Rebecca Dobash (1988), we need to strip societies of those conditions that have traditionally provided the material and ideolog-ical foundations for the battering of women and other forms of violence and "replace them with conditions that reject such violence unequivocally" (cited in Heise, 1989:9). The task is to suggest actions and transformational pro-cesses that lead to the creation of social arrangements that increase human empowerment while decreasing structural violence, the incidence and prev-alence of battering, and other forms of violent interaction. We need to initi-ate processes directed toward ending gender stratification and inequality that can initially exist alongside programs for the survivors of violence and for the empowerment of women. Such programs might at first coexist with the intrapersonal, interpersonal, and community-coordinated responses to bat-tering explored and critiqued in Chapters 7, 8, and 9, yet have the potential to reach beyond these responses (as the DAIP program does) and reduce the need for them.

We need a proactive, before-the-battering, needs-based, primary preven-tion, public health (Bowen and Sedlak, 1985; Mercy and O'Carroll, 1988), social structural approach to battering. We need to replace the core cultural and structural arrangements that support battering; to create a society with much less violence and much less spiritual, emotional, and behavioral power exercise; to make a world where individuals develop a sense of personhood that does not necessitate the diminishment, objectification, or control of others.

A primary prevention approach to battering must address the core con-texts within which decisions to batter are imposed. It requires an awareness of historical, cross-cultural, and social arrangement alternatives. It necessi-tates creating a transcendent future and acting to bring about fundamental change in our current cultural and social arrangements. Primary prevention is a process.

Primary prevention of social problems requires each of us to discover our values and truths and commit ourselves to living in greater accord with them.[2] It requires that we make choices and create social arrangements infused with a willingness to take risks and a recognition of the necessity to co-create enriching and nurturant social environments compatible with our developmental needs.[3]

This version of a primary prevention approach has at its root understanding and creating social arrangements attentive to the essential human needs for (1) harmony with and acclimation to our natural environment; (2) a physiologically natural environment—"clean," nonpolluted air, nutritious, non-chemically-poisoned food and water, etc.; (3) a healthful balance of sociality and privacy; and (4) a social life that is noncoercive in thought, expression, movement, association, or action and in which our perceived harms, conflicts, and injustices will not spiral into disputes that lay us open to external imposition and the reassertion of hierarchy and structural violence. It is an approach concerned with how needs might be most thoroughly met to foster the highest degree of individual and collective health, safety, diversity, well-being, and empowerment (Tifft and Stevenson, 1985).

Primary Prevention with Interconnecting Sources

Violence and the acceptance of violence permeate our culture in all spheres of interaction—intrapersonal, interpersonal, social policy, institutional, national, and global. The causal dimensions or sources of battering, especially the battering of women by men (Gil, 1979b:77–78), are located in a set of interrelated levels of social interaction:

1. On the *global* level, violence is accepted in the maintenance and restoration of geopolitical, ecopolitical, global capitalist, and religious arrangements. Here the politics of hunger, the feminization and exploitation of labor, and the ravages of war batter women and thwart their development.

2. On the *societal* level, the interplay of values and economic and political processes shape the social policies through which the needs, "rights," and lives of women are defined, constrained, and diminished. Here the social construction of gender, gender socialization, the definition of women's "rights" and needs, and the extent to which our society accepts power exercise and the use of violence shape arrangements that place women in positions of subordination and limited participation.

3. On the *institutional* level, policies and practices that form the broad array of "educational," work, and social "welfare" organizations distort women's development and ensure their dependency.
4. On the *interpersonal* level or in the family interaction sphere (e.g., in child care arrangements or in the expression of intimacy), interaction hierarchies harm women. Distress (dis-ease) results from isolation and economic and political deprivation.
5. On the *intrapersonal* level, expressions of intrapsychic conflict, confusion, depression, and struggles for psychic survival are rooted in the foregoing spheres of social life.

An exploration of the different and interacting sources for the transmission and support of the use of violence against women might initially focus on battering within any of the aforementioned spheres of interaction—child care practices, the social organization of work, gender hierarchy and socialization, global corporate exploitation, or violent state foreign policy (e.g., U.S. foreign policy in Central America [Tifft and Markham, 1991]). Although the battering of intimates, especially the battering of women by men, at any specific level may be more closely related to one, rather than another, source, none of these levels is independent; each influences and is influenced by the others (Gil, 1979b).

Because there is multiple interaction among these dimensions, programs and processes that negate power exercise and violence at any level have the potential to spread to other realms of social organization (Brock-Utne, 1985; Gil, 1989) and reduce their "power grip." Primary prevention programs and processes that negate power and diminish the acceptance of violence between adult intimates have the potential to initiate processes of negating power, ending violence, and diminishing the acceptance of violence in interactions between adults and children. They also have the potential to set in motion processes for the negation of power, battering, and the acceptance of violence in the workplace, in social policy, and in national and global levels of social organization. Correspondingly, resolving disputes without using violence or decreasing the acceptance of violence in the global economic and nation-state spheres can set in motion processes that have the potential to end violence in the family and on the street.

Transforming inegalitarian social philosophies, value premises, and hierarchical relationships based on gender into egalitarian ones may result in a corresponding modification of the position of women (and men) in our society in each sphere of social life (Brock-Utne, 1985; Gil, 1989). This transformation would tend to result in an increase in the rights of women, a decrease in the degree of alienation at work, and a rejection of the use of force and violence in both child care practices and adult intimate relations. Such changes would tend to positively influence psychological well-being and minimize the processes that trigger battering as expressions of domination and control, anger, psychic survival, or validation. Primary prevention programs aimed at restructuring the prevailing gender-based inegalitarian practices of child care and relations among intimates may, in turn, tend to reduce the acceptability of violence in the other spheres of interaction.

To illustrate, physical punishment plays a crucial role in teaching people to accept violence. As stated earlier, physical punishment within many families begins in infancy, before speech is developed. The primacy of this learning is built into the deepest layers of these children's emerging personalities (Straus and Smith, 1990:517). When children are exposed to direct violence and an acceptance of violence from the mouths and hands of their parents, they perhaps effectively learn to avoid certain dangers (e.g., fires, cars), but they may also learn to associate love, care, or protection with violence. They learn that those who love and care most deeply about them use physical violence or the threat of it and claim this violence is morally necessary to exercise power, discipline, teach, or control them (Straus, 1977:202). Furthermore, they learn that the use of force or physical violence is an acceptable method for "getting one's way." Moreover, they learn to respond to conflict with verbal attack, withdrawal, anger, or violence rather than with problem raising and solving, negotiation, apology, accommodation, understanding, compromise, and change. Such conflict "resolution" styles may later be instituted with partners or children and form part of a set of factors that differentiate violent from nonviolent relationships (Margolin, Sibner, and Gleberman, 1988; Lloyd, 1990).

It is these connections and lessons that some men who choose to act violently learn and generalize from their experiences as children (as survivors of violence and/or as witnesses of or identifiers with the person using violence) to their later relationships with other adults in the family or to spheres outside the family. We must recognize that the lessons, justifications, neutralizations, and ideologies of violence within the family are extraordinarily similar to those presented to us to legitimate violence between nation-states. This is not to suggest that those who accept or undertake violence for "reasons of state," for reasons of "national defense," or for the purpose of "making the world safe for democracy" learned their justifications for violence at home as children. Justifications for violence for reasons of state or for reasons of profit are institutionalized, positively valued, and readily learned within the organizations and hierarchies for which these persons work and from which they receive positive reward.

If, however, a significant number of us were, in our interactions and decision-making practices with our intimate partners and children, to imagine ourselves as individually unique (with differing talents, skills, developed abilities, and potential) but in different phases of the life cycle, we could imagine democratic, participatory family arrangements for maintaining the household, for making decisions about it, and for taking responsibility for both ourselves and one another (see Figure 1.1). If we were to institute these relations (a neverending process), we might feel that we are listened to; that our ideas, feelings, desires, and choices are valued; that we make a contribution to the culture of the family; and that our voice does count. If we were to create patterns of family interaction and conflict resolution that, regardless of sex and age, reflected dignity, equality, individual preciousness, and self-worth, then we could, with considerable energy, carry our positive sense of self and our ideals into our social, classroom, workplace, and political discourse. These more egalitarian and participatory processes of conflict resolution, decisionmaking, care of children, and division of labor in the family might lead to workplace democracy or to workplaces that would reflect "production for need" (e.g., cooperatives, producer-consumer federations) as opposed to "production for profit."

Experiencing violence, domination, and indignity at work has an enormous effect on an individual's interaction in other life spheres. As has been noted (Chapter 2), many survivors of objectification, indignity, and violence in the work setting who themselves subscribe to dominance norms frequently become victimizers in other spheres (e.g., batterers) (Gil, 1989; Barling and Rosenbaum, 1986; Straus, 1980c; Margolin, Sibner, and Gleberman, 1988). Inverting this relationship by creating programs and processes that increase participation in the workplace and reflect dignity and equality might carry over to the family sphere. However, egalitarian work arrangements would have to be generalized to sex and age equality, not an easy transfer. In fact, in the short run, during social arrangement and interpersonal transition, conflict may tend to increase until and unless those involved become comfortable with egalitarian social arrangements (Margolin, Sibner, and Gleberman, 1988:99).

It is, of course, possible that we may enter or co-create a workplace that is participatory, where decisions are discussed, where our ideas are respected and solicited within a work group, where we decide what we will produce or provide and who will do what tasks. Such places of work would tend to arrange work so that each individual is doing what he or she really enjoys doing—even when this changes or a variety of tasks can be chosen. These work arrangements (Gil, 1986:143–146; Gil, 1989:48–53) would increase the level at which needs are met and pain is diminished. They would foster a strong sense of self, dignity, and empowerment that might reinforce or spill over to the nature of intimate relationships within the family. If the collective culture and the social arrangements of the family and workplace reinforce one another, fostering neither structural nor interrelational violence, then these experiences may be contagious to our collective decision-making processes and organizational arrangements in other spheres of collective life.

Primary Prevention with an Individual Focus

A comprehensive primary prevention approach must recognize that battering is expressed in varying patterns of behavior in differently composed intimate relationships. As previously presented, different forms of battering may well be associated with distinct sets of persons and involve different causal dimensions, motivations (domination and control, expressive anger, validation of self, etc.), meanings, and consequences.[4]

Similar to primary prevention of disease, primary prevention of battering requires that the recipient of intervention be identified (Bowen and Sedlak, 1985:3). Unlike disease, however, battering involves more than one person for whom intervention is necessary. The effects of battering are not limited to the "person with the presenting problem." In the instance of battering of women by men, the person with the presenting problem of injury, safety, disempowerment, distress, confusion, depression, rage, betrayal, and need is the survivor. It is of vital importance that we listen to survivors, attempt to help them meet their needs, and collectively provide restorative justice (Zehr, 1990). Supporting this position, yet attempting to establish a focus appropriate for primary prevention, I have not principally focused on women, on women as survivors, or on interventions for survivors, even though intervening with the person who chooses to batter is in many instances intervening for the survivor. Rather, I have focused on men who batter women—on their violence, their choice to threaten and control, their need to stop battering, and their need for empowerment—because men are the persons with the presenting problem. Moreover, I have strongly asserted that the social arrangements and cultural structures that form the context within which interpersonal battering takes place are the most essential target for our intervention. Ultimately, these structures are the primary presenting problem.

That battering involves multiple recipients for public health intervention has implications not only for "targeting the population or arrangements for intervention" but also for delineating stages of preventive intervention. Specifically intervening with women who are survivors of battering (*secondary prevention*) and generally intervening to aid all women of all ages to empower themselves (*primary prevention*) may lead to intrapersonal, interpersonal, and social arrangement changes that would have a *primary preventive* effect on their children (providing an environment for them that would enhance, rather than diminish, their developmental potential). Gary Bowen and Andrea Sedlak (1985:3) point out that specifically intervening with a husband to end his battering (*tertiary prevention*) and generally aiding men of all ages to empower themselves (*primary-prevention*) may result in intrapersonal, interpersonal, and, most important, social arrangement changes that would have a *primary preventive* effect on battering by his, especially male, children when they become adults (Carter, Stacey, and Shupe, 1988: 270).

This issue requires further exploration. Violence in the family of origin is believed by many to be one of the more significant sources of subsequent violence. Research examining the intergenerational learning and transfer of battering indicates some support for the thesis that the presence of aggression in a person's family of origin has an impact on the development of subsequent aggressive relationships in that person's family of procreation.[5] Many researchers argue that men who witness or experience family violence during childhood are more likely to both approve of the use of violence and resort to violence to "resolve" family conflicts in adulthood. Jack Carter, William Stacey, and Anson Shupe assert that

> previous research (e.g., Jayaratne, 1977; Rosenbaum and O'Leary, 1981; Stacey and Shupe, 1983) has seriously questioned the empirical basis for a "generational transfer" of violence from a woman's family of orientation to her own, as far as her victimization is concerned. This study, however, suggests that the cycle of violence theory may have merit in terms of males' behavior. Socialization experiences of wife batterers, whether involving neglect, outright abuse, or merely witnessing parental/sibling abuse, appear to be directly related to the severity of their later adult violence in the family. Whether adult violence is measured by *how* these men batter women, or with what *effect*, or by some

combination of the two dimensions that yields a better overall picture of the violence's severity, the results are the same. Merely witnessing interparental violence seems the most important of the early "sources" of adult violence.
(1988:270)

Similarly, Gerald Hotaling and David Sugarman's study (1986) of risk
markers in husband-to-wife violence and Debra Kalmuss's (1984) research
on marital aggression suggest that witnessing violence as a child is a more
consistent risk marker for wife battering than is being the object of violence.
Attempting to specify the nature of these experiences and their later effects,
Lynn Caesar (1988) has obtained both the details of exposure to events (or
practices) of physical violence and the meanings attached to these experiences. She has found that men who had battered their partners were more
likely than men who had not (a nonbattering comparison group) to have
been abused as children and to have witnessed their fathers battering their
mothers. Her data also indicate that men who had battered their partners
were more likely to describe themselves as having been disciplined as a child
with corporal punishment, which in most cases was considered a standard,
justified practice, even when it was harsh.

Extending this research, Nancy Shields, George McCall, and Christine
Hanneke (1988) interviewed men involved in distinctly different patterns of
violence against adults—those involved in "family only" violence; those involved in "nonfamily only" violence, and those involved in both family and
nonfamily violence (the "generally" violent). Their research indicates that
the "generally" violent and "nonfamily only" violent men used more violence
and held much stronger positive attitudes about the use of violence than did
the "family only" violent men. "Family only" violent men were, however,
more likely to have experienced victimization by their fathers when they
were children. This finding

that fathers of "family only" husbands were more likely to have been violent
with them as children was consistent with the large body of family violence literature that suggests that acceptance of the use of violence against family
members is passed on from one generation to the next (Kalmuss, 1984). That
"family only" husbands were relatively more violent with family compared with
nonfamily members further suggests that, for this violence pattern, socialization *to acceptance of violence may rather be specific to particular targets.*
Among this group, higher levels of remorse following violence may also indicate that the "cycle of violence" is a value system learned in the home. ...

In general, our findings support a social-cultural theory of violence (Gelles, 1974) as well as a social-structural theory of violence (Straus et al., 1980), in that those men who were involved in the most violence, used the most severe · forms of violence overall, and held the most favorable attitudes toward the use of violence (i.e., our "generally" and "nonfamily only" groups) also appeared to be involved in a deviant lifestyle organized around illegal activities that often involves violence. The values and attitudes regarding the use of interpersonal violence are probably learned and supported by the social groups in which these men participate.

In other words, our findings support the notion that violence is culturally transmitted. Acceptance of the use of violence seems to be passed on to younger generations of the family, as well as by social groups outside the family (Shupe et al., 1986). Some men probably receive support for the use of violence inside and outside the home, while others have learned to view the use of violence as acceptable only with certain targets.

It is also probable that "generally" violent and "nonfamily only" violent husbands learn violent behavior from nonfamily social groups of which they are a part. Although our data do not directly address this issue, it seems plausible that violent men may learn from family members that the use of violence outside the home is justified, and that some violent men may receive social support from nonfamily groups for the use of violence against family members. Perhaps it is socialization to a "subculture of violence" that shapes one's general attitudes about and participation in violence (Shupe et al., 1986), while it is one's specific "family culture" that inclines him toward or against violence at home (Fagan, 1987). (1988:92–93) (italics added)

Other researchers agree that battering is affected by affiliation with those who approve the use of violence and the assertion of dominance, especially male dominance (Cappell and Heiner, 1990; MacEwen and Barling, 1988; Stark and Flitcraft, 1985; Kurz, 1989). These researchers suggest that the association of violence in the family of origin and violence in the current family is neither as pervasive as was previously thought nor as lacking in complexity. Indeed, Stark and Flitcraft (1985:168) conclude that the vast majority of persons from violent childhoods do not become physically violent and that the vast majority of men who batter women do not come from physically violent families of origin. The intergenerational transfer of violence is a very complex process, and interpersonal violence in the family of origin is but one source among many for the battering of women.

Most unfortunately, the intergenerational transfer research does not indicate the presence of structural violence within the family of origin or procreation and is therefore seriously flawed. Future researchers must collect these data and also investigate (1) the nature of the conflict resolution strategies used in different relationships (Lloyd, 1990); (2) the full involvement of batterers in different types of battering, violence, and controlling behaviors (Pence, 1985, 1989); and (3) the scope of men's (and women's) violence as it is related to participation in different social groups and spheres.

Primary Prevention Interventions and Processes

Primary prevention awareness interventions can be instituted to increase consciousness of how different forms of violence (e.g., battering, child abuse, U.S. foreign policy, and global corporate violence) interconnect. Awareness interventions can also raise consciousness about how gender conceptions, gender socialization experiences, and personal development opportunities based on gender diminish the dignity and potentiality of all women and all men.

Raising people's awareness of battering as a social problem has been a major objective of many domestic violence groups and of the battered women's movement. Made-for-television movies and documentaries, public-speaking engagements, outreach-education classes, task force hearings, conferences, shelter-based information programs, brochures, and posters are just a few ways in which the nature and pervasiveness of battering, the public health threat it poses, the immediate and perhaps intergenerational consequences of battering, and the availability of programs for those involved have been brought to public attention (Goolkasian, 1986:117–118). Media exposure and consciousness-raising programs have helped reframe battering as a social problem that involves the very core of our lives—the way we think and act toward one another, make decisions affecting others, and organize our lives. Women who have survived battering are learning that they are not alone and can find help in their communities. Men who batter are being informed that their violence, whatever its pattern or form, is both unacceptable and illegal. They are being told that their battering has effects not only on their intimate relationships but also on themselves and on us. Those who are not so directly affected by battering are at least becoming sensitive to the issue and exploring how they are implicated in battering via their values, behaviors, and relationships. The secrecy involved in battering is being disclosed, laying bare, for those willing to break through the mystifications, the fact that domination, mystification, isolation, and alienation are present in many spheres of our lives.

Awareness programs are also being created and developed for specific sets of persons: for medical, mental health, and criminal justice workers; for clergy and teachers who are likely to come into contact with batterers, survivors, and witnesses of battering; and for women who have been battered or who are in violent relationships. Primary prevention programs are also being established for adolescents who are about to enter intimate adult relationships and for teenage mothers (Schinke et al., 1986) and other parents. These programs provide information about gender expectations, nonhierarchical relationships, problem-solving strategies, personal validation skills, stress management skills, dating and marital expectations and realities, listening and communication skills, healthy ways of dealing with "negative" emotions, violence and the acceptance of it, and healthy ways of resolving conflicts and cooperating with others (Levy, 1984).

Problem-solving, peace education, and conflict resolution programs are also being created for children. To illustrate, a primary prevention program designed to teach children prosocial behavior that would be reinforced by parents and nursery school teachers has been instituted at a community mental health center in Philadelphia (Flaste, 1987). When problems and conflicts arise, children are taught to think about the points of view of other children and of as many ways as possible of dealing with the situation. Three months are spent encouraging this kind of thinking in make-believe situations such as puppet shows or stories. The children are also encouraged to think about the consequences of each alternative. (There is no emphasis on how "correct" any specific alternative might be.) Then, for a month or two, the children are urged to use in real situations what they have learned. Those children who at the age of four or five are able to think of alternatives and consequences demonstrate an increased concern for others. When these children see someone in a corner crying, they now more frequently than before try to help. The children also become less aggressive and impulsive in their behavior. They learn to practice how to get along with others in creative, imaginative, and friendly ways. For example, a child who has been left out of a group spends some time trying to think of a way to join. Finally, instead of pushing her way into the group, she shouts, "If you need a fireman, I'm right here." In response, one of the children in the group just happens to spot a pretend fire.

The entire fall-winter (1991) issue of the *Peace Reporter* presents a number of models of peace education. A major focus of these various programs is to teach nonviolent conflict resolution skills to parents, teachers, and schoolchildren. Many programs are based on the Community Board Program of San Francisco. In these programs faculty and staff become volunteer coordinators and train students as conflict managers. At the elementary school level, the emphasis is on deescalating incidents and bringing about agreement. Pairs of conflict managers wear "Conflict Manager" T-shirts on the playground and in the lunchroom and help resolve disputes through a four-step intervention process. At the middle and high school levels, there is a more formal process of dispute definition and resolution.

In New York City, the Resolving Conflicts Creatively Program involves more than thirty-five hundred students and twelve hundred teachers in 120 schools. Peace education and conflict resolution are framed as central to the process by which young people become responsible decision-makers and active participants in society. Instruction takes place on three levels: through the organization of the classroom (classroom management), through the teaching of conflict resolution skills directly, and through an infusion of conflict analysis into subject areas such as literature and social studies.

Like many school systems, Montgomery County, Maryland, incorporates conflict resolution into its school curriculum but in addition offers mediation in Spanish, Vietnamese, and English. In Rochester, New York, the Conciliation Task Force of the Judicial Process Commission offers "peaceful problem solving skills" to preschoolers and elementary school students. In 1991 alone, one hundred teachers, five hundred elementary school students, and one hundred preschool students were helped to identify feelings, articulate emotions, and engage in problem solving through cooperation.

Such programs and processes help teachers, children, and parents develop an increased sensitivity to others and recognize that conflict can be an occasion for growth. They also learn that there are many alternatives for defining and dealing with problems rather than discovering the one "right" answer or having one imposed. Perhaps most important, participants in these programs discover that the skills necessary to solve problems and bring about a more peaceful world can be learned (Allers, 1992).

Let me add, however, that these programs and processes are likely to have little effect when they are countered by the modes of learning, the curricula, or the social organization of the classroom or home. Unless what is learned is experientially reinforced—that is, practiced in a relationship, family, school, classroom, or work setting to restructure the social arrangements—it is likely to have little impact. Extensions of these programs and processes are being developed for school administrators, teachers, and teachers in training. In addition, predating and premarriage education programs as well as prebirthing, parenting education programs and support groups for new parents need to be more extensively developed and implemented. Pre-life-transition education programs could also be developed. Yet changing a phenomenon as deeply embedded in our society as battering is a vast undertaking. A broad public understanding of and commitment to change are necessary if we, as individuals and as groups, are to attend to structural change in each sphere of social life (Straus, 1980b:231).

Again, violence and battering between intimates are *not* an inevitable part of human interaction. They are largely a reflector and generator of specific values and social arrangements, gender arrangements, economic arrangements, age arrangements, and decision-making arrangements within the family and in other units of the society, especially as these arrangements justify the use of violence and the exercise of power. The prevalence and incidence of battering can be significantly decreased if we choose to transform, rather than react to or accommodate, the social arrangements that constitute structural violence (Gil, 1977:29). We need to develop programs and policies that support nonviolence in families and reduce internal and external stress and inequalities (Gelles and Straus, 1988:194). The prevalence and incidence of battering can be significantly reduced if we eliminate cultural supports for the use of violence as a means of resolving disagreements, perceived injustices, and conflicts while providing alternative values and problem-solving processes (Gelles and Straus, 1988:194; Pence, 1987). Furthermore, battering can be decreased if public policy changes that address the many sources of battering are implemented (Brock-Utne, 1985; Straus, 1980b).

As indicated throughout this book, the existing social organization of work must be reconceptualized and transformed into a nonviolent process and experience (Gil, 1986). Productive resources must become far more accessible to everyone. Work and production should be geared toward meeting people's needs. Poverty and "worklessness" must be eliminated as they undermine individuals' self-assessments and directly limit their ability to cope with social and psychological stress (Gelles and Straus, 1988:202). Individuals should cooperatively participate to select, design, direct, and perform work as a means to sustain existence and enhance the quality of life (Gil, 1977:30). When the context of work and social life becomes democratic, cooperative, and intrinsically rewarding, socialization at home and at school will no longer initiate authoritarian and punitive processes of interaction and learning (Gil, 1977:30, 1979a).

Recognized human rights must be expanded. Women and children must be regarded as persons entitled to the full protection of the Constitution, including the integrity and inviolability of their minds and bodies (Gil, 1986:147). Sexism in all its forms, in all spheres of social life, must be eliminated. The organization of work, the division of labor within the family, and decision-making processes within society must reflect sex equality (Brock-Utne, 1985; Straus, 1980b). The changes suggested in Figure 1.1 must be developed. Adequate health maintenance and medical care must be provided to all persons. Comprehensive and quality child care arrangements must be established (Straus, 1980b; Gil, 1986:147). The marital relationship, indeed all intimate relationships, must be redefined "as one in which any use of physical force is as unacceptable as it is between oneself and those with whom one works, bowls, or plays tennis" (Straus, 1980b:229).

As battering reflects societal violence, we must reduce by the maximum amount possible the use of physical force as an instrument of governance (Straus, 1980b:229). A first step in this process might be to pass legislation (such as that enacted in Scandinavian countries) that bans capital punishment, corporal punishment, and the use of spanking by parents (Gelles and Straus, 1988:198). Violence in the media must be limited to as much as is consistent with preserving freedom of expression and artistic integrity (e.g., developing nonviolent programming for children, banning commercials advertising war toys or violence-related toys, or at least allowing advertising to counter the message of violent toys and games [Straus, 1980b; Gelles and Straus, 1988:199]). Educational programs that teach noncoercive and nonviolent means of caring for children need to be implemented. Parent education programs that provide parents with alternatives to violence for resolving conflicts need to be organized and supported (Straus, 1980b; Gelles and Straus, 1988:199). The list of suggestions is endless.

Conclusion

What is clear from this inquiry into the nature and primary prevention of battering is that battering is a social problem deeply embedded in the cultural and social organization of our society. All too often it is easier to confront others about their actions than to challenge our own. It seems safer to ask others to change than to do so ourselves. Nonetheless, if we are to end battering and pursue our full individual and collective potential, we must confront ourselves—our values and our participation at all levels of social life. Only then, while in the process of changing ourselves, and with the support of others, can we begin to creatively alter the gender, age, economic, and political hierarchies within which most of us now interact and communicate.

Notes

Chapter 1

1. This statement has considerable validity when victimization by a "stranger" is illegal, as when a person is robbed while walking down the street. We are, however, much more likely to be seriously victimized by a different kind of stranger (e.g., a corporate executive)—one whose behavior is legal but whose actions and decisions substantially appropriate our health, our freedom of choice, and perhaps even the duration of our lives (Reiman, 1979, 1984; Elias, 1986; Kramer, 1989).

This statement is also significant in that national crime victimization surveys have only rarely included victimization by intimates. As a consequence, researchers have consistently found women's fear of violent crime to be much greater than their measured chances of being violently victimized. When researchers count women's experiences of intimate violence, women's fear of violent crime shows a factual, experiential basis (Smith, 1988).

2. There is a voluminous literature on violence and the acceptance of violence in our society. The following references generally focus on family violence and forms of societal violence that constitute a context for family violence: Straus (1973, 1977); Hotaling and Sugarman (1986); Bowker (1983); Dobash and Dobash (1979); Flitcraft and Stark (1978); Horton and Williamson (1988); Martin (1981); Schechter (1982); Bograd (1984); Brock-Utne (1985); Giles-Sims (1983); Wardell, Gillespie, and Leffler (1983); Quinney (1991); Pepinsky (1991, 1991a); Pepinsky and Quinney (1991); Pagelow and Johnson (1988); Smith (1990); Breines and Gordon (1983); Tifft and Sullivan (1980); Sullivan (1980); Lobel (1986); and Pence (1987, 1988a, 1989).

3. See the following references for this history: Oppenlander (1981); Pleck (1987); Pagelow (1988a); Schechter (1982); NiCarthy (1986); Taub and Schneider (1982); Davidson (1977); and Saline (1984).

4. Definitional dissensus concerning what behaviors constitute battering and who is defined as an intimate partner or victim has impeded research, public policy formulation, and intervention (Margolin, Sibner, and Gleberman, 1988; Bowen and Sedlak, 1985; Strach, Jervey, Hornstein, and Porat, 1986; Weis, 1988; Yllö, 1988). Some definitions have limited battering to the most extreme manifestations of physical violence and victim inclusion to a select set of battered persons. Benjamin and Adler (1980), for example, define battering as injuries that either are visible for some period of time or

require medical attention. Freeman (1979) asserts that a woman is battered when she has suffered persistent or serious physical violence at the hands of her partner.

These definitions imply that some degree of physical or psychological abuse is socially and/or legally acceptable (McGillivray, 1987; Cecere, 1986:28) and that only specific "victims" are deserving of protection (Merwine, 1987). Such definitions exclude the threat of violence, sexual violence (Kelly, 1988, 1988a), isolation, psychological (Tolman, 1989) or emotional violence (Follingstad et al., 1990), intimidation, threat of disclosure (Hart, 1986a), and the destruction of personal property or pets (Pence, 1985:24–25, 32, 1989:40), although these patterns of behavior are frequently experienced by many battered women (NiCarthy, 1986; Lobel, 1986; Hart, 1986a; Dziggel, 1986:66–68; Pharr, 1986; Marie, 1984; Pence, 1985). The full range of behaviors utilized by batterers is illustrated in Figure 1.2.

Definitions limited to overt physical violence have been charged with creating a distorted and class-based image of battering that has to some extent diverted research, policy, and intervention to a limited set of "victims" and "assailants" (Freeman, 1980; Adams, Jackson, and Lauby, 1988; see also Morash, 1986). Definitions that exclude intimates of the same sex (Lobel, 1986) have had similar distortive effects. See Chapter 1, note 24.

Most definitions, including those used in many state protection order laws, limit the victim of battering to the spouse or former spouse, cohabitee or former cohabitee of the batterer (Freeman, 1980; Merwine, 1987; Morash, 1986; for legislative limitations, see Lerman, Livingston, and Jackson, 1983; Lengyel, 1990; Finn, 1991; for exceptions, see Goolkasian, 1986). Many victims are consequently excluded from legal protection. Women who have never lived with the battering partner do not meet protection eligibility requirements in most states (Lerman, Livingston, and Jackson, 1983; Merwine, 1987), and in some states battered women who establish a legal residence separate from the batterer may forfeit civil protection.

Lerman (1984) suggests that "domestic violence" should refer to any overt acts, attempts, or threats, including battery, assault, coercion, sexual assault, harassment, unlawful imprisonment, unlawful entry, damage to property, and theft, where the perpetrator and the victim have or have had an ongoing personal relationship or living arrangement. Terms such as "family violence" and "wife abuse" are rejected as distractive (Lerman, 1984:67) and exclusionary (Lobel, 1986). See Lerman (1984) for a model statute that attempts to resolve definitional and legislative issues. See McGillivray (1987); Bowen and Sedlak (1985); Lobel (1986); Tifft (1989); Liddle (1989); Straus (1991); Rosenbaum (1988); the text; and Chapter 1, note 13 for further discussions of definitional issues.

Battering can be defined as acts, processes, or social arrangements that obstruct an intimate's potential to develop freely and fully (Gil, 1977, 1979b, 1986, 1987, 1989; Galtung, 1980; Tifft, 1989). This is the definition presented and developed in this book (see Chapters 10 and 11). In concert with this definition of battering, Gil (1979b:69) defines child abuse in the following manner: "This definition views child abuse as inflicted gaps or deficits between circumstances of living which would facilitate the optimal development of children, to which they should be entitled, and their actual circumstances, irrespective of the sources or agents of the deficit.

"Every child, despite his/her individual differences and uniqueness, is to be considered of equal intrinsic worth, and hence should be entitled to equal social, economic, civil, and political rights, so that he/she may fully realize his/her inherent potential and share equally in life, liberty, and happiness. Obviously, these value premises are rooted in the humanistic philosophy of our Declaration of Independence.

"In accordance with these value premises, then, any act of commission or omission by individuals, institutions, or society as a whole, and any conditions resulting from such acts or inactions, which deprive children of equal rights and liberties, and/or interfere with their optimal development, constitute, by definition, abusive or neglectful acts or conditions."

5. National victimization research findings and estimates of the prevalence of battering over the course of marital relationships can be found in the following references: Straus, Gelles, and Steinmetz (1980); Straus and Gelles (1986); Feld and Straus (1989); Straus and Smith (1990); Straus (1991); Walker (1979); and Russell (1982).

6. Ellis (1989) suggests that the greater likelihood of the battering of women in these arrangements is a function, not of the nature of these arrangements, but of the specific concentration of individuals within these "marital status" categories who have had certain kinds of experiences and group affiliations and who occupy specific locations within the social organization of our current society. For example, he suggests that men who are currently cohabiting are more likely to batter their female partners because they are more committed to patriarchal norms and values, more likely to experience a disjunction between these norms and existential or economic conditions in the household, more likely to bring past experiences of violence between intimates into the relationship, and more likely to belong to social groups characterized by high levels of interpersonal violence and an acceptance of it.

7. See Heise (1989); NiCarthy (1989); Campbell (1985); Levinson (1988, 1989); Straus (1983a); and Ulrich (1989).

8. See Steinmetz and Lucca (1988); Masumura (1979); Lester (1980); Yllö (1983); Straus (1983a); and Levinson (1988, 1989).

9. See Levinson (1988); Yllö (1983, 1984); Coleman and Straus (1986); and Hornung, McCullough, and Sugimuto (1981).

10. See Gil (1977); Flitcraft and Stark (1978); Brock-Utne (1985); Schecter (1982); Dobash and Dobash (1979); Bograd (1984); Pence (1987, 1988a, 1989); and Tifft and Markham (1991).

11. For references on the decontextualization of battering, see Bograd (1984); Dobash and Dobash (1979); Stanko (1988); Lobel (1986); Gordon (1988); and Pence (1989). For references presenting the history of the women's movement against battering, see Tierney (1982); Schechter (1982); Pence (1988a); and Davis (1988).

12. I use the phrases *the batterer* and *the battered woman* interchangeably with *the person who batters* and *the person who is battered.* My use of the former terms does not imply that these persons are radically different or specific psychological types.

13. Many researchers (Breines and Gordon, 1983:511–512; Saunders, 1986:48; Hart, 1986a; Levinson, 1988) contend that acts of violence or "marital violence events" should be studied in their context and that extreme caution is needed in the application of particular labels or meanings to simple counts of acts or events. Furthermore, because battering can be most fruitfully conceptualized as a dynamic process (Chapters 3–5), a comprehensive understanding is not well captured through quantitative research methodologies (Williams and Hawkins, 1989a; Ferraro, 1988; Kelly, 1988, 1988a; Follingstad et al., 1990).

The initial studies of marital violence were incidence surveys from which incidence and prevalence rates were computed. (The *incidence rate* is the proportion of new incidents that occur within a period of time within a specific relationship; the *prevalence rate* is the proportion of a population experiencing battering in intimate relationships at a specific time.) These studies indicated that husbands and wives committed similar rates of violent acts (Steinmetz and Lucca, 1988; McNeely and Robinson-Simpson, 1987). The data led some researchers to label violence by women "husband abuse," "mutual combat," or "mutual couple violence" and to infer that women were as violent as men (Straus, 1991), an inference challenged by many (McLeod, 1984; Stark and Flitcraft, 1988; Pleck et al., 1978).

Incidence surveys do not ascertain either the cultural or interaction context of these acts or the meanings these acts have to the persons involved (Denzin, 1984; Marie, 1984; O'Toole and Webster, 1988). They fail to explore the intention (e.g., attack or self-defense) (Saunders, 1988; Ptacek, 1988a), consequences (e.g., the degree of psychological or physical injury), pattern, history, duration (Feld and Straus, 1989; Fagan, 1988), or extent of these acts (Stark and Flitcraft, 1988). They fail to distinguish real violence, clearly understood by all persons involved, from spurious, playful, accidental, or paradoxical violence (Denzin, 1984). To infer from simple counts of acts that men and women are similarly violent imposes meanings that may or may not be those of the persons involved and takes these actions out of the power context within which they take place (Breines and Gordon, 1983:505). Stark and Flitcraft (1988:312) conclude that "husband and wife abuse appear similar only so long as all acts of force are equated irrespective of their social, historical, and political context and consequence."

To infer that the experiences of men who are victimized by violence or a pattern of violence in the home are similar to the experiences of women who are battered is capricious and pernicious (Berk et al., 1983). The "mutual combat" characterization and the "husband abuse syndrome" equivalency characterization are crude empirical distortions. According to Stark and Flitcraft (1988:312), "there are no clinical reports of battering syndrome among men similar to the profile identified among women." See Chapter 8, note 1.

An exploration of the meanings of violent acts and their consequences (Marie, 1984) must be undertaken to fully grasp the personal and cultural realities of these experiences (Stets, 1988; Denzin, 1984, 1984a; Lobel, 1986; Levinson, 1988; Campbell, 1985; Ferraro and Johnson, 1983; Ptacek, 1988a, 1988b; Follingstad et al., 1990). Although most research indicates that women much more frequently report physical battering (Dobash and Dobash, 1977; Straus, 1976; Berk et al., 1983), this may reflect meaning differences, propensity to report differences, and, of course, experience differences.

Even if women's violence against men does not as frequently result in reportable violence or even if it does not constitute a comparable battering pattern, this form of violence should neither be unexplored nor denied nor minimized (Steinmetz and Lucca, 1988; McNeely and Robinson-Simpson, 1987; Straus, 1991). To focus on battered women exclusively deflects attention from the reality that some women, too, are caught up in domination and control, that our society glorifies violence, and that we need to recognize and change violence-producing sociocultural conditions. Denial, silence, and secrecy regarding any form of violence cannot break the cycle of violence.

14. For a critique of this research, see Dobash and Dobash (1984); Mayer and Johnson (1988); Ferraro and Johnson (1983); Denzin (1984, 1984a); Stets (1988); Johnson and Ferraro (1988); and Arias and Johnson (1989).

15. There is evidence of a trend toward official criminal sanction against batterers and the availability of greater protective measures for a more comprehensive population of victims (Goolkasian, 1986a:4–5; Micklow, 1988:411–417; Finn, 1991; Cahn and Lerman, 1991; Lengyel, 1990; Law Enforcement Training Project, 1989). Due primarily to the organizing efforts of battered women's advocates (Schechter, 1982; Pence, 1988a:19; Fagan, 1988) and following the Attorney General's Task Force on Family Violence report (1984), Goolkasian's *Confronting Domestic Violence* (1986), and significant court litigation (Moore, 1985), agencies within the criminal justice system have begun to show a clearer responsibility for taking legal action against domestic violence. Most states have developed an ex parte protective order for battered women. Some states require consideration of domestic violence in child custody decisions, and some states have passed laws against mediation for battered women. Preferred arrest laws and even mandatory arrest laws contain "primary aggressor" language to prevent wholesale arrest of battered women (Osmundson, 1992). The Attorney General's Task Force report (1984:22) recommends that "every law enforcement agency should establish arrest as the preferred response in cases of family violence."

Legislation in a number of states (Lerman, Livingston, and Jackson, 1983; Lengyel, 1990) and policy development in many communities have (1) forced police agencies to define guidelines for arrest practices, (2) mandated data collection and reporting, (3) required domestic violence training programs, (4) provided for victim assistance and protection (e.g., pretrial release restrictions), and (5) authorized the use of civil orders of protection (Finn, 1991). Additionally, some states have legislated standards for batterer's programs and issued sentencing guidelines intended to give the clear messages that this violence will not be tolerated, that offenders will be held accountable for their battering, and that the needs of victims and other family members will be met (Goolkasian, 1986a:2–5; Lengyel, 1990; Finn, 1991; Cahn and Lerman, 1991; Law Enforcement Training Project, 1989).

Arrest is not, however, the *practice* of police departments (Ferraro, 1989; Steinman, 1988; Steinman, ed., 1991). Police are more likely to "handle the immediate situation" and respond to the batterer's "characteristics" (e.g., prior arrests, alcohol abuse, and excessive verbal abuse) (Gondolf and McFerron, 1989) in deciding whether to arrest. Infrequent arrest practice leads many of those who batter to expect few official negative consequences for their violence and leads many victims to conclude that there is little reason to report battering to the police (Stafne, 1989). The National Family Violence Surveys indicate that only about 7 percent of assaults between spouses are reported to the police and that these rarely result in arrest (Straus and Smith, 1990:512).

Unfortunately, the message that violence against women in the home is not serious is infrequently contradicted by decision-makers in the agencies that follow the police within the criminal justice process (Sedlak, 1988a:345). According to Schmidt and Steury (1989), the decision to issue a criminal charge is primarily related to the defendant's appearance and use of drugs or alcohol at the time of violence and only secondarily to the degree of injury, prior offenses, and prior abuse of the particular victim. (For a more comprehensive discussion of the effects of differing police and criminal justice agency intervention policies, see Sherman and Berk, 1985; Berk and Newton, 1985; Jaffe et al., 1986; Berk, Newton, and Berk, 1986; Schmidt, 1987; Fagan, 1988; Steinman, 1988, 1989, 1990; Steinman, ed., 1991; Williams and Hawkins, 1989a; Ferraro, 1989; Mederer and Gelles, 1989; Sedlak, 1988a; Dunford, Huizinga, and Elliott, 1989; Hirschel and Hutchinson, 1991; Ford, 1991; Davis, 1988; Eisikovits and Edleson, 1989; Saunders and Parker, 1989; Schmidt and Steury, 1989; Straus and Lincoln, 1985; Straus and Smith, 1990; Gondolf and McFerron, 1989; Stafne, 1989; Dutton, 1988a; Stith, 1990; Caputo, 1988; and Binder and Meeker, 1988.)

Criminalization indicates a shift from defining battering as a personal or relational problem to recognizing battering as a violent social problem and an issue of human (women's) rights. Abolishing the spousal exemption in sexual assault laws has similarly indicated not only that sexual assault is unacceptable violence but also that the issue of consent is meaningful regardless of marital status (Lerman, 1984:65; Lipsman, 1985; Woods and Paulsen, 1987; Cahn and Lerman, 1991; Pagelow, 1988a). Furthermore, community-coordinated intervention projects (Pence, 1985, 1989; Steinman, ed., 1991) have demonstrated that changing the official policies and procedures of the criminal justice response to battering can undermine at least this official, significant reinforcement for the acceptance of battering and violence against women.

Attempts to go beyond altering the official criminal justice system's reinforcement of battering are in their initial stages of development (Pence, 1988a, 1989). (See Chapter 9.) Unfortunately, legislative and programmatic change has in many communities had unanticipated backlash effects on women. Batterers have raced their partners to court to apply for injunctions, and mutual injunctions have become a favorite neutralizing tactic for some judges. Battered women have been arrested along with their abusers under the preferred and mandatory arrest laws. Furthermore, the growing "men's rights" movement has effectively manipulated some of the best work of legislators and activists for women's rights (Osmundson, 1992).

16. According to Denzin (1984:503), a system of battering instituted again and again is an attempt not merely to destroy but also to systematically deconstruct the other as a person. Battering processes distort, erode, and diminish the person's existential presence (Wilson et al., 1987). As the structure of battering emerges in our understanding, we are looking at the structure of unmaking, uncreating. Battering processes graphically objectify a step-by-step, backward movement along the path by which language and existential presence once came into being and which, in the battering experience, is being reversed or uncreated—deconstructed (Scarry, 1985:20, 1988). Loss of the ability to observe self (Mills, 1985), to express self, and to identify self is often accompanied by depression, debility, dependency, and dread. Battering processes uncreate the survivor's spiritual and material world and deconstruct the culture and existence of self. This critical conceptualization is elaborated in Chapter 3.

17. Even though members of the clergy are the most frequently and often the initial "professional" contacted by battered women, the theological perspective on women's roles advanced by many clergy and religious doctrines inhibits involvement in the problem of the battering of women. In a survey of Protestant pastors, Alsdurf (1985) found support for the claim that pastors hold a patriarchal attitude toward women that results in a "distrustful, even subtly accusatory manner" of response toward survivors whom they counsel. A majority of pastors felt either that the abuse must be "severe" to justify separation or that no amount of abuse justified separation. (For a full discussion of the role of the clergy and of religious ideology in family violence, see Pagelow and Johnson, 1988; Bowker, 1988a; and Horton and Williamson, 1988.)

18. For a general review of individual correlates research, see the following references: Edleson, Eisikovits, and Guttman (1985); Hotaling and Sugarman (1986); Hastings and Hamberger (1988); Hamberger and Hastings (1986a, 1988a); Dutton (1988, 1988a); Adams (1990); and Smith (1990). For information on difficulties with intimacy, see Allen et al. (1989); Purdy and Nickle (1981); Claes and Rosenthal (1990); Gondolf and Hanneken (1987); and Gondolf (1987).

19. For references regarding jealousy, see the following: Bowker (1983); Davidson (1978); Dobash and Dobash (1979); and Adams (1990). For references on exposure to violence, see the following: Browne (1987); Hamberger and Hastings (1988); Hotaling and Sugarman (1986); Sugarman and Hotaling (1989); Caesar (1988); and Seltzer and Kalmuss (1988).

20. See Stets (1988); Berkowitz (1983); Denzin (1984, 1984a); Breines and Gordon (1983); O'Toole and Webster (1988); and Ferraro (1988).

21. Taub and Schneider (1982:123) point out that law has operated directly and explicitly to prevent women from attaining self-support and influence in the public sphere, thereby institutionally reinforcing dependence upon men. At the same time, the absence of law from the private sphere to which many women have been relegated has not only left individual women without formal remedies but has also devalued and discredited women as a "group."

22. The prevalence of battering has fluctuated with different modes of production and participation between and within specific historical periods. It has also varied within differently constituted and organized "families" within these conditions. (See Ellis, 1989; Barrett, 1985; Dobash and Dobash, 1979; Zaretsky, 1976; and Pharr, 1988.)

23. See Marie (1984); Hart (1986a); NiCarthy (1986); Lobel (1986); Brand and Kidd (1986); Renzetti (1988, 1989); and Pharr (1988).

24. I was unable to locate research on the incidence and prevalence of battering among gay and lesbian intimates. Frequently gay and lesbian intimates are excluded by the language of domestic violence statutes from eligibility for programs aiding survivors of battering. Twenty-four states currently restrict domestic abuse legislation to persons of the "opposite sex" (Lengyel, 1990:63–64). Several survivor programs for gays have been established. Yet as recently as 1987 there were no programs for gays who were perpetrators of this form of violence. MOVE, a program offering counseling for gay and straight men who batter, has sought to meet this need in San Francisco. The premises of this program are that violence is a men's issue and that battering occurs in gay relationships as frequently as in nongay relationships.

Violence among gay and lesbian intimates must be understood in the larger cultural and social structural context of violence, antigay/antilesbian violence, homophobia, and sexism (Pharr, 1988). At the center of violence against gays and lesbians is ethnoviolence, a concept defined by Ehrlich (1990:361) as referring to an act or attempted act in which the actor is motivated to do psychological or physical harm to another where the "other" is perceived as a group representative or is identified with a group and where the motivation for the act is group prejudice. (For an excellent introduction to the context and ecology of antigay violence see Herek, 1990; Ehrlich, 1990; and articles in the *Journal of Interpersonal Violence* 5, no. 3 [1990]. For information on antilesbian violence and battering among lesbian intimates, see Chapter 1, note 28, especially Lobel, 1986.)

25. Piercy (1976) and Le Guin (1974) illustrate how language is symbolic of our values and social arrangements. If we desire to bring about a society without hierarchy based on gender and without possessive (ownership) relations, we must create language that reflects these desires, values, and arrangements. In this quote *person* and the pronoun *per* replace pronouns that designate sex (e.g., "him," "her"); *the partner* replaces language that designates sex and possession (ownership) (e.g., "my wife or husband").

26. For references on the differing dimensions and patterns of battering, see Pence (1985, 1987, 1989); Russell (1982); Kelly (1988, 1988a); Sonkin, Martin, and Walker (1985); Tolman (1989); Patrick-Hoffman (1982); Denzin (1984, 1984a); NiCarthy (1986); and Dziggel (1986).

27. For references to differing motivations, see the following: Wallerstein and Kelly (1980); Pillemer (1985); Ellis and DeKeseredy (1989); Ferraro (1988); Gondolf (1985, 1988c); Gondolf and Fisher (1988); Allen et al. (1989); Ptacek (1988a, 1988b); and Tolman (1989). For references to differing sources or "causal" dimensions, see the following: Bowen and Sedlak (1985); Gondolf (1985, 1988, 1988a, 1988b, 1988c); Dutton (1988, 1988a); Shields and Hanneke (1983); Hotaling and Sugarman (1986); Carter, Stacey, and Shupe (1988); Shields, McCall, and Hanneke (1988); and Caesar (1988).

28. It is clear that women who are differently situated within age, class, ethnic or cultural group, sex-relational, and organizational context are differentially at risk to victimization and injury. Differently situated women vary in their survivor strategies and empowerment needs and therefore require different programmatic supports if we are to aid them in making healthful decisions about their own lives. (For a discussion of this literature, see Schwartz, 1988, 1988a, 1990; McGillivray, 1987; Lockhart, 1987; Lockhart and White, 1989; Coley and Beckett, 1988, 1988a; Torres, 1987; Ellis, 1989; Feyen, 1989; Kurdek and Schmitt, 1986; Krestan and Bepko, 1980; Renzetti, 1988, 1989; Pharr, 1986, 1988; Vargo, 1987; Pearlman, 1987; Engelhardt and Triantafillou, 1987; Lobel, 1986; Campbell, 1985; Levinson, 1988, 1989; Gondolf, Fisher, and McFerron, 1988; and Gelles, 1988.)

29. According to Hart (1986), there are no personal attributes or circumstances that permit reliable prediction or identification of the lesbian who will batter her intimate partner. Preliminary research indicates that she is (1986:20–25) (1) perhaps the partner who is physically stronger, and perhaps not; (2) perhaps the partner who has more personal power and greater access to resources, and perhaps not; (3) perhaps the partner who experienced violence as a child, and perhaps not; (4) perhaps the partner who is acutely homophobic, and perhaps not; (5) perhaps the partner who holds contempt for women or who identifies with men, and perhaps not; (6) perhaps the partner who perceives herself to be victimized by the world and misused or controlled by the victim, and perhaps not; (7) perhaps the partner who has anger control or communication problems, and perhaps not.

30. See NiCarthy (1986); Sedlak (1988a); Pence (1987); Margolin, Sibner, and Gleberman (1988); Sonkin, Martin, and Walker (1985); and Sonkin and Durphy (1982) for a review of programs that provide support, advocacy, and safety for the victims of battering. Today, a strong network of domestic violence programs crisscrosses the country. Yet within the context of a fiscal crisis for all social programs, community shelters face increasing competition for funding and referrals from state-run services, which include programs for men who batter and victim support services structurally linked with the criminal justice system (Currie, 1990:90). Social change programs are

increasingly endangered. Funding is tenuous in spite of the passage of legislation creating local, state, and national funding. Many shelters have become United Way agencies or supplement funding by raising private contributions. The National Network of
Women's Funds estimates that 5 percent of charitable giving is directed to programs
specifically serving women and girls (Osmundson, 1992:8).

As programs have become institutionalized, funders have exerted their power. As
paying jobs have developed, applicants are required to have degrees; formerly
battered women and lesbians are no longer qualified. Pressure by funders has led to
other changes. "Battered women" have become "family violence." Advocates and organizers have become counselors and therapists. Antiracism and homophobia work
has become risky (Osmundson, 1992:8). As the need to maintain funding for services
has become paramount, social change organizers and critical thinkers have been
driven out of some shelters. Some shelters have opted for the mental health model,
while others are struggling to maintain their vision for social justice. Today, shelters are
interminably full, and yet many battered women do not have transportation to reach
them. Some rural women must travel hundreds of miles. Women with disabilities,
mental health, and substance abuse problems are all too frequently denied shelter
(Osmundson, 1992:8).

Many shelters limit residence to a month or so. Lack of affordable housing, day
care, medical care, and jobs that pay decent wages makes it virtually impossible for
survivors to get by on their own. To meet the need, some shelters have developed tran-
sitional housing programs, day care centers, and job training programs. But each of
these services is expensive. Funding buildings and services has in many places become
the goal, while organizing for social change to end the "war" against women has taken a
back seat (Osmundson, 1992:8).

In spite of these conditions, many women activists continue to organize, and many
community-coordinated intervention organizers and participants recognize the necessity of altering the social arrangements and cultural values that underlie and foster battering (Pence, 1985, 1987, 1988a, 1989). (Community-coordinated intervention programs are discussed in Chapter 9. Extensive social change recommendations are given
by Brock-Utne, 1985:72–142; Gil, 1977, 1986, 1989; Straus, 1980c; Straus and Smith,
1990; and Gelles and Straus, 1988. Primary prevention programs are discussed in
Chapter 11.)

Chapter 2

1. These contexts are explored in the following references: Gil (1987, 1989);
Flitcraft and Stark (1978); Dobash and Dobash (1984); Schwartz (1988, 1988a);
Carlson (1984); Eisikovits and Edleson (1989); Straus (1983); and Giles-Sims (1983).

2. The following references review the history and development of the movement
and programs: Schechter (1982); Pence (1983, 1985, 1989); Soler and Martin (1983);
and Gamache, Edleson, and Schock (1988).

Chapter 3

1. Walker's (1979a) identification of the calm, loving stage is perhaps, in part, a direct result of the fact that she interviewed only women. Stets (1988:102) reports from interviews with men who battered and women who were battered that the loving stage appeared almost exclusively in women's accounts. A majority of the women indicated that their partners were apologetic and loving after a violent incident.

Two interpretations can be made regarding the fact that men in general do not mention a loving stage. On the one hand, the loving stage may exist only from the battered woman's perspective. Because her partner's behavior after an incident becomes very salient to her, she may focus all her attention on him, especially on how he will behave next. She may interpret any act of kindness as a display of his love for her, particularly as she may have viewed his violence as a lack of love. Thus, she may experience a contrast effect, which places her in a double bind.

Ferraro and Johnson (1983:332) suggest that when these periods of remorse and solicitude occur, they deepen the emotional bonds and make rejection more difficult. (It should be noted, however, that not all men who batter experience or express remorse [Adams, 1989:84]). Ferraro and Johnson also suggest that as battering progresses in a relationship, periods of remorse may shorten, or disappear, thereby eliminating the basis for maintaining a positive outlook on the marriage. After a number of episodes of violence, the batterer may realize that his partner will not retaliate or escape, and thus he feels no need to express remorse. Extended periods devoid of kindness or love may alter a woman's feelings toward her partner so much that she may eventually begin to define herself as a victim of abuse.

On the other hand, the batterer may be affectionate, caring, or loving to his partner after an incident, not because he wants to express how he truly feels about her, but because he wants to relieve himself of his guilt for the violence. In this sense, this phase of the violence cycle is not a loving stage so much as it is a forgiveness phase (Stets, 1988:102–103, 127). The batterer may not reveal his loving and apologetic behavior after an incident because this would be admitting, both to himself and perhaps to the researcher, that he is sorry for what he did. In turn, this sorrow might imply that he was responsible for the injury he inflicted or that the battering episode was his fault, and this, perhaps, he does not want to admit.

The person who chooses to batter and the person who is battered tend to focus on different aspects of the violent episode because of their differing positions in it. Those who are battered tend to remember the specifics of these incidents because they received the pain. Those who batter consistently underestimate the amount of violence, its frequency, and its severity (Edleson and Brygger, 1986; O'Leary and Arias, 1988; Szinovacz, 1983; Browning and Dutton, 1986). They may be more likely to forget specifics and even whole episodes to preserve their self-esteem or construct a self-concept that does not include this violence. They are more likely to feel shame and guilt, which they do not wish to relive by recalling the episode. Moreover, these men are aware that their actions are unacceptable, at least to the audience who is asking them for an account, if not to themselves or their partners. If they did not feel that their actions were normatively unacceptable, they would not deny, minimize, and rationalize them (Dutton and Browning, 1988a).

Batterers are more likely to focus on their feelings—my emotions were out of control, that was not my real self, it was the booze—rather than on their partners' feelings. Note, however, that if a batterer states he was out of control emotionally and therefore denies responsibility for the violence, he is at the same time admitting that he is the "type of person" who is out of control—not an especially positive attribute, especially for males in our present culture. If a batterer says he was in control—that he could have inflicted a more severe injury had he been less in control—he is suggesting that he is not "a really violent" person or "such a bad person" and that he is a person who takes control. Men who batter are more likely to focus on the fact that they were seemingly able to regain control over their partners, that violence was successful in enforcing submission, and that they did not suffer in relative terms from using violence. Shifting the focus from the victim/damage/wound to the weapon and the effects of its use on the inflictor are essential linguistic techniques in the language of pain infliction, justification, and legitimation (Scarry, 1985, 1988). They are essentials of exercising power.

2. Men who batter do not frequently place themselves in their mates' circumstances (Coates and Leong, 1988:194). If they imagined their victims' position, they might not be able to undertake the violence (Stets, 1988:36). Stets feels that batterers may have low role-taking ability, just as rape assailants do (Franks, 1985). Note, however, that this is not necessarily a personality attribute; it is more likely an attribute of being in a position to exercise power.

Events in many nations repeatedly demonstrate that thinking of others as members of a category, rather than as diverse individuals, can create indifference to extreme violence against those categorized. Making sweeping derogatory generalizations about all people in a particular age, sex, race, color, national, religious, political, or other category is a first step toward treating them inhumanly (Glaser, 1986:23). In this instance many "batterers" think of their partners as members of the category "wife," not as the distinctively separate individuals (with names and identities) they are. A "wife" is supposed to act a certain way, not any way she chooses.

Dissociation allows someone exercising power to not focus on the person controlled as a person. The torturer does not think about, or focus on the pain he is inflicting on, the person tortured. Like the batterer, he is focused on himself. Those who institutionally exercise power, inflict pain, or obstruct others' development organizationally distance themselves. They learn or are taught that they cannot do their jobs if they think about what they are doing to other persons. If we think of all prisoners as in the same category and derogate that category, we can then talk ourselves into acceptably violating them. We can incarcerate, kill, or inhumanely house them; thwart their needs; or make them suffer. We can place them in out-of-the-way locations so we do not have to see the pain they receive. We can isolate them from one another, from their loved ones, from their culture.

Chapter 5

1. These issues are discussed in Chapters 8 and 9. For a detailed discussion of the effects of these programs, see the following references: Ptacek (1988a, 1988b); Gondolf (1987a, 1988, 1988a, 1988b, 1988c); Gondolf and Russell (1986); Tolman and Saunders (1988); Edleson (1988); Margolin, Sibner, and Gleberman (1988); Pence (1985, 1989); Hart (1986, 1988); and Hamberger and Hastings (1988b).

2. These programs are discussed in Chapters 8 and 9. For the details of these programs, see the following references: Pence (1985, 1987, 1988a, 1989); Gondolf and Russell (1986); Gondolf (1985); Sonkin (1988); Jennings (1987); and Adams (1989).

Chapter 6

1. This section is specifically focused on interventions with men who batter women. Most of the literature on battering and responses to battering reflects a definition of the problem as principally the battering of women by their male intimate partners. Even though we have clearly established that in our culture battering is a significant social problem within all adult intimate relationships, most programmatic interventions with assailants have focused on men who batter women. As was mentioned in Chapter 1, note 24, there are only a few intervention programs for men who batter their intimate male partners. There are also only a few programs for either women who batter their intimate female partners or for women who batter their intimate male partners.

2. These issues are specifically discussed in Chapters 7–9. For general sources on research addressing successful interventions with men who batter women, see the following references: Margolin, Sibner, and Gleberman (1988); Eisikovits and Edleson (1989); Edleson and Syers (1990); Gondolf (1987, 1987a, 1987b); Gondolf and Hanneken (1987); and Jennings (1987).

Chapter 7

1. For exposure to violence as children, see the following: Rosenbaum and O'Leary (1981); Roy (1977); Straus, Gelles, and Steinmetz (1980); Walker and Browne (1985); and Hastings and Hamberger (1988). For issues related to alcohol abuse, see Rounsaville (1978); Feazell, Mayers, and Deschner (1984); Berk, Berk, Loseke, and Rauma (1983); and Taylor and Leonard (1983). For further information on adherence to patriarchal expectations, see Davidson (1978); Rosenbaum and O'Leary (1981); Telch and Lindquist (1984); Walker (1979); and Saunders (1984). On low self-esteem,

see Ball and Wyman (1978); Goldstein and Rosenbaum (1985); Neidig, Friedman, and Collins (1985); and Walker (1979). On excessive dependency, see Weitzman and Dreen (1982). On jealousy, see Dewsbury (1975); Rounsaville (1978a); and Scott (1974). On approval of violence, see Straus (1980c). On lack of assertiveness, see O'Leary and Curley (1986).

Chapter 8

1. Gender analysis of battering must not be avoided. Most batterers are men, and most survivors are women. In the face of this experiential reality, terms such as "battering couples," "conjugal violence," "domestic violence," "spouse abuse," and "spousal assaults" are not acceptable (Pence, 1989:1).

To begin meeting the needs of those women who have been severely violated and deconstructed, we must "rescue" and protect them. This does not in any way imply that these women are helpless or that they lack or do not exhibit enormous personal strength in the face of structural and interpersonal terror. According to Pence et al. (1984:479), "We live in a society which decorates policemen, firemen, and concerned citizens who bravely rescue people from burning buildings or raging floods. But when women rescue other women from life threatening violent situations at the hands of their husbands or lovers, suddenly rescuing is equated with home wrecking." (For a discussion and summary of interventions for women who have been battered, see Sedlak, 1988a; Margolin, Sibner, and Gleberman, 1988; and the references in Chapter 1, note 3.)

Chapter 9

1. Community-coordinated interventions are presented in the following references: Pence (1983, 1985, 1987, 1989); Pence and Shepard (1988); Edleson (1991); Gamache, Edleson, and Schock (1988); Brygger and Edleson (1987); and Soler and Martin (1983).

2. I have selected the DAIP program to illustrate community-coordinated interventions because it has served as a model for more than twenty coordinated interventions in other cities (e.g., Milwaukee and Baltimore) (Pence and Shepard, 1988: 294). The DAIP, which has been comprehensively described (Pence, 1987, 1989), represents the most thoughtful, thorough, and practical implementation of programs directly addressing battering as both an interpersonal and a social structural problem.

This remarkable program has with considerable success implemented principles of collective decision-making, participation, empowerment, and equality in its own decision-making processes, in the content and implementation of its programs, in participation in cooperative policy formulation with other agencies, and in follow-up, evaluation, and change procedures. The DAIP embodies choice, openness to change (Pence and Shepard, 1988), and sensitivity to the needs of persons who identify with special groups (e.g., Vietnam-era veterans, Native Americans) (Pence, 1989). It is the most constructive and hopeful intervention program I have been able to locate.

Chapter 10

1. Gondolf (1985:321) points out that we must go much deeper than the issues of anger control and the restraint of oppression. We must confront our cultural notions of who we are and why we are this way. We must go beyond pat therapies and decisive interventions to discover the "real self."

2. Pain, suffering, and distress can result from usual and desired events (e.g., the birth of a child, marriage, career advancements). Periods of life transition can be overwhelming and disruptive of relationships and of the lives of those from whom we receive our most essential support. These life transitions are both natural to our human existence and specific to our cultural and social arrangements.

According to Levinson (1986), we make life choices, build structures around them, and pursue our daily lives within these structures. Then we begin to question and reappraise these structures and values, explore the possibilities for personal and life-direction change, and move toward a commitment to different core choices, which then form the basis of our new life structures. No life structure is permanent—life structure change is as natural as is biological change through the human life span.

Chapter 11

1. See Gill (1977, 1979b, 1986, 1989); Figure 1.1; Pence (1985, 1987, 1989); Brock-Utne (1985); Sullivan (1980); Tifft (1979); Tifft and Sullivan (1980); Tifft and Stevenson (1985); and Tifft and Markham (1991).

2. Bowen and Sedlak (1988:2–5) point out that from a public health perspective, there are three different levels of preventive effort: (1) *primary prevention*—to prevent the disease or condition either by doing something to the at-risk population that strengthens its immunity and resistance to the problem or by doing something to eliminate the noxious or infectious agent and its source; (2) *secondary prevention*—to minimize the impact and duration of the disease or condition by performing early diagnosis and treatment and by channeling efforts to curtail the spread of the problem; and (3) *tertiary prevention*—to keep the disease or condition from getting worse and to rehabilitate the client.

3. For a full introduction to this perspective, see the following references: Gil (1973, 1977, 1979, 1979a, 1979b, 1986, 1987, 1989); Brock-Utne (1985); Straus (1980b, 1980c); Sullivan (1980); Quinney (1991); Pepinsky (1991, 1991a); Tifft and Stevenson (1985); Tifft and Sullivan (1980).

4. These issues are discussed in the following references: Bowen and Sedlak (1985:3–4); Gondolf (1985:319–320); Shields and Hanneke (1983); Hotaling and Sugarman (1986); Carter, Stacey, and Shupe (1988); Shields, McCall, and Hanneke (1988); and Caesar (1988).

5. See Kalmuss (1984); Straus (1974a); Gelles (1974); Straus, Gelles, and Steinmetz (1980); MacEwen and Barling (1988); and Cappell and Heiner (1990).

References

Adams, David. 1989. "Stages of Anti-sexist Awareness and Change for Men Who Batter," pp. 61–98 in Leah J. Dickstein and Carol C. Nadelson, eds., *Family Violence.* Washington, DC: American Psychiatric Press.

_____. 1990. "Identifying the Assaultive Husband in Court: You Be the Judge." *Response* 13:13–16.

Adams, David, Jann Jackson, and Mary Lauby. 1988. "Family Violence Research: Aid or Obstacle to the Battered Women's Movement?" *Response* 11:14–18.

Adams, David C., and Andrew J. McCormick. 1982. "Men Unlearning Violence: A Group Approach Based on the Collective Model," pp. 170–197 in Maria Roy, ed., *The Abusive Partner.* New York: Van Nostrand.

Albee, George W. 1982. "Preventing Psychopathology and Promoting Human Potential." *American Psychologist* 37: 1043–1050.

_____. 1986. "Toward a Just Society." *American Psychologist* 41: 891–898.

Allen, Kathryn, Donald A. Calsyn, Peter A. Fehrenbach, and Gary Benton. 1989. "A Study of the Interpersonal Behaviors of Male Batterers." *Journal of Interpersonal Violence* 4: 79–89.

Allers, Uta. 1992. "Peace and Conflict Resolution Initiatives in U.S. Schools." *Justicia: Newsletter of Greater Rochester Community of Churches Judicial Process Commission,* February, 3–4.

Alsdurf, Jim M. 1985. "Wife Abuse and the Church: The Response of Pastors." *Response* 8:9–11.

Amnesty International. 1973. *Report on Torture.* London: Duckworth/Amnesty International.

Archer, Naomi Hilton. 1989. "Battered Women and the Legal System: Past, Present, and Future." *Law and Psychology Review* 13:145–163.

Arias, Ileana, and Patti Johnson. 1989. "Evaluations of Physical Aggression Among Intimate Dyads." *Journal of Interpersonal Violence* 4:298–307.

Arias, Ileana, Mary Samios, and K. Daniel O'Leary. 1987. "Prevalence and Correlates of Physical Aggression During Courtship." *Journal of Interpersonal Violence* 2:82–90.

Armstrong, Louise. 1983. *The Home Front: Notes on the Family War Zone.* New York: McGraw-Hill.

Athens, Lonnie H. 1977. "Violent Crime: A Symbolic Interactionist Study." *Journal of Symbolic Interaction* 1:56–70.

———. 1980. *Violent Criminal Acts and Actors: A Symbolic Interactionist Study.* Boston: Routledge and Kegan Paul.

———. 1986. "Types of Violent Persons: Toward the Development of a Symbolic Interactionist Theory of Violent Criminal Behavior." *Studies in Symbolic Interaction* 7:367–389.

Attorney General's Task Force on Family Violence. 1984. *Attorney General's Task Force on Family Violence, Final Report.* Washington, DC: U.S. Department of Justice.

Bagarozzi, Dennis A. 1982. "The Family Therapist's Role in Treating Families in Rural Areas: A General Systems Approach." *Journal of Marital and Family Therapy* 8:51–58.

———. 1983. "Methodological Developments in Measuring Social Exchange Perceptions in Marital Dyads (SIDCARB): A New Tool for Clinical Intervention," pp. 79–104 in Dennis A. Bagarozzi, Anthony P. Jurich, and Robert W. Jackson, eds., *Marital and Family Therapy: New Perspectives in Theory, Research, and Practice.* New York: Human Sciences.

Bagarozzi, Dennis A., and C. Winter Giddings. 1983. "Conjugal Violence: A Critical Review of Current Research and Clinical Practices." *American Journal of Family Therapy* 11:3–15.

Bagarozzi, Dennis A., and John S. Wodarski. 1977. "A Social Exchange Typology of Conjugal Relationships and Conflict Development." *Journal of Marriage and Family Counseling* 3:53–60.

Bailey, Roy, and Mike Brake. 1975. *Radical Social Work.* London: Edward Arnold.

Ball, Patricia P., and Elizabeth Wyman. 1978. "Battered Wives and Powerlessness: What Can Counselors Do?" *Victimology* 2:545–552.

Barling, Julian, and Alan Rosenbaum. 1986. "Work Stressors and Wife Abuse." *Journal of Applied Psychology* 71:346–348.

Barrett, Michelle. 1985. *Women's Oppression Today: Problems in Marxist Feminist Analysis.* London: Verso.

Beck, Aaron T. 1978. *Cognitive Therapy and the Emotional Disorders.* New York: International Universities Press.

Bedrosian, Richard C. 1982. "Using Cognitive and Systems Intervention in the Treatment of Marital Violence," pp. 117–138 in Laurence R. Barnhill, ed., *Clinical Approaches to Family Violence.* Rockville, MD: Aspen.

Bell, Daniel. 1985. "Domestic Violence: Victimization, Police Intervention, and Disposition." *Journal of Criminal Justice* 13:525–534.

Benedek, Elissa. 1989. "Baseball, Apple Pie, and Violence: Is It American?" pp. 1–14 in Leah J. Dickstein and Carol C. Nadelson, eds., *Family Violence.* Washington, DC: American Psychiatric Press.

Benjamin, Michael, and Susan Adler. 1980. "Wife Abuse: Implications for Socio-legal Policy and Practice." *Canadian Journal of Family Law* 3:339–368.

Berk, Richard A., Sarah F. Berk, Donileen R. Loseke, and David Rauma. 1983. "Mutual Combat and Other Family Violence Myths," pp. 197–212 in David Finkelhor et al., eds., *The Dark Side of Families*. Newbury Park, CA: Sage.

Berk, Richard A., and Phyllis J. Newton. 1985. "Does Arrest Really Deter Wife Battery? An Effort to Replicate the Findings of the Minneapolis Spouse Abuse Experiment." *American Sociological Review* 50:253–262.

Berk, Richard A., Phyllis J. Newton, and Sarah F. Berk. 1986. "What a Difference a Day Makes: An Empirical Study of the Impact of Shelters for Battered Women." *Journal of Marriage and the Family* 48:481–490.

Berkowitz, Leonard. 1983. "The Goals of Aggression," pp. 166–181 in David Finkelhor et al., eds., *The Dark Side of Families*. Newbury Park, CA: Sage.

Bernard, Jessie L., and M. L. Bernard. 1984. "The Abusive Male Seeking Treatment: Jekyll and Hyde." *Family Relations* 33:543–547.

Binder, Arnold, and James W. Meeker. 1988. "Experiments as Reforms." *Journal of Criminal Justice* 16:347–358.

Blackman, Julie. 1989. *Intimate Violence: A Study of Injustice*. New York: Columbia University Press.

Blumstein, Philip, and Pepper Schwartz. 1983. *American Couples*. New York: Morrow.

Bograd, Michele. 1982. "Battered Women, Cultural Myths, and Clinical Interventions: A Feminist Analysis." *Women and Therapy* 1:69–77.

_____. 1984. "Family Systems Approaches to Wife Battering: A Feminist Critique." *American Journal of Orthopsychiatry* 54:558–568.

_____. 1988. "How Battered Women and Abusive Men Account for Domestic Violence: Excuses, Justifications, or Explanations?" pp. 60–77 in Gerald T. Hotaling et al., eds., *Coping with Family Violence*. Newbury Park, CA: Sage.

Bolton, Frank G., and Susan R. Bolton. 1987. *Working with Violent Families*. Beverly Hills, CA: Sage.

Bookchin, Murray. 1986. *The Modern Crisis*. Philadelphia: New Society.

Boston Lesbian Psychologies Collective, eds. 1987. *Lesbian Psychologies: Explorations and Challenges*. Urbana: University of Illinois Press.

Boulette, Teresa Ramirez, and Susan M. Andersen. 1985. "'Mind Control' and the Battering of Women." *Community Mental Health Journal* 21:109–118.

Bowen, Gary L., and Andrea J. Sedlak. 1985. "Toward a Domestic Violence Surveillance System: Issues and Prospects." *Response* 8:2–7.

Bowker, Lee H. 1983. *Beating Wife Beating*. Lexington, MA: D. C. Heath.

_____. 1988. "The Effect of Methodology on Subjective Estimates of the Differential Effectiveness of Personal Strategies and Help Sources Used by Battered

Women," pp. 80–92 in Gerald T. Hotaling et al., eds., *Coping with Family Violence.* Newbury Park, CA: Sage.

————. 1988a. "Religious Victims and Their Religious Leaders: Services Delivered to One Thousand Battered Women," pp. 229–234 in Anne L. Horton and Judith A. Williamson, eds., *Abuse and Religion.* Lexington, MA: Lexington Books.

Brammer, Lawrence M., and Everett L. Shostrom. 1982. *Therapeutic Psychology,* 4th ed. Englewood Cliffs, NJ: Prentice-Hall.

Brand, Pamela A., and Aline H. Kidd. 1986. "Frequency of Physical Aggression in Heterosexual and Female Homosexual Dyads." *Psychological Reports* 59:1307–1313.

Breines, Wini, and Linda Gordon. 1983. "The New Scholarship on Family Violence." *Signs* 8:490–531.

Brisson, Norman. 1982. "Helping Men Who Batter Women." *Public Welfare* 40:29–47.

Brock-Utne, Brigit. 1985. *Educating for Peace: A Feminist Perspective.* New York: Pergamon Press.

Brown, Bruce W. 1980. "Wife-Employment, Marital Equality, and Husband-Wife Violence," pp. 176–187 in Murray A. Straus and Gerald T. Hotaling, eds., *The Social Causes of Husband-Wife Violence.* Minneapolis: University of Minnesota Press.

Browne, Angela. 1987. *When Battered Women Kill.* New York: Free Press.

Browning, James J., and Donald G. Dutton. 1986. "Assessment of Wife Assault with the Conflict Tactics Scale: Using Couple Data to Quantify the 'Differential Reporting Effort.'" *Journal of Marriage and the Family* 48:375–379.

Brownmiller, Susan. 1975. *Against Our Will: Men, Women, and Rape.* New York: Simon and Schuster.

Brygger, Mary P., and Jeffrey L. Edleson. 1987. "The Domestic Abuse Project: A Multisystems Intervention in Woman Battering." *Journal of Interpersonal Violence* 2:324–336.

Bureau of Justice. 1984. *Bureau of Justice Statistics Special Report: Family Violence.* Washington, DC: U.S. Department of Justice.

Burris, Carole A., and Peter Jaffe. 1983. "Wife Abuse as a Crime: The Impact of Police Laying Charges." *Canadian Journal of Criminology* 25:309–318.

Butler, Marylou. 1985. "Guidelines for Feminist Therapy," pp. 32–38 in Lynne Bravo Rosewater and Lenore E.A. Walker, eds., *Handbook of Feminist Therapy.* New York: Springer.

Buzawa, Eve S. 1988. "Explaining Variations in Police Response to Domestic Violence: A Case Study in Detroit and New England," pp. 169–182 in Gerald T. Hotaling et al., eds., *Coping with Family Violence.* Beverly Hills, CA: Sage.

Caesar, P. Lynn. 1988. "Exposure to Violence in the Families-of-Origin Among Wife Abusers and Maritally Nonviolent Men." *Violence and Victims* 3:49–63.

Cahn, Naomi R., and Lisa G. Lerman. 1991. "Prosecuting Woman Abuse," pp. 95–112 in Michael Steinman, ed., *Woman Battering.* Cincinnati: Anderson.

Campbell, Jacquelyn. 1985. "Beating of Wives: A Cross-cultural Perspective." *Victimology* 10:174–185.

Cantor, Aviva. 1983. "The Club, the Yoke, and the Leash." *Ms. Magazine* (August): 27–29.

Cappell, Charles, and Robert B. Heiner. 1990. "The Intergenerational Transmission of Family Aggression." *Journal of Family Violence* 5:135–152.

Caputo, Richard K. 1988. "Managing Domestic Violence in Two Urban Police Districts." *Social Casework* 69:498–504.

Carlson, Bonnie E. 1984. "Causes and Maintenance of Domestic Violence: An Ecological Analysis." *Social Service Review* 58:569–586.

———. 1987. "Dating Violence: A Research Review and Comparison with Spouse Abuse." *Social Casework* 68:16–23.

Carson, Barbara A. 1986. "Parents Who Don't Spank: Deviation in the Legitimation of Physical Force." Ph.D. diss., University of New Hampshire.

Carter, Jack, William A. Stacey, and Anson W. Shupe. 1988. "Male Violence Against Women: Assessment of the Generational Transfer Hypothesis." *Deviant Behavior* 9:259–273.

Case, Laurie. 1980. "Mass Psychogenic Illness." *Science for the People* 12:18–19.

Cecere, Donna J. 1986. "The Second Closet: Battered Lesbians," pp. 21–31 in Kerry Lobel, ed., *Naming the Violence.* Seattle: Seal Press.

Check, James V.P. 1988. "Hostility Toward Women: Some Theoretical Considerations," pp. 29–42 in Gordon W. Russell, ed., *Violence in Intimate Relationships.* New York: PMA.

Claes, Jacalyn A., and David M. Rosenthal. 1990. "Men Who Batter Women: A Study in Power." *Journal of Family Violence* 5:215–224.

Coates, Carolie J., and Deborah J. Leong. 1988. "A Psychosocial Approach to Family Violence: Application of Conceptual Systems Theory," pp. 177–201 in Gordon W. Russell, ed., *Violence in Intimate Relationships.* New York: PMA.

Cohen, Pennie. 1984. "Violence in the Family: An Act of Loyalty?" *Psychotherapy* 21:249–253.

Cohn, Ellen G. 1987. "Changing the Domestic Violence Policies of Urban Police Departments: Impact of the Minneapolis Experiment." *Response* 10:22–24.

Coleman, Diane H., and Murray A. Straus. 1986. "Marital Power, Conflict, and Violence in a Nationally Representative Sample of American Couples." *Violence and Victims* 1:141–157.

Coleman, Karen H. 1980. "Conjugal Violence: What 33 Men Report." *Journal of Marriage and Family Counseling* 6: 207–213.

Coley, Soraya M., and Joyce O. Beckett. 1988. "Black Battered Women: Practice Issues." *Social Casework* 69:483–492.

———. 1988a. "Black Battered Women: A Review of Empirical Literature." *Journal of Counseling and Development* 66:266–270.

Conrad, Fran. 1979. "Society May Be Dangerous to Your Health." *Science for the People* 11:14–19, 32–38.

Cook, David R., and Anne Frantz-Cook. 1984. "A Systematic Treatment Approach to Wife Battering." *Journal of Marital and Family Therapy* 10:83–93.

Corenblum, Barry. 1988. "Alcohol and Spouse Abuse: A Social Cognition Perspective," pp. 217–237 in Gordon W. Russell, ed., *Violence in Intimate Relationships.* New York: PMA.

Corsini, Raymond J., ed. 1984. *Current Psychotherapies,* 3rd ed. Itasca, IL: Peacock.

Crouter, Ann C. 1984. "Spillover from Family to Work: The Neglected Side of the Work-Family Interface." *Human Relations* 37:425–442.

Currie, Dawn H. 1990. "Battered Women and the State: From the Failure of Theory to a Theory of Failure." *Journal of Human Justice* 1:77–96.

Davidson, Terry. 1977. "Wifebeating: A Recurring Phenomenon Throughout History," pp. 2–34 in Maria Roy, ed., *Battered Women.* New York: Van Nostrand Reinhold.

_____. 1978. *Conjugal Crime: Understanding and Changing the Wifebeating Problem.* New York: Hawthorne Books.

Davis, Fred. 1961. "Deviance Disavowal: The Management of Strained Interaction by the Visibly Handicapped." *Social Problems* 9:120–132.

Davis, Liane V. 1987. "Battered Women: The Transformation of a Social Problem." *Social Work* 32:306–311.

Davis, Nanette J. 1988. "Battered Women: Implications for Social Control." *Contemporary Crises* 12:345–372.

Del Oma, Rosa. 1975. "Limitations for the Prevention of Violence: The Latin American Reality and Its Criminological Theory." *Crime and Social Justice* 3:21–29.

DeMaris, Alfred. 1989. "Attrition in Batterers' Counseling: The Role of Social and Demographic Factors." *Social Service Review* 63:142–154.

Denzin, Norman K. 1984. "Toward a Phenomenology of Domestic, Family Violence." *American Journal of Sociology* 90:483–513.

_____. 1984a. *On Understanding Emotions.* San Francisco: Jossey-Bass.

Deschner, Jeanne P. 1984. *The Hitting Habit: Anger Control for Battering Couples.* New York: Free Press.

Dewsbury, Anton R. 1975. "Family Violence Seen in General Practice." *Royal Society of Health Journal* 95:290–295.

Dickstein, Leah J., and Carol C. Nadelson, eds. 1989. *Family Violence: Emerging Issues of a National Crisis.* Washington, DC: American Psychiatric Press.

Dietrich, Mary Lou. 1986. "Nothing Is the Same Anymore," pp. 155–162 in Kerry Lobel, ed., *Naming the Violence.* Seattle: Seal Press.

Dobash, Rebecca Emerson. 1988. "Violence Against Women—A Worldwide View." Paper presented at the Welsh Women's Aid International Conference, Cardiff, Wales, October 21–23.

Dobash, Rebecca Emerson, and Russell P. Dobash. 1977. "Wives: The 'Appropriate Victims' of Marital Violence." *Victimology* 2:436–442.

_____. 1979. *Violence Against Wives: A Case Against the Patriarchy.* New York: Free Press.

_____. 1983. "Patterns of Violence in Scotland," pp. 147–158 in Richard J. Gelles and Clair P. Cornell, eds., *International Perspectives on Family Violence.* Lexington, MA: Lexington Books.

_____. 1984. "The Nature and Antecedents of Violent Events." *British Journal of Criminology* 24:269–288.

_____. 1988. "Research as Social Action: The Struggle for Battered Women," pp. 51–74 in Kersti Yllö and Michele Bograd, eds., *Feminist Perspectives on Wife Abuse.* Newbury Park, CA: Sage.

Dunford, Franklyn W., David Huizinga, and Delbert S. Elliott. 1990. "The Role of Arrest in Domestic Assault: The Omaha Police Experiment." *Criminology* 28:183–206.

Dutton, Donald G. 1988. *The Domestic Assault of Women: Psychological and Criminal Justice Perspectives.* Newton, MA: Allyn and Bacon.

_____. 1988a. "Profiling of Wife Assaulters: Preliminary Evidence for a Trimodal Analysis." *Violence and Victims* 3:5–29.

_____. 1988b. "Research Advances in the Study of Wife Assault: Etiology and Prevention," pp. 161–220 in David N. Weisstub, ed., *Law and Mental Health: International Perspectives,* vol. 4. New York: Pergamon Press.

Dutton, Donald G., and James J. Browning. 1988. "Concern for Power, Fear of Intimacy, and Aversive Stimuli for Wife Assault," pp. 163–175 in Gerald T. Hotaling et al., eds., *Family Abuse and Its Consequences.* Newbury Park, CA: Sage.

_____. 1988a. "Power Struggles and Intimacy Anxieties as Causative Factors of Wife Assault," pp. 163–175 in Gordon W. Russell, ed., *Violence in Intimate Relationships.* New York: PMA.

Dutton, Donald G., and Barbara M.S. McGregor. 1991. "The Symbiosis of Arrest and Treatment for Wife Assault: The Case for Combined Intervention," pp. 131–154 in Michael Steinman, ed., *Woman Battering.* Cincinnati: Anderson.

Dutton, Donald G., and Susan Lee Painter. 1981. "Traumatic Bonding: The Development of Emotional Attachments in Battered Women and Other Relationships of Intermittent Abuse." *Victimology* 6:139–155.

Dutton, Donald G., and Catherine E. Strachan. 1987. "Motivational Needs for Power and Spouse-specific Assertiveness in Assaultive and Nonassaultive Men." *Violence and Victims* 2:145–156.

Dworkin, Andrea. 1983. *Right-Wing Women.* New York: Perigee Books.

Dziggel, Cory. 1986. "The Perfect Couple," pp. 62–69 in Kerry Lobel, ed., *Naming the Violence.* Seattle: Seal Press.

Edleson, Jeffrey L. 1984. "Working with Men Who Batter." *Social Work* 29:237–242.

_____. 1985. "Violence Is the Issue: A Critique of Neidig's Assumptions." *Victimology* 9:483–489.

_____. 1988. "Judging Success in Intervention: The Case of Men Who Batter." Paper presented at the American Enterprise Institute for Public Policy Conference on Family Violence Research, Washington, DC.

_____. 1991. "Coordinated Community Responses," pp. 203–220 in Michael Steinman, ed., *Woman Battering*. Cincinnati: Anderson.

Edleson, Jeffrey L., and Mary P. Brygger. 1986. "Gender Differences in Reporting of Battering Incidents." *Family Relations* 35:377–382.

Edleson, Jeffrey L., Zvi C. Eisikovits, and Edna Guttmann. 1985. "Men Who Batter Women: A Critical Review of the Evidence." *Journal of Family Issues* 6:229–247.

Edleson, Jeffrey L., David M. Miller, and Gene W. Stone. 1983. *Counseling Men Who Batter: A Group Leader's Handbook*. Albany, NY: Men's Coalition Against Battering.

Edleson, Jeffrey L., and Maryann Syers. 1990. "Relative Effectiveness of Group Treatments for Men Who Batter." *Social Work Research Abstracts* 26:10–17.

Ehrlich, Howard J. 1990. "The Ecology of Anti-gay Violence." *Journal of Interpersonal Violence* 5:359–365.

Eisikovits, Zvi C., and Jeffrey L. Edleson. 1989. "Intervening with Men Who Batter: A Critical Review of the Literature." *Social Service Review* 63:384–414.

Elbow, Margaret. 1977. "Theoretical Considerations of Violent Marriages." *Social Casework* 58:515–526.

Elias, Robert. 1986. *The Politics of Victimization: Victims, Victimology and Human Rights*. New York: Oxford University Press.

Elliot, Frank A. 1977. "The Neurology of Explosive Rage: The Dyscontrol Syndrome," pp. 98–109 in Maria Roy, ed., *Battered Women*. New York: Van Nostrand.

Ellis, Albert. 1962. *Reason and Emotion in Psychotherapy*. Secaucus, NJ: Citadel Press.

_____. 1976. "Techniques of Handling Anger in Marriage." *Journal of Marriage and Family Counseling* 2:305–315.

Ellis, Desmond. 1989. "Male Abuse of a Married or Cohabiting Female Partner: The Application of Sociological Theory to Research Findings." *Violence and Victims* 4:235–256.

Ellis, Desmond, and Walter DeKeseredy. 1989. "Marital Status and Woman Abuse: The DAD model." *International Journal of Sociology and the Family* 19:67–87.

Engelhardt, Bonnie J., and Katherine Triantafillou. 1987. "Mediation for Lesbians," pp. 327–343 in Boston Lesbian Psychologies Collective, eds., *Lesbian Psychologies*. Urbana: University of Illinois Press.

Everett, Aub. 1988. "The Role of Personality in Violent Relationships," pp. 135–148 in Gordon W. Russell, ed., *Violence in Intimate Relationships*. New York: PMA.

Fagan, Jeffrey A. 1987. "Cessation of Family Violence: Deterrence and Dissuasion," pp. 377–426 in Lloyd Ohlin and Michael Tonry, eds., *Crime and Justice*. Chicago: University of Chicago Press.

————. 1988. "Contributions of Family Violence Research to Criminal Justice Policy on Wife Assault: Paradigms of Science and Social Control." *Violence and Victims* 3:159–203.

Fagan, Jeffrey, and Sandra Wexler. 1987. "Crime at Home and in the Streets: The Relationship Between Family and Stranger Violence." *Violence and Victims* 2:5–23.

Farber, Bernard. 1964. *Family Organization and Interaction*. San Francisco: Chandler.

Farrington, Keith. 1986. "The Application of Stress Theory to the Study of Family Violence: Principles, Problems, and Proposals." *Journal of Family Violence* 1:131–147.

Faulk, M. 1974. "Men Who Assault Their Wives." *Medicine, Science and the Law* 14:180–183.

Feazell, Carann S., Raymond S. Mayers, and Jeanne Deschner. 1984. "Services for Men Who Batter: Implications for Programs and Policies." *Family Relations* 33:217–223.

Feld, Scott L., and Murray A. Straus. 1989. "Escalation and Desistance of Wife Assault in Marriage." *Criminology* 27: 141–161.

Ferguson, Harv. 1987. "Mandating Arrests for Domestic Violence." *FBI Law Enforcement Bulletin* 56:6–11.

Ferraro, Kathleen J. 1988. "An Existential Approach to Battering," pp. 126–138 in Gerald T. Hotaling et al., eds., *Family Abuse and Its Consequences*. Newbury Park, CA: Sage.

————. 1989. "Policing Woman Battering." *Social Problems* 36:61–74.

Ferraro, Kathleen, and John M. Johnson. 1983. "How Women Experience Battering." *Social Problems* 30:325–339.

Feyen, Carol. 1989. "Battered Rural Women: An Exploratory Study of Domestic Violence in a Wisconsin County." *Wisconsin Sociologist* 26:17–32.

Finkelhor, David, Richard J. Gelles, Gerald T. Hotaling, and Murray A. Straus, eds. 1983. *The Dark Side of Families: Current Family Violence Research*. Newbury Park, CA: Sage.

Finn, Peter. 1991. "Civil Protection Orders: A Flawed Opportunity for Intervention," pp. 155–190 in Michael Steinman, ed., *Woman Battering*. Cincinnati: Anderson.

Flaste, Richard. 1977. "Teach Kindness: There's a Lesson in It for Parents." *New York Times*, October 28, p. 18.

Fleming, Jennifer Baker. 1979. *Stopping Wife Abuse*. Garden City, NY: Anchor Books.

Flitcraft, Anne, and Evan Stark. 1978. "Notes on the Social Construction of Battering." *Antipode* 10:73–93.

————. 1984. *Medical Therapy as Repression: The Case of the Battered Woman. Wife Abuse: The Facts*. Washington, DC: Center for Women Policy Studies.

Fogarty, Thomas F. 1979. "On Emptiness and Closeness," pp. 70–90 in Eileen C. Pendagast, ed., *The Family: Compendium One, The Best of the Family, 1973–1978.* New Rochelle, NY: Center for Family Learning.

Follingstad, Diane R., Larry L. Rutledge, Barbara J. Berg, Elizabeth S. Hause, and Darlene S. Polek. 1990. "The Role of Emotional Abuse in Physically Abusive Relationships." *Journal of Family Violence* 5:107–120.

Ford, David A. 1991. "Preventing and Provoking Wife Battery Through Criminal Sanctions: A Look at the Risks," pp. 191–210 in Dean D. Knudsen and Jo Ann L. Miller, eds., *Abused and Battered.* New York: Aldine De Gruyter.

Ford, Peter. 1966. "Libertarian Psychiatry: An Introduction to Existential Analysis." *Anarchy* 70:353–375.

Frankl, Viktor E. 1965. *The Doctor and the Soul.* New York: Knopf.

Franks, David D. 1985. "Role-taking, Social Power and Imperceptiveness." *Studies in Symbolic Interaction* 6: 229–259.

Freeman, Michael D.A. 1979. *Violence in the Home.* Westmea, England: Saxon House.

_____. 1980. "Violence Against Women: Does the Legal System Provide Solutions or Itself Constitute the Problem?" *Canadian Journal of Family Law* 3:377–401.

Frieze, Irene Hanson. 1979. "Perceptions of Battered Wives," pp. 79–108 in Irene Hanson Frieze, Daniel Bar-Tal, and John S. Carroll, eds., *New Approaches to Social Problems: Applications of Attribution Theory.* San Francisco: Jossey-Bass.

Galtung, Johann. 1980. *The True Worlds: A Transnational Perspective.* New York: Free Press.

Gamache, Denise J., Jeffrey L. Edleson, and Michael D. Shock. 1988. "Coordinated Police, Judicial, and Social Service Response to Woman Battering: A Multiple-Baseline Evaluation Across Three Communities," pp. 193–209 in Gerald T. Hotaling et al., eds., *Coping with Family Violence.* Newbury Park, CA: Sage.

Ganley, Anne. 1981. *Court-Mandated Counseling for Men Who Batter.* Washington, DC.: Center for Women Policy Studies.

Garnet, Shelley, and Doris Moss. 1982. "How to Set Up a Counseling Program for Self-referred Batterers: The AWAIC Model," pp. 267–276 in Maria Roy, ed., *The Abusive Partner.* New York: Van Nostrand.

Gelles, Richard J. 1974. *The Violent Home: A Study of Physical Aggression Between Husbands and Wives.* Newbury Park, CA: Sage.

_____. 1975. "Violence and Pregnancy: A Note on the Extent of the Problem and Needed Services." *Family Coordinator* 24:81–86.

_____. 1978. "Violence Toward Children in the United States." *American Journal of Orthopsychiatry* 48:580–592.

_____. 1982. "Domestic Criminal Violence," pp. 201–235 in Marvin E. Wolfgang and Neil A. Weiner, eds., *Criminal Violence.* Newbury Park, CA: Sage.

_____. 1982a. "An Exchange/Social Control Approach to Understanding Intra-family Violence." *Behavior Therapist* 5:5–8.

_____. 1988. "Violence and Pregnancy: Are Pregnant Women at Greater Risk of Abuse?" *Journal of Marriage and the Family* 50:841–847.

Gelles, Richard J., and Clair P. Cornell. 1983. *International Perspectives on Family Violence*. Lexington, MA: Lexington Books.

Gelles, Richard J., and John W. Harrop. 1989. "Violence, Battering, and Psychological Distress Among Women." *Journal of Interpersonal Violence* 4:400–420.

Gelles, Richard J., and Murray A. Straus. 1979. "Violence in the American Family." *Journal of Social Issues* 35:15–39.

_____. 1988. *Intimate Violence*. New York: Simon and Schuster.

Gibbs, Jack P. 1989. "Conceptualization of Terrorism." *American Sociological Review* 54:329–340.

Gil, David G. 1973. *Unravelling Social Policy*. Cambridge, MA: Schenkman.

_____. 1977. "Societal Violence and Violence in Families," pp. 14–33 in John M. Eckelaar and Sanford M. Katz, eds., *Family Violence*. Toronto: Butterworths.

_____. 1979. *Child Abuse and Violence*. New York: AMS.

_____. 1979a. "The Hidden Success of Schooling in the United States." *The Humanist* 39:32–37.

_____. 1979b. "Unravelling Child Abuse," pp. 69–79 in Richard Bourne and Eli H. Newberger, eds., *Critical Perspectives on Child Abuse*. Lexington, MA: Lexington Books.

_____. 1985. "The Political and Economic Context of Child Abuse," pp. 9–19 in Eli H. Newberger and Richard Bourne, eds., *Unhappy Families*. Littleton, MA: PSG.

_____. 1986. "Sociocultural Aspects of Domestic Violence," pp. 124–149 in Mary Lystad, ed., *Violence in the Home*. New York: Brunner/Mazel.

_____. 1987. "Individual Experience and Critical Consciousness: Sources of Social Change in Everyday Life." *Journal of Sociology and Social Welfare* 14:5–20.

_____. 1989. "Work, Violence, Injustice and War." *Journal of Sociology and Social Welfare* 16:39–53.

Giles-Sims, Jean. 1983. *Wife-Battering: A Systems Theory Approach*. New York: Guilford.

Glaser, Daniel. 1986. "Violence in Society," pp. 5–31 in Mary Lystad, ed., *Violence in the Home*. New York: Brunner/Mazel.

Goffman, Jerry M. 1984. *Batterers Anonymous: Self-Help Counseling for Men Who Batter*. San Bernardino, CA: B. A. Press.

Goldstein, Diane, and Alan Rosenbaum. 1985. "An Evaluation of the Self-Esteem of Maritally Violent Men." *Family Relations* 34:425–428.

Gondolf, Edward W. 1985. "Anger and Oppression in Men Who Batter: Empiricist and Feminist Perspectives and Their Implications for Research." *Victimology* 10:311–324.

_____. 1985a. "Fighting for Control: Clinical Assessment of Men Who Batter." *Social Casework* 66:48–54.

_____. 1985b. *Men Who Batter: An Integrated Approach to Stopping Wife Abuse.* Holmes Beach, FL: Learning Publications.

_____. 1987. "Changing Men Who Batter: A Developmental Model for Integrated Interventions." *Journal of Family Violence* 2:335–349.

_____. 1987a. "Evaluating Programs for Men Who Batter: Problems and Perspectives." *Journal of Family Violence* 2:95–108.

_____. 1987b. "Seeing Through Smoke and Mirrors: A Guide to Batterer Program Evaluations." *Response* 10:16–19.

_____. 1988. "Dealing with the Abuser: Issues, Options, and Procedures," pp. 101–111 in Anne L. Horton and Judith A. Williamson, eds., *Abuse and Religion.* Lexington, MA: D. C. Heath.

_____. 1988a. "How Some Men Stop Their Abuse: An Exploratory Program Evaluation," pp. 129–144 in Gerald T. Hotaling et al., eds., *Coping with Family Violence.* Newbury Park, CA: Sage.

_____. 1988b. "The State of the Debate: A Review Essay on Woman Battering." *Response* 11:3–8.

_____. 1988c. "Who Are Those Guys? Toward a Behavioral Typology of Batterers." *Violence and Victims* 3:187–203.

_____. 1990. "The Human Rights of Women Survivors." *Response* 13:6–8.

Gondolf, Edward W., and Ellen R. Fisher. 1988. *Battered Women as Survivors: An Alternative to Treating Learned Helplessness.* Lexington, MA: Lexington Books.

Gondolf, Edward W., Ellen R. Fisher, and J. Richard McFerron. 1988. "Racial Differences Among Shelter Residents: A Comparison of Anglo, Black, and Hispanic Battered." *Journal of Family Violence* 3:39–51.

Gondolf, Edward W., and James Hanneken. 1987. "The Gender Warrior: Reformed Batterers on Abuse, Treatment, and Change." *Journal of Family Violence* 2:177–191.

Gondolf, Edward W., and Richard J. McFerron. 1989. "Handling Battering Men: Police Action in Wife Abuse Cases." *Criminal Justice and Behavior* 16:429–439.

Gondolf, Edward W., and David Russell. 1986. "The Case Against Anger Control Treatment Programs for Batterers." *Response* 9:2–5.

Goode, William J. 1971. "Force and Violence in the Family." *Journal of Marriage and the Family* 33:624–636.

Goolkasian, Gail A. 1986. *Confronting Domestic Violence: A Guide for Criminal Justice Agencies.* Washington, DC: U.S. Department of Justice.

_____. 1986a. "The Judicial System and Domestic Violence—An Expanding Role." *Response* 9:2–7.

Gordon, Linda. 1988. *Heroes of Their Own Lives: The Politics and History of Family Violence, Boston, 1880–1960.* New York: Viking Press.

Hamberger, L. Kevin, and James E. Hastings. 1986. "Characteristics of Spouse Abusers: Predictors of Treatment Acceptance." *Journal of Interpersonal Violence* 1:363–375.

_____. 1986a. "Personality Correlates of Men Who Abuse Their Partners: A Cross-Validation Study." *Journal of Family Violence* 1: 323–341.

_____. 1988. "Characteristics of Male Spouse Abusers Consistent with Personality Disorders." *Hospital and Community Psychiatry* 39:763–770.

_____. 1988a. "Exposure to Violence in the Families-of-Origin Among Wife Abusers and Maritally Nonviolent Men." *Violence and Victims* 3:49–63.

_____. 1988b. "Skills Training for Treatment of Spouse Abusers: An Outcome Study." *Journal of Family Violence* 3:121–130.

_____. 1989. "Counseling Male Spouse Abusers: Characteristics of Treatment Completers and Dropouts." *Violence and Victims* 4:275–286.

Hart, Barbara. 1986. "Lesbian Battering: An Examination." *Aegis* 41:19–28.

_____. 1986a. "Lesbian Battering: An Examination," pp. 173–189 in Kerry Lobel, ed., *Naming the Violence*. Seattle: Seal Press.

_____. 1988. *Safety for Women: Monitoring Batterers' Programs*. Harrisburg: Pennsylvania Coalition Against Domestic Violence.

Hastings, James E., and L. Kevin Hamberger. 1988. "Personality Characteristics of Spouse Abusers: A Controlled Comparison." *Violence and Victims* 3:31–47.

Heise, Lori. 1989. "International Dimensions of Violence Against Women." *Response* 12:3–11.

Herek, Gregory M. 1990. "The Context of Anti-gay Violence: Notes on Cultural and Psychological Heterosexism." *Journal of Interpersonal Violence* 5:316–333.

Hirschel, J. David, and Ira Hutchinson. 1991. "Police-preferred Arrest Policies," pp. 49–72 in Michael Steinman, ed., *Woman Battering*. Cincinnati: Anderson.

Hornung, Carleton A., B. Clair McCullough, and Taichi Sugimoto. 1981. "Status Relationships in Marriage: Risk Factors in Spouse Abuse." *Journal of Marriage and the Family* 42:675–692.

Horton, Anne L., and Judith A. Williamson, eds. 1988. *Abuse and Religion: When Prayer Is Not Enough*. Lexington, MA: Lexington Books.

Hotaling, Gerald T., and David B. Sugarman. 1986. "An Analysis of Risk Markers in Husband to Wife Violence: The Current State of Knowledge." *Violence and Victims* 1:101–124.

_____. 1990. "A Risk Marker Analysis of Assaulted Wives." *Journal of Family Violence* 5:1–13.

Hotaling, Gerald T., David Finkelhor, John T. Kirkpatrick, and Murray A. Straus, eds. 1988. *Coping with Family Violence: Research and Policy Perspectives*. Newbury Park, CA: Sage.

_____. 1988a. *Family Abuse and Its Consequences: New Directions in Research*. Newbury Park, CA: Sage.

Jaffe, Peter, David A. Wolfe, Anne Telford, and Gary Austin. 1986. "The Impact of Police Charges in Incidents of Wife Abuse." *Journal of Family Violence* 1:37–49.

Jayaratne, Srinika. 1977. "Child Abusers as Parents and Children: A Review." *Social Work* 22:5–9.

Jennings, Jerry L. 1987. "History and Issues in the Treatment of Battering Men: A Case for Unstructured Group Therapy." *Journal of Family Violence* 2:193–213.

————. 1990. "Preventing Relapse Versus 'Stopping' Domestic Violence: Do We Expect Too Much Too Soon from Battering Men?" *Journal of Family Violence* 5:43–60.

Johnson, John M. 1988. "Media Manslaughter." *Studies in Symbolic Interaction* 9:201–208.

Johnson, John M., and Kathleen J. Ferraro. 1988. "Courtship Violence: Survey vs. Empathetic Understandings of Abusive Conduct." *Studies in Symbolic Interaction* 9:175–186.

Johnston, Mildred E. 1988. "Correlates of Early Violence Experience Among Men Who Are Abusive Toward Female Mates," pp. 192–202 in Gerald T. Hotaling et al., eds., *Family Abuse and Its Consequences*. Newbury Park, CA: Sage.

Kalmuss, Debra. 1984. "The Intergenerational Transmission of Marital Aggression." *Journal of Marriage and the Family* 46:11–19.

Kalmuss, Debra, and Judith A. Seltzer. 1986. "Continuity of Marital Behavior in Remarriage: The Case of Spouse Abuse." *Journal of Marriage and the Family* 48:113–120.

Kanter, Rosabeth Moss. 1977. *Work and Family in the United States: A Critical Review and Agenda for Research and Policy*. New York: Russell Sage Foundation.

Kelly, Liz. 1988. "How Women Define Their Experiences of Violence," pp. 114–132 in Kersti Yllö and Michele Bograd, eds., *Feminist Perspectives on Wife Abuse*. Newbury Park, CA: Sage.

————. 1988a. *Surviving Sexual Violence*. Cambridge: Polity Press.

Kessler, Marc, and George W. Albee. 1975. "Primary Prevention." *Annual Review of Psychology* 26:557–591.

Knudsen, Dean D., and Jo Ann L. Miller, eds. 1991. *Abused and Battered: Social and Legal Responses to Family Violence*. New York: Aldine De Gruyter.

Kramer, Ronald C. 1989. "Criminologists and the Social Movement Against Corporate Crime." *Social Justice* 16: 146–165.

Krestan, Jo-Ann, and Claudia S. Bepko. 1980. "The Problem of Fusion in the Lesbian Relationship." *Family Process* 19: 277–290.

Kropotkin, Peter. 1924. *Ethics*. New York: Mother Earth Publications.

Kübler-Ross, Elisabeth. 1975. *Death: The Final Stage of Growth*. Englewood Cliffs, NJ: Prentice-Hall.

Kurdek, Lawrence A., and J. Patrick Schmitt. 1986. "Relationship Quality of Partners in Heterosexual Married, Heterosexual Cohabiting, and Gay and Lesbian Relationships." *Journal of Personality and Social Psychology* 51:711–720.

Kurz, Demie. 1987. "Responses to Battered Women: Resistance to Medicalization." *Social Problems* 34:501–513.

_____. 1989. "Social Science Perspectives on Wife Abuse: Current Debates and Future Directions." *Gender and Society* 3:489–505.

Laing, R. D. 1965. *The Divided Self*. London: Tavistock.

Langer, Ellen. 1982. *The Psychology of Control*. Beverly Hills, CA: Sage.

Langley, Roger, and Richard G. Levy. 1977. *Wifebeating: The Silent Crisis*. New York: Dutton.

Law Enforcement Training Project of the Victim Services Agency of New York City. 1989. "State Legislation Providing for Law Enforcement Response to Family Violence." *Response* 12:6–9.

Le Guin, Ursula K. 1974. *The Dispossessed*. New York: Avon.

Leidig, Marjorie W. 1981. "Violence Against Women: A Feminist-psychological Analysis," pp. 190–205 in Sue Cox, ed., *Female Psychology: The Emerging Self*. New York: St. Martin's Press.

_____. 1992. "The Continuum of Violence Against Women: Psychological and Physical Consequences." *Journal of American College Health* 40:149–155.

Lein, Laura. 1986. "The Changing Role of the Family," pp. 32–50 in Mary Lystad, ed., *Violence in the Home*. New York: Brunner/Mazel.

Lengyel, Linda B. 1990. "Survey of State Domestic Violence Legislation." *Legal Reference Services Quarterly* 10:59–82.

Leonard, Linda. 1983. *The Wounded Woman*. Athens, OH: Swallow Press.

Leonard, Peter. 1975. "Towards a Paradigm for Radical Practice," pp. 46–61 in Roy Bailey and Mike Brake, eds., *Radical Social Work*. London: Edward Arnold.

Lerman, Lisa G. 1984. "A Model State Act: Remedies for Domestic Abuse." *Harvard Journal on Legislation* 21:61–144.

Lerman, Lisa G., Franci Livingston, and Vicky Jackson. 1983. "State Legislation and Domestic Violence." *Response* 6:1–28.

Lerner, Michael. 1987. "Public-Interest Psychotherapy: A Cure for the Pain of Powerlessness." *Utne Reader* 20:39–47.

Lester, David. 1980. "A Cross-cultural Study of Wife Abuse." *Aggressive Behavior* 6:361–364.

Levinson, Daniel J. 1986. "A Conception of Adult Development." *American Psychologist* 41:3–13.

Levinson, David. 1983. "Physical Punishment of Children and Wifebeating in Cross-cultural Perspective," pp. 73–78 in Richard J. Gelles and Clair P. Cornell, eds., *International Perspectives on Family Violence*. Lexington, MA: Lexington Books.

_____. 1988. "Family Violence in Cross-cultural Perspective," pp. 435–455 in Vincent B. Van Hasselt et al., eds., *Handbook of Family Violence*. New York: Plenum Press.

_____. 1989. *Family Violence in Cross-cultural Perspective*. Newbury Park, CA: Sage.

Levy, Barrie. 1984. *Skills for Violence-free Relationships: Curriculum for Young People Ages 13–18.* Santa Monica, CA: California Coalition on Battered Women.

Lewin, Kurt. 1986. "'Everything Within Me Rebels': A Letter from Kurt Lewin to Wolfgang Kohler, 1933." *Journal of Social Issues* 42:39–48.

Lewis, Glen. 1983. *Real Men Like Violence: Australian Men, Media, and Violence.* Sidney: Kangaroo Press.

Liddle, A. Mark. 1989. "Feminist Contributions to an Understanding of Violence Against Women—Three Steps Forward, Two Steps Back." *Canadian Review of Sociology and Anthropology* 26:759–775.

Liou, Kuo-Tsai, Ronald D. Sylvia, and Gregory Brunk. 1990. "Non-work Factors and Job Satisfaction Revisited." *Human Relations* 43:77–86.

Lipsman, Julie A. 1985. "Criminal Law: Domestic Violence." *1985 Annual Survey of American Law*, 839–862.

Lloyd, Sally A. 1990. "Conflict Types and Strategies in Violent Marriages." *Journal of Family Violence* 5:269–284.

Lobel, Kerry, ed. 1986. *Naming the Violence: Speaking Out About Lesbian Battering.* Seattle: Seal Press.

Lockhart, Lettie L. 1987. "A Reexamination of the Effects of Race and Social Class on the Incidence of Marital Violence: A Search for Reliable Differences." *Journal of Marriage and the Family* 49:603–610.

Lockhart, Lettie L., and Barbara W. White. 1989. "Understanding Marital Violence in the Black Community." *Journal of Interpersonal Violence* 4:421–436.

Loseke, Donileen R., and Spencer E. Cahill. 1984. "The Social Construction of Deviance: Experts on Battered Women." *Social Problems* 31:296–310.

Lystad, Mary, ed. 1986. *Violence in the Home: Interdisciplinary Perspectives.* New York: Brunner/Mazel.

MacEwen, Karyl E., and Julian Barling. 1988. "Multiple Stressors, Violence in the Family of Origin, and Marital Aggression: A Longitudinal Investigation." *Journal of Family Violence* 3:73–87.

Makepeace, James M. 1983. "Life Events, Stress, and Courtship Violence." *Family Relations* 32:101–109.

Margolin, Gayla. 1979. "Conjoint Marital Therapy to Enhance Anger Management and Reduce Spouse Abuse." *American Journal of Family Therapy* 7:13–23.

————. 1988. "Interpersonal and Intrapersonal Factors Associated with Marital Violence," pp. 203–217 in Gerald T. Hotaling et al., eds., *Family Abuse and Its Consequences.* Newbury Park, CA: Sage.

Margolin, Gayla, Linda Gorin Sibner, and Lisa Gleberman. 1988. "Wife Battering," pp. 89–118 in Vincent B. Van Hasselt et al., eds., *Handbook of Family Violence.* New York: Plenum.

Marie, Susan. 1984. "Lesbian Battering: An Inside View." *Victimology* 9:16–20.

Martin, Del. 1981. *Battered Wives.* San Francisco: Volcano Press.

_____. 1981a. "Battered Women: Scope of the Problem," pp. 190–201 in Burt Galaway and Joe Hudson, eds., *Perspectives on Crime Victims*. St. Louis: Mosby.

_____. 1985. "Domestic Violence: A Sociological Perspective," pp. 1–32 in Daniel J. Sonkin, Del Martin, and Lenore E.A. Walker, eds., *The Male Batterer.* New York: Springer.

Masumura, Wilfred T. 1979. "Wife Abuse and Other Forms of Aggression." *Victimology* 4:46–59.

Matza, David. 1964. *Delinquency and Drift.* New York: Wiley.

_____. 1969. *Becoming Deviant.* Englewood Cliffs, NJ: Prentice-Hall.

May, Rollo, and Irwin Yalom. 1984. "Existential Psychotherapy," pp. 354–391 in Raymond J. Corsini, ed., *Current Psychotherapies,* 3rd ed. Itasca, IL: Peacock.

Mayer, Lawrence J., and John M. Johnson. 1988. "Courtship Violence and the Emotional Career of Betrayal." *Studies in Symbolic Interaction* 9:187–199.

McCall, George J., Michael M. McCall, Norman K. Denzin, Gerald D. Suttles, and Sue B. Kurth. 1970. *Social Relationships.* Chicago: Aldine.

McCall, George, and Nancy Shields. 1986. "Social and Structural Factors in Family Violence," pp. 98–123 in Mary Lystad, ed., *Violence in the Home.* New York: Brunner/Mazel.

McGillivray, Anne. 1987. "Battered Woman: Definition, Models, and Prosecutorial Policy." *Canadian Journal of Family Law* 6:15–45.

McGrath, Colleen. 1979. "The Crisis of Domestic Order." *Socialist Review* 43:11–22.

McLeod, Maureen. 1984. "Women Against Men: An Examination of Domestic Violence Based on an Analysis of Official Data and National Victimization Data." *Justice Quarterly* 1:171–194.

McNeely, R. L., and Gloria Robinson-Simpson. 1987. "The Truth About Domestic Violence: A Falsely Framed Issue." *Social Work* 32:485–490.

Meador, Betty D., and Carl R. Rogers. 1984. "Person-centered Therapy," pp. 142–195 in Raymond J. Corsini, ed., *Current Psychotherapies,* 3rd ed. Itasca, IL: Peacock.

Mederer, Helen J., and Richard J. Gelles. 1989. "Compassion or Control: Intervention in Cases of Wife Abuse." *Journal of Interpersonal Violence* 4:25–43.

Meichenbaum, Donald. 1977. *Cognitive-Behavior Modifications: An Integrative Approach.* New York: Plenum Press.

Mercy, James A., and Patrick W. O'Carroll. 1988. "New Directions in Violence Prediction: The Public Health Arena." *Violence and Victims* 3:285–301.

Meridith, Nikki. 1987. "Psychotherapy: Everybody's Doin' It, But Does It Work?" *Utne Reader* 20:26–33.

Merwine, Connie J. 1987. "Pennsylvania's Protection from Abuse Act: A Decade in Existence Generates Judicial Interpretation and New Changes in House Bill 2026." *Dickinson Law Review* 91:805–832.

Micklow, Patricia L. 1988. "Domestic Abuse: The Pariah of the Legal System," pp. 407–433 in Vincent B. Van Hasselt et al., eds., *Handbook of Family Violence.* New York: Plenum Press.

Miller, David. 1976. *Social Justice.* Oxford: Oxford University Press.

Miller, Jenny. 1982. "Psychiatry as a Tool of Repression." *Science for the People* 15:14–17.

Miller, Walter P. 1958. "Lower Class Culture as a Generating Milieu of Gang Delinquency." *Journal of Social Issues* 14:5–19.

Mills, C. Wright. 1956. *The Power Elite.* Oxford: Oxford University Press.

Mills, Trudy. 1985. "The Assault on the Self: Stages in Coping with Battering Husbands." *Qualitative Sociology* 8:103–123.

Moore, Jamie M. 1985. "Landmark Court Decision for Battered Women." *Response* 8:5–8.

Morash, Merry. 1986. "Wife Battering." *Criminal Justice Abstracts* 18:252–271.

Morrell, Lisa. 1984. "Violence in Premarital Relationships." *Response* 7:17–18.

Nadelhaft, Jerome. 1987. "Wife Torture: A Known Phenomenon in Nineteenth-Century America." *Journal of American Culture* 10:39–59.

National Coalition Against Domestic Violence. 1991. *The 1991 National Directory of Domestic Violence Programs.* Washington, DC: NCADV.

National Woman Abuse Prevention Project. 1988. *Domestic Violence Fact Sheets.* Washington DC: NWAPP.

Neidig, Peter H. 1984. "Women's Shelters, Men's Collectives and Other Issues in the Field of Spouse Abuse." *Victimology* 9:464–476.

Neidig, Peter H., Dale H. Friedman, and Barbara S. Collins. 1985. "Domestic Conflict Containment: A Spouse Abuse Treatment Program." *Social Casework* 66:195–204.

Newberger, Eli H., and Richard Bourne, eds. 1985. *Unhappy Families: Clinical and Research Perspectives on Family Violence.* Littleton, MA: PSG.

Newman, Graeme. 1979. *Understanding Violence.* New York: Lippincott.

NiCarthy, Ginny N. 1986. *Getting Free: A Handbook for Women in Abusive Relationships,* 2nd ed. Seattle: Seal Press.

————. 1989. "From the Sounds of Silence to the Roar of a Global Movement: Notes on the Movement Against Violence Against Women." *Response* 12:3–10.

Norwood, Robin. 1985. *Women Who Love Too Much.* New York: Pocket Books.

Ohlin, Lloyd, and Michael Tonry, eds. 1988. *Crime and Justice: A Review of Research, Volume 11, Family Violence.* Chicago: University of Chicago Press.

Okun, Lewis. 1986. *Woman Abuse: Facts Replacing Myths.* Albany, NY: SUNY Press.

————. 1988. "Termination or Resumption of Cohabitation in Woman Battering Relationships: A Statistical Study," pp. 107–119 in Gerald T. Hotaling et al., eds., *Coping with Family Violence.* Newbury Park, CA: Sage.

O'Leary, K. Daniel, and Ileana Arias. 1988. "Assessing Agreement of Reports of Spouse Abuse," pp. 218–227 in Gerald T. Hotaling et al., eds., *Family Abuse and Its Consequences.* Newbury Park, CA: Sage.

_____. 1988a. "Prevalence, Correlates and Development of Spouse Abuse," pp. 104–127 in Ray DeV Peters and Robert J. McMahon, eds., *Social Learning and Systems Approaches to Marriage and the Family.* New York: Brunner/Mazel.

O'Leary, K. Daniel, Julian Barling, Ileana Arias, Alan Rosenbaum, Jean Malone, and Andrea Tyree. 1989. "Prevalence and Stability of Physical Aggression Between Spouses: A Longitudinal Analysis." *Journal of Consulting and Clinical Psychology* 57:263–268.

O'Leary, K. Daniel, and Alison D. Curley. 1986. "Assertion and Family Violence: Correlates of Spouse Abuse." *Journal of Marital and Family Therapy* 12:281–290.

Oppenlander, Nan. 1981. "The Evolution of Law and Wife Abuse." *Law and Policy Quarterly* 3:382–405.

Osmundson, Linda A. 1992. "Nothing Short of a Revolution: Anti-Battering Movement at a Crossroad." *Peace and Justice Journal* 6:1, 8.

O'Toole, Richard, and Steven Webster. 1988. "Differentiation of Family Mistreatment: Similarities and Differences by Status of the Victim." *Deviant Behavior* 9:347–368.

Pagelow, Mildred D. 1981. *Woman-Battering: Victims and Their Experiences.* Beverly Hills, CA: Sage.

_____. 1984. *Family Violence.* New York: Praeger.

_____. 1988. "The Incidence and Prevalence of Criminal Abuse of Other Family Members," pp. 263–313 in Lloyd Ohlin and Michael Tonry, eds., *Crime and Justice.* Chicago: University of Chicago Press.

_____. 1988a. "Marital Rape," pp. 207–232 in Vincent B. Van Hasselt et al., eds., *Handbook of Family Violence.* New York: Plenum Press.

Pagelow, Mildred D., and Pam Johnson. 1988. "Abuse in the American Family: The Role of Religion," pp. 1–12 in Anne L. Horton and Judith A. Williamson, eds., *Abuse and Religion.* Lexington, MA: Lexington Books.

Parsons, Patricia. 1982. "Radical Therapy: Living from the Inside Out." *Science for the People* 14:17–20.

Patrick-Hoffman, Patricia A. 1982. "Psychological Abuse of Women by Spouses and Live-in Lovers." Ph.D. diss., Union for Experimenting Colleges and Universities.

Patterson, Cecil Holden. 1986. *Theories of Counseling and Psychotherapy.* New York: Harper and Row.

Pearlman, Sarah F. 1987. "The Saga of Continuing Clash in Lesbian Community, or Will an Army of Ex-lovers Fail?" pp. 313–326 in Boston Lesbian Psychologies Collective, eds., *Lesbian Psychologies.* Urbana: University of Illinois Press.

Pence, Ellen. 1983. "The Duluth Domestic Abuse Intervention Project." *Hamline Law Review* 6:247–275.

_____. 1985. *The Justice System's Response to Domestic Assault Cases: A Guide for Policy Development.* Duluth: MN: Domestic Abuse Intervention Project, Minnesota Program Development.

_____. 1987. *In Our Best Interest: A Process for Personal and Social Change*. Duluth: Minnesota Program Development.

_____. 1988. *Batterers Programs: Shifting from Community Collusion to Community Confrontation*. Duluth: Minnesota Program Development.

_____. 1988a. "The Role of Advocacy Groups in Police Reforms." *Response* 11:19.

_____. 1989. *The Justice System's Response to Domestic Assault Cases: A Guide for Policy Development*, rev. ed. Duluth: Domestic Abuse Intervention Project, Minnesota Program Development.

Pence, Ellen et al. 1984. "Response to Peter Neidig's Article: 'Women's Shelters, Men's Collectives and Other Issues in the Field of Spouse Abuse.'" *Victimology* 9:477–482.

Pence, Ellen, and Melanie Shepard. 1988. "Integrating Feminist Theory and Practice: The Challenge of the Battered Women's Movement," pp. 282–298 in Kersti Yllö and Michele Bograd, eds., *Feminist Perspectives on Wife Abuse*. Newbury Park, CA: Sage.

Pepinsky, Harold E. 1991. *The Geometry of Violence and Democracy*. Bloomington: Indiana University Press.

_____. 1991a. "Peacemaking in Criminology and Criminal Justice," pp. 299–327 in Harold E. Pepinsky and Richard Quinney, eds., *Criminology as Peacemaking*. Bloomington: Indiana University Press.

Pepinsky, Harold E., and Richard Quinney, eds. 1991. *Criminology as Peacemaking*. Bloomington: Indiana University Press.

Peterson, David. 1991. "Physically Violent Husbands of the 1890s and Their Resources." *Journal of Family Violence* 6:1–15.

Peterson-Lewis, Sonja, Charles W. Turner, and Afesa M. Adams. 1988. "Attribution Processes in Repeatedly Abused Women," pp. 107–130 in Gordon W. Russell, ed., *Violence in Intimate Relationships*. New York: PMA.

Pfouts, Jane H. 1978. "Violent Families: Coping Responses of Abused Wives." *Child Welfare* 57:101–111.

Pharr, Suzanne. 1986. "The Connection Between Homophobia and Violence Against Women." *Aegis* 41:35–37.

_____. 1986a. "Two Workshops on Homophobia," pp. 202–222 in Kerry Lobel, ed., *Naming the Violence*. Seattle: Seal Press.

_____. 1988. *Homophobia: A Weapon of Sexism*. Little Rock, AR: Chardon Press.

Piercy, Marge. 1976. *Woman on the Edge of Time*. New York: Fawcett Crest.

Pillemer, Karl. 1985. "The Dangers of Dependency: New Findings on Domestic Violence Against the Elderly." *Social Problems* 33:146–158.

Pirog-Good, Maureen A., and Jan E. Stets. 1989. *Violence in Dating Relationships*. New York: Praeger.

Pirog-Good, Maureen A., and Jan E. Stets-Kealey. 1985. "Male Batterers and Battering Prevention Programs: A National Survey." *Response* 8:8–12.

Plachta, Leslie R. 1989. "Torture and Health Care Professionals." *New York State Journal of Medicine* 89:143–148.

Pleck, Elizabeth. 1987. *Domestic Tyranny: The Making of Social Policy Against Family Violence from Colonial Times to the Present.* New York: Oxford University Press.

Pleck, Elizabeth, Joseph H. Pleck, Marilyn Grossman, and Pauline B. Bart. 1978. "The Battered Data Syndrome: A Comment on the Steinmetz' Article." *Victimology* 2:680–684.

Ptacek, James. 1985. "Wifebeaters' Accounts of Their Violence: Loss of Control as Excuse and as Subjective Experience." Unpublished paper, University of New Hampshire.

———. 1988. "The Clinical Literature on Men Who Batter: A Review and Critique," pp. 149–161 in Gerald T. Hotaling et al., eds., *Family Abuse and Its Consequences.* Newbury Park, CA: Sage.

———. 1988a. "How Men Who Batter Rationalize Their Behavior," pp. 247–258 in Anne L. Horton and Judith A. Williamson, eds., *Abuse and Religion.* Lexington, MA: Lexington Books.

———. 1988b. "Why Do Men Batter Their Wives?" pp. 133–157 in Kersti Yllö and Michele Bograd, eds., *Feminist Perspectives on Wife Abuse.* Newbury Park, CA: Sage.

Purdy, Frances, and Norm Nickle. 1981. "Practice Principles for Working with Groups of Men Who Batter." *Social Work with Groups* 4:111–122.

Quinney, Richard. 1991. "The Way of Peace: On Crime, Suffering, and Service," pp. 3–13 in Harold E. Pepinsky and Richard Quinney, eds., *Criminology as Peacemaking.* Bloomington: Indiana University Press.

Rainone, Francine Lea. 1987. "Beyond Community: Politics and Spirituality," pp. 344–354 in Boston Lesbian Psychologies Collective, eds. *Lesbian Psychologies.* Urbana: University of Illinois Press.

Reiman, Jeffery. 1979. *The Rich Get Richer and the Poor Get Prison.* New York: Wiley.

———. 1984. *The Rich Get Richer and the Poor Get Prison,* 2nd ed. New York: Wiley.

Renzetti, Claire M. 1988. "Violence in Lesbian Relationships: A Preliminary Analysis of Causal Factors." *Journal of Interpersonal Violence* 3:381–399.

———. 1989. "Building a Second Closet: Third Party Responses to Victims of Lesbian Partner Abuse." *Family Relations* 38:157–163.

Resick, Patricia A., and Donnis Reese. 1986. "Perception of Family Social Climate and Physical Aggression in the Home." *Journal of Family Violence* 1:71–83.

Response. 1986. "The Use and Enforcement of Civil Protection Orders for Domestic Violence Cases." *Response* 9:24.

Rich, Adrienne. 1979. *Lies, Secrets, and Silence.* New York: Norton.

Roberts, Albert R. 1982. "A National Survey of Services for Batterers," pp. 230–243 in Maria Roy, ed., *The Abusive Partner.* New York: Van Nostrand.

———. 1984. *Battered Women and Their Families: Intervention Strategies and Treatment Programs.* New York: Springer.

———. 1984a. "Police Intervention," pp. 116–128 in Albert R. Roberts, ed., *Battered Women and Their Families.* New York: Springer.

Robinson, Stephen. 1982. "Critical Psychiatry?" *Radical Science Journal* 12:100–111.

Rogers, Carl R. 1972. *Bringing Together the Cognitive and the Affective-Experiential.* Handout #5. La Jolla, CA: Center for Studies of the Person.

Romero, Mary. 1985. "A Comparison Between Strategies Used on Prisoners of War and Battered Wives." *Sex Roles* 13:537–547.

Rosenbaum, Alan. 1988. "Methodological Issues in Marital Violence Research." *Journal of Family Violence* 3:91–104.

Rosenbaum, Alan, and K. Daniel O'Leary. 1981. "Marital Violence: Characteristics of Abusive Couples." *Journal of Consulting and Clinical Psychology* 49:63–71.

———. 1986. "Treatment of Marital Violence," pp. 385–406 in Neil S. Jacobson and Alan S. Gurman, eds., *Clinical Handbook of Marital Therapy.* New York: Guilford.

Rosewater, Lynne Bravo, and Lenore E.A. Walker, eds. 1985. *Handbook of Feminist Therapy: Women's Issues in Psychotherapy.* New York: Springer.

Rounsaville, Bruce J. 1978. "Battered Wives: Barriers to Identification and Treatment." *American Journal of Orthopsychiatry* 48:487–494.

———. 1978a. "Theories of Marital Violence: Evidence from a Study of Battered Women." *Victimology* 3:11–31.

Roy, Maria. 1977. "A Current Survey of 150 Cases," pp. 25–44 in Maria Roy, ed., *Battered Women.* New York: Van Nostrand.

———. 1982. "Four Thousand Partners in Violence: A Trend Analysis," pp. 17–35 in Maria Roy, ed., *The Abusive Partner.* New York: Van Nostrand.

Roy, Maria, ed. 1977. *Battered Women: A Psychological Study of Domestic Violence.* New York: Van Nostrand.

———. 1982. *The Abusive Partner: An Analysis of Domestic Battering.* New York: Van Nostrand.

Russell, D. 1984. *Facing Up to Spouse Abuse: A Theme-centered Program for Batterers.* Unpublished paper from the Second Step Program, Pittsburgh, Pennsylvania.

Russell, Diana E.H. 1982. *Rape in Marriage.* New York: Macmillan.

Russell, Gordon W., ed. 1988. *Violence in Intimate Relationships.* New York: PMA.

Russell, Mary. 1988. "Wife Assault Theory, Research, and Treatment: A Literature Review." *Journal of Family Violence* 3:193–208.

Saline, Carol. 1984. "Bleeding in the Suburbs." *Philadelphia Magazine* 75:1ff.

Saunders, Daniel G. 1982. "Counseling the Violent Husband," pp. 16–29 in Peter A. Keller and Lawrence G. Ritt, eds., *Innovations in Clinical Practice.* Sarasota, FL: Professional Resource Exchange.

References

209

_____. 1984. "Helping Husbands Who Batter." *Journal of Contemporary Social Work* 65:347–353.

_____. 1986. "When Battered Women Use Violence: Husband-Abuse or Self-Defense?" *Violence and Victims* 1:47–60.

_____. 1988. "Wife Abuse, Husband Abuse, or Mutual Combat? A Feminist Perspective on the Empirical Findings," pp. 90–113 in Kersti Yllö and Michele Bograd, eds., *Feminist Perspectives on Wife Abuse.* Newbury Park, CA: Sage.

Saunders, Daniel G., and Darald Hanusa. 1986. "Cognitive-behavioral Treatment of Men Who Batter: The Short Term Effects of Group Therapy." *Journal of Family Violence* 1:357–372.

Saunders, Daniel G., and Jennifer C. Parker. 1989. "Legal Sanctions and Treatment Follow-through Among Men Who Batter: A Multivariate Analysis." *Social Work Research Abstracts* 25:21–29.

Scarry, Elaine. 1985. *The Body in Pain: The Making and Unmaking of the World.* New York: Oxford University Press.

_____. 1988. "Introduction," pp. vii–xxvii in Elaine Scarry, ed., *Literature and the Body.* Baltimore, MD: Johns Hopkins University Press.

Schaef, Anne Wilson. 1986. *Co-dependence.* New York: Harper and Row.

Schauss, Alexander G. 1982. "Effects of Environmental and Nutritional Factors on Potential and Actual Batterers," pp. 76–90 in Maria Roy, ed., *The Abusive Partner.* New York: Van Nostrand.

Schechter, Susan. 1982. *Women and Male Violence: The Visions and Struggles of the Battered Women's Movement.* Boston: South End Press.

Schinke, Steven Paul, Robert F. Schilling II, Richard P. Barth, Lewayne D. Gilchrist, and Josie Solseng Maxwell. 1986. "Stress-Management Intervention to Prevent Family Violence." *Journal of Family Violence* 1:13–26.

Schmidt, Janell. 1987. "Replication of the Minneapolis Experiment." *Response* 10:23.

Schmidt, Janell, and Ellen Hochstedler Steury. 1989. "Prosecutorial Discretion in Filing Charges in Domestic Violence Cases." *Criminology* 27:487–510.

Schwartz, Martin D. 1988. "Ain't Got No Class: Universal Risk Theories of Battering." *Contemporary Crises* 12:373–392.

_____. 1988a. "Marital Status and Woman Abuse Theory." *Journal of Family Violence* 3:239–248.

_____. 1990. "Work Status, Resource Equality, Injury and Wife Battery: The National Crime Survey Data." *Free Inquiry in Creative Sociology* 18:57–61.

Scott, P. D. 1974. "Battered Wives." *British Journal of Psychiatry* 125:433–441.

Sedlak, Andrea J. 1988. "The Effects of Personal Experiences with Couple Violence on Calling It Battering and Allocating Blame," pp. 31–59 in Gerald T. Hotaling et al., eds., *Coping with Family Violence.* Newbury Park, CA: Sage.

_____. 1988a. "Prevention of Wife Abuse," pp. 319–358 in Vincent B. Van Hasselt et al., eds., *Handbook of Family Violence.* New York: Plenum Press.

Seltzer, Judith A., and Debra Kalmuss. 1988. "Socialization and Stress Explanations for Spouse Abuse." *Social Forces* 67:473–491.

Shainess, Natalie. 1977. "Psychological Aspects of Wife Battering," pp. 111–118 in Maria Roy, ed., *Battered Women*. New York: Van Nostrand.

Shepard, Melanie, and Ellen Pence. 1988. "The Effect of Battering on the Employment Status of Women." *Affilia* 3:55–61.

Sherman, Lawrence W. 1984. *The Impact of the Minneapolis Domestic Violence Experiment: Wave I Findings*. Washington, DC: Police Foundation.

Sherman, Lawrence W., and Richard A. Berk. 1985. "The Specific Deterrent Effects of Arrest for Domestic Assault." *American Sociological Review* 49:261–272.

Sherman, Lawrence W., and Ellen G. Cohn. 1986. *Police Policy on Domestic Violence: A National Survey*. Washington, DC: Crime Control Institute.

Shields, Nancy M., and Christine R. Hanneke. 1983. "Attribution Processes in Violent Relationships: Perceptions of Violent Husbands and Their Wives." *Journal of Applied Social Psychology* 13:515–527.

Shields, Nancy M., George J. McCall, and Christine R. Hanneke. 1988. "Patterns of Family and Nonfamily Violence: Violent Husbands and Violent Men." *Violence and Victims* 3:83–97.

Shupe, Anson, William A. Stacey, and Lonnie R. Hazelwood. 1986. *Violent Men, Violent Couples: The Dynamics of Domestic Violence*. Lexington, MA: Lexington Books.

Small, Martin. 1966. "Freud, Anarchism and Experiments in Living." *Anarchy* 70:300–319.

Smith, Christine, and Murray A. Straus. 1988. "Cohabiting, Commitment, and Social Control." Durham: University of New Hampshire, Family Research Laboratory.

Smith, Michael D. 1988. "Women's Fear of Violent Crime: An Exploratory Test of a Feminist Hypothesis." *Journal of Family Violence* 3:29–38.

————. 1990. "Patriarchal Ideology and Wife Beating: A Test of a Feminist Hypothesis." *Violence and Victims* 5:257–273.

Snell, John E., Richard J. Rosenwald, and Ames Robey. 1964. "The Wife-Beater's Wife." *Archives of General Psychiatry* 11:107–112.

Soler, Esta, and Sue Martin. 1983. *Domestic Violence Is a Crime*. San Francisco: Family Violence Project.

Sonkin, Daniel J. 1988. "The Male Batterer: Clinical and Research Issues." *Violence and Victims* 3:65–79.

Sonkin, Daniel J., and Michael Durphy. 1982. *Learning to Live Without Violence: A Handbook for Men*. San Francisco: Volcano Press.

Sonkin, Daniel J., Del Martin, and Lenore E.A. Walker. 1985. *The Male Batterer: A Treatment Approach*. New York: Springer.

Stacey, William A., and Anson Shupe. 1983. *The Family Secret: Domestic Violence in America*. Boston: Beacon Press.

Stafne, Gigi. 1989. *The Wisconsin Mandatory Arrest Monitoring Project: Final Report.* Madison: Wisconsin Coalition Against Domestic Violence.

Stanko, Elizabeth A. 1985. *Intimate Intrusions: Women's Experience of Male Violence.* London: Routledge and Kegan Paul.

_____. 1988. "Fear of Crime and the Myth of the Safe Home: A Feminist Critique of Criminology," pp. 75–89 in Kersti Yllö and Michele Bograd, eds., *Feminist Perspectives on Wife Abuse.* Newbury Park, CA: Sage.

Star, Barbara. 1982. "Programs for Assaulters: Nationwide Trends," pp. 76–86 in Jerry P. Flanzer, ed., *The Many Faces of Family Violence.* Springfield, IL: Charles C. Thomas.

_____. 1983. *Helping the Abuser.* New York: Family Service Association of America.

Stark, Evan, and Anne Flitcraft. 1985. "Woman Battering, Child Abuse and Social Heredity: What Is the Relationship?" pp. 147–171 in Norman Johnson, ed., *Marital Violence.* London: Routledge and Kegan Paul.

_____. 1988. "Violence Among Intimates," pp. 293–317 in Vincent B. Van Hasselt et al., eds., *Handbook of Family Violence.* New York: Plenum Press.

Statham, Daphine. 1978. *Radicalism and Social Work.* London: Routledge and Kegan Paul.

Steiner, Claude. 1981. "Radical Psychiatry," pp. 724–735 in Raymond J. Corsini, ed., *Handbook of Innovative Psychotherapies.* New York: Wiley.

Steinman, Michael. 1988. "Anticipating Rank and File Police Reactions to Arrest Policies Regarding Spouse Abuse." *Criminal Justice Research Bulletin* 4.

_____. 1989. "The Effects of Police Responses on Spouse Abuse." *American Journal of Police* 8:1–19.

_____. 1990. "Lowering Recidivism Among Men Who Batter Women." *Journal of Police Science and Administration* 17:124–132.

_____. 1991. "Coordinated Criminal Justice Interventions and Recidivism Among Batterers," pp. 221–236 in Michael Steinman, ed., *Woman Battering.* Cincinnati: Anderson.

Steinman, Michael, ed. 1991. *Woman Battering: Policy Responses.* Cincinnati: Anderson.

Steinmetz, Suzanne K. 1978. "The Battered Husband Syndrome." *Victimology* 2:499–509.

Steinmetz, Suzanne K., and Joseph S. Lucca. 1988. "Husband Battering," pp. 233–246 in Vincent B. Van Hasselt et al., eds., *Handbook of Family Violence.* New York: Plenum Press.

Stets, Jan E. 1988. *Domestic Violence and Control.* New York: Springer-Verlag.

Stets, Jan E., and Murray A. Straus. 1989. "The Marriage License as a Hitting License: A Comparison of Assaults in Dating, Cohabiting, and Married Couples." *Journal of Family Violence* 4:161–180.

Stith, Sandra M. 1990. "Police Response to Domestic Violence: The Influence of Individual and Familial Factors." *Violence and Victims* 5:37–49.

Stordeur, Richard A., and Richard Stille. 1989. *Ending Men's Violence Against Their Partners: One Road to Peace.* Newbury Park, CA: Sage.

Strach, Ann, Nan Jervey, Susan J. Hornstein, and Nomi Porat. 1986. "Lesbian Abuse: The Process of the Lesbian Abuse Issues Network (LAIN)," pp. 88–94 in Kerry Lobel, ed., *Naming the Violence.* Seattle: Seal Press.

Straus, Murray A. 1973. "A General Systems Theory Approach to a Theory of Violence Between Family Members." *Social Science Information* 12:105–125.

———. 1974. "Cultural and Social Organization Influences on Violence Between Family Members," pp. 53–69 in Raymond Price and Dorothy Barrier, eds., *Configurations: Biological and Cultural Factors in Sexuality and Family Life.* Lexington, MA: Lexington Books.

———. 1974a. "Leveling, Civility, and Violence in the Family." *Journal of Marriage and the Family* 36:13–29.

———. 1976. "Sexual Inequality, Cultural Norms, and Wife-Beating." *Victimology* 1:54–76.

———. 1977. "A Sociological Perspective on the Prevention and Treatment of Wifebeating," pp. 194–238 in Maria Roy, ed., *Battered Women.* New York: Van Nostrand.

———. 1980. "The Marriage License as a Hitting License: Evidence From Popular Culture, Law, and Social Science," pp. 39–50 in Murray A. Straus and Gerald T. Hotaling, eds., *The Social Causes of Husband-Wife Violence.* Minneapolis: University of Minnesota Press.

———. 1980a. "Social Stress and Marital Violence in a National Sample of American Families." *Annals of the New York Academy of Sciences* 347:229–250.

———. 1980b. "A Sociological Perspective on the Prevention of Wife-Beating," pp. 211–232 in Murray A. Straus and Gerald T. Hotaling, eds., *The Social Causes of Husband-Wife Violence.* Minneapolis: University of Minnesota Press.

———. 1980c. "Victims and Aggressors in Marital Violence." *American Behavioral Scientist* 23:681–704.

———. 1983. "Ordinary Violence, Child Abuse, and Wife Beating: What Do They Have in Common?" in David Finkelhor et al., eds., *The Dark Side of Families.* Newbury Park, CA: Sage.

———. 1983a. "Societal Morphogenesis and Intrafamily Violence in Cross-cultural Perspective," pp. 27–43 in Richard J. Gelles and Clair P. Cornell, eds., *International Perspectives on Family Violence.* Lexington, MA: Lexington Books.

———. 1991. "Conceptualization and Measurement of Battering: Implications for Public Policy," pp. 19–48 in Michael Steinman, ed., *Woman Battering.* Cincinnati: Anderson.

_____. 1991a. "Physical Violence in American Families: Incidence Rates, Causes, and Trends," pp. 17–34 in Dean D. Knudsen and Jo Ann L. Miller, eds., *Abused and Battered*. New York: Aldine De Gruyter.

Straus, Murray A., and Richard J. Gelles. 1986. "Societal Change and Change in Family Violence from 1975 to 1985 as Revealed by Two National Surveys." *Journal of Marriage and the Family* 48:465–479.

Straus, Murray A., Richard J. Gelles, and Suzanne K. Steinmetz. 1980. *Behind Closed Doors: Violence in the American Family*. New York: Doubleday/Anchor.

Straus, Murray A., and Alan J. Lincoln. 1985. "A Conceptual Framework for Understanding Crime and the Family," pp. 5–23 in Murray A. Straus and Alan J. Lincoln, eds., *Crime and the Family*. Springfield, IL: Charles C. Thomas.

Straus, Murray A., and Christine Smith. 1990. "Family Patterns and Primary Prevention of Family Violence," pp. 507–526 in Murray A. Straus, Richard J. Gelles, and Christine Smith, eds., *Physical Violence in American Families*. New Brunswick, NJ: Transaction Books.

Straus, Murray A., and Gerald T. Hotaling, eds. 1980. *The Social Causes of Husband-Wife Violence*. Minneapolis: University of Minnesota Press.

Straus, Murray A., Richard J. Gelles, and Christine Smith, eds. 1990. *Physical Violence in American Families: Risk Factors and Adaptations to Violence in 8,145 Families*. New Brunswick, NJ: Transaction Books.

Strube, Michael J. 1988. "The Decision to Leave an Abusive Relationship," pp. 93–106 in Gerald T. Hotaling et al., eds., *Coping with Family Violence*. Newbury Park, CA: Sage.

Strube, Michael J., and Linda S. Barbour. 1983. "The Decision to Leave an Abusive Relationship: Economic Dependence and Psychological Commitment." *Journal of Marriage and the Family* 45:785–793.

_____. 1984. "Factors Related to the Decision to Leave an Abusive Relationship." *Journal of Marriage and the Family* 46:837–844.

Sugarman, David B., and Gerald T. Hotaling. 1989. "Violent Men in Intimate Relationships: An Analysis of Risk Markers." *Journal of Applied Social Psychology* 19:1034–1048.

Sullivan, Dennis C. 1980. *The Mask of Love: Corrections in America; Toward a Mutual Aid Alternative*. Port Washington, NY: Kennikat Press.

_____. 1987. "The True Cost of Things, the Loss of the Commons, and Radical Change." *Social Anarchism* 6:20–26.

"Surgeon General's Workshop on Violence and Public Health: Recommendations for the Working Group." 1985. Unpublished report, October.

Symonds, Martin. 1978. "The Psychodynamics of Violence-prone Marriages." *American Journal of Psychoanalysis* 38:213–222.

Szinovacz, Maximiliane E. 1983. "Using Couple Data as a Methodological Tool: The Case of Marital Violence." *Journal of Marriage and the Family* 45:633–644.

Taub, Nadine, and Elizabeth M. Schneider. 1982. "Perspectives on Women's Subordination and the Law," pp. 117–171 in David Kairys, ed., *The Politics of Law: A Progressive Critique*. New York: Pantheon Books.

Taylor, John W. 1984. "Structured Conjoint Therapy for Spouse Abuse Cases." *Social Casework* 65:11–18.

Taylor, Shelley E., and Susan T. Fiske. 1978. "Salience, Attention and Attribution: Top of the Head Phenomena," pp. 249–288 in Leonard Berkowitz, ed., *Advances in Experimental Social Psychology*, vol. 11. New York: Academic Press.

Taylor, Stuart P., and Kenneth E. Leonard. 1983. "Alcohol and Human Physical Aggression," pp. 77–102 in Russell G. Green and Edward I. Donnerstein, eds., *Aggression: Theoretical and Empirical Reviews*. New York: Academic Press.

Telch, Christy F., and Carol Ummels Lindquist. 1984. "Violent Versus Nonviolent Couples: A Comparison of Patterns." *Psychotherapy* 21:242–248.

Tierney, Kathleen J. 1982. "The Battered Women Movement and the Creation of the Wife Beating Problem." *Social Problems* 29:207–213.

Tifft, Larry L. 1979. "The Coming Redefinition of Crime: An Anarchist Perspective." *Social Problems* 26:392–402.

———. 1982. "Capital Punishment Research, Policy, and Ethics: Defining Murder and Placing Murderers." *Crime and Social Justice* 17:61–68.

———. 1989. "Stopping the Violence: The Battering of Women and Interventions with Men Who Batter Women—A Critical Assessment." Master's paper, Central Michigan University.

Tifft, Larry L., and Lyn. Markham. 1991. "Battering Women and Battering Central Americans," pp. 114–153 in Harold E. Pepinsky and Richard Quinney, eds., *Criminology as Peacemaking*. Bloomington: Indiana University Press.

Tifft, Larry L., and Lois Stevenson. 1985. "Humanistic Criminology: Roots from Peter Kropotkin." *Journal of Sociology and Social Welfare* 22:488–520.

Tifft, Larry L., and Dennis C. Sullivan. 1980. *The Struggle to be Human: Crime, Criminology, and Anarchism*. Over-the-water, Sanday, Orkney, Scotland: Cienfuegos Press.

Tolman, Richard M. 1989. "The Development of a Measure of Psychological Maltreatment of Women by Their Male Partners." *Violence and Victims* 4:159–177.

Tolman, Richard M., and Larry W. Bennett. 1990. "A Review of Quantitative Research on Men Who Batter." *Journal of Interpersonal Violence* 5:87–118.

Tolman, Richard M., and Daniel G. Saunders. 1988. "The Case for the Cautious Use of Anger Control with Men Who Batter." *Response* 11:15–20.

Torres, Sara. 1987. "Hispanic-American Battered Women: Why Consider Cultural Differences?" *Response* 10:20–21.

Turner, Susan F., and Constance Hoenk Shapiro. 1986. "Battered Women: Mourning the Death of a Relationship." *Social Casework* 31:372–376.

Ulrich, Yvonne Campbell. 1989. "Cross-cultural Perspective on Violence Against Women." *Response to the Victimization of Women and Children* 12:21–23.

U.S. Commission on Civil Rights. 1982. *Under the Rule of Thumb: Battered Women and the Administration of Justice.* Washington, DC: U.S. Commission on Civil Rights.

U.S. Department of Justice. 1980. *Intimate Victims: A Study of Violence Among Friends and Relatives.* Washington, DC: Government Printing Office.

Van Hasselt, Vincent B., Randall L. Morrison, Alan S. Bellack, and Michel Hersen, eds. 1988. *Handbook of Family Violence.* New York: Plenum Press.

Vargo, Sue. 1987. "The Effects of Women's Socialization on Lesbian Couples," pp. 161–174 in Boston Lesbian Psychologies Collective, eds., *Lesbian Psychologies.* Urbana: University of Illinois Press.

Waisbrooker, Lois. 1985. *A Sex Revolution.* Philadelphia: New Society.

Walker, Lenore E.A. 1979. *The Battered Woman.* New York: Harper and Row.

———. 1979a. "How Battering Happens and How to Stop It," pp. 59–78 in Donna M. Moore, ed., *Battered Women.* Beverly Hills, CA: Sage.

———. 1983. "Victimology and the Psychological Perspective of Battered Women." *Victimology* 8:82–104.

———. 1984. *The Battered Woman Syndrome.* New York: Springer.

———. 1985. "Feminist Therapy with Victim/Survivors of Interpersonal Violence," pp. 203–214 in Lynne Bravo Rosewater and Lenore E.A. Walker, eds., *Handbook of Feminist Therapy.* New York: Springer.

———. 1985a. "What Counselors Should Know About the Battered Woman," pp. 150–166 in Daniel J. Sonkin, Del Martin, and Lenore E.A. Walker, eds., *The Male Batterer.* New York: Springer.

———. 1988. "The Battered Woman Syndrome," pp. 139–148 in Gerald T. Hotaling et al., eds., *Family Abuse and Its Consequences.* Newbury Park, CA: Sage.

Walker, Lenore E.A., and Angela Browne. 1985. "Gender and Victimization by Intimates." *Journal of Personality* 53:179–193.

Wallerstein, Judith S., and Joan Berlin Kelly. 1980. *Surviving the Breakup.* New York: Basic Books.

Wardell, Laurie, Dair L. Gillespie, and Ann Leffler. 1983. "Science and Violence Against Wives," pp. 69–84 in David Finkelhor et al., eds., *The Dark Side of Families.* Newbury Park, CA: Sage.

Watts, Deborah L., and Christine A. Courtois. 1981. "Trends in the Treatment of Men Who Commit Violence Against Women." *Personnel and Guidance Journal* 60:245–249.

Weis, Joseph G. 1988. "Family Violence Research Methodology and Design," pp. 117–162 in Lloyd Ohlin and Michael Tonry, eds., *Crime and Justice.* Chicago: University of Chicago Press.

Weitzman, Jack, and Karen Dreen. 1982. "Wife Beating: A View of the Marital Dyad." *Social Casework* 63:259–265.

Welch, I. David, and George H. Tate. 1985. "Carl Rogers: Quiet Revolutionary of the Helping Professionals," pp. 16–32 in Donald L. Avila and Arthur W. Combs, eds., *Perspectives on Helping Relationships and the Helping Professions.* Boston: Allyn and Bacon.

Wetzel, Laura, and Mary Anne Ross. 1983. "Psychological and Social Ramifications of Battering: Observations Leading to a Counseling Methodology for Victims of Domestic Violence." *Personnel and Guidance Journal* 61:423–428.

Wexler, Sandra. 1982. "Battered Women and Public Policy," pp. 184–204 in Ellen Boneparth, ed., *Women, Power, and Policy.* New York: Pergamon Press.

Williams, Kirk R., and Richard Hawkins. 1989. "Controlling Male Aggression in Intimate Relationships." *Law and Society* 23:591–612.

_____. 1989a. "The Meaning of Arrest for Wife Assault." *Criminology* 27:163–181.

Williams-White, Deborah. 1989. "Self-Help and Advocacy: An Alternative Approach to Helping Battered Women," pp. 45–60 in Leah J. Dickstein and Carol C. Nadelson, eds., *Family Violence.* Washington, DC: American Psychiatric Press.

Wilson, Elizabeth. 1980. "Feminism and Social Work," pp. 26–42 in Roy Bailey and Mike Brake, eds., *Radical Social Work and Practice.* London: Edward Arnold.

Wilson, Melvin N., A. J. Baglioni, Jr., and Deborah Downing. 1989. "Analyzing Factors Influencing Readmission to a Battered Women's Shelter." *Journal of Family Violence* 4:275–284.

Wilson, Melvin N., W. John Curtis, Lori Abercrombie, Nina Reau Veau, and Richard Folley. 1987. "Wife-Battering: A Case of Deindividuation." *Practice: Journal of Political, Economic, Psychological, and Sociological Culture* 5:88–97.

Woods, Laurie, and Anita Paulsen. 1987. "Annual Review of Family Law." *Clearinghouse Review* 20:1192–1201.

Ylhö, Kersti. 1983. "Sexual Equality and Violence Against Wives in American States." *Journal of Comparative Family Studies* 14:67–86.

_____. 1984. "The Status of Women, Marital Equality and Violence Against Wives." *Journal of Family Issues* 5:307–320.

_____. 1988. "Political and Methodological Debates in Wife Abuse Research," pp. 28–50 in Kersti Ylhö and Michele Bograd, eds., *Feminist Perspectives on Wife Abuse.* Newbury Park, CA: Sage.

Ylhö, Kersti, and Michele Bograd, eds. 1988. *Feminist Perspectives on Wife Abuse.* Newbury Park, CA: Sage.

Zaretsky, Eli. 1976. *Capitalism, the Family, and Personal Life.* London: Pluto.

Zehr, Howard. 1990. *Changing Lenses: A New Focus for Crime and Justice.* Scottdale, PA: Herald Press.

About the Book
and Author

Why have most interventions failed to decrease domestic violence in this country? Larry Tifft provides reasons—and suggests possible solutions—in this revealing study of the cultural, social structural, and interpersonal dynamics that support a man's choice to batter his intimate partner.

Tifft addresses the cultural underpinnings of violence against women, including the gender hierarchy evident in the basic structure of our society and in our institutions. Through an analysis of the stages in the battering process, he explores the context, meanings, and decision-making processes that lead men to batter women and encourage women to choose various coping, resistance, and survival strategies. What emerges from Tifft's study are not only patterns of physical violence, but also patterns of sexual, psychological, and spiritual violence that the batterer uses to control his partner's thoughts, to annihilate her voice, and to deconstruct her sense of self and reality.

Intrapersonal and interpersonal interventions have failed to decrease the prevalence of battering in our society. Primary prevention strategies designed to change the social structural arrangements that foster violence are likely to be much more effective. Tifft explains why and how these community-coordinated interventions, which challenge our most basic assumptions, are our best hope for reducing the prevalence of battering.

Larry L. Tifft is professor of sociology at Central Michigan University. He is author, with Dennis Sullivan, of *The Struggle to Be Human: Crime, Criminology, and Anarchism* and the forthcoming *The Social Structural Roots of Crime.*

Index

Child abuse, 1, 11, 34, 35, 98, 153, 166,
    172–173(n4)
  control and, 91
  impact of, 36
  intrafamily violence and, 3
  See also Corporal punishment
Child care, 28, 43, 92, 93, 159, 161
  development of, 180(n30)
  nonviolent, 170
  women and, 31, 160
Children
  conflict resolution programs for, 167
  disciplining, 1–3, 28–29, 35, 113, 164
  empowerment and, 93
  inferiority of, 144
  mediation by, 76
  protecting, 76, 80, 169, 175(n15)
  rights of, 173(n4)
  socialization of, 156, 170
  violence and, 11, 33, 64, 76, 129, 163,
    165, 179(n29)
  withdrawal by, 73
  See also Spanking
Civil protection, 130
  forfeiting, 172(n4)
Class structures, 147
  impact of, 146
Codependence, 5, 94
Cognitive restructuring, 66, 108, 109–116
Collective emergence, 137, 141
Communication
  abusive, 114
  battering and, 105
  nonviolent, 113
Communication skills, 108, 118
  developing, 107, 111, 113
Community Board Program (San
    Francisco), 167
Community-coordinated intervention,
    125–126, 133, 157, 163, 176(n15),
    180(n30), 184–185(n2)
  development of, 132

effects of, 134
  police and, 130–131
  See also Intervention
Conciliation Task Force (Judicial Process
    Commission, Rochester, N.Y.), 168
Conflict resolution, 111, 147, 160, 161,
    166
  for children, 167
  family, 163–164
  teaching, 168
Conflict Tactics Scale, Physical
    Aggression Subscale of, 6
Confronting Domestic Violence
    (Goolkasian), 131
Consciousness-raising, 147, 149, 166. *See
    also* Awareness
Control, 2, 13, 20, 25, 35, 140, 160, 162,
    175(n13)
  acceptance of, 121
  accountability for, 83
  benefits of, 152
  ending, 49–50, 119, 128, 133, 157
  exploring, 121, 128, 130
  increasing, 107, 120
  limiting, 69, 134–135
  loss of, 44, 46–47
  maintaining, 26–27, 42–43, 49, 50
  need for, 118
  patterns of, 29, 30, 83
  regaining, 47, 48, 64, 84, 182(n1)
  right to, 90, 128
  as social ideal, 144
  submitting to, 49
  tactics of, 94
  violence and, 42, 47, 48, 82
  See also Domination
Controller, description of, 100
Corporal punishment, 35
  ban on, 170
  cultural acceptance of, 28–29
  See also Child abuse
Correlates research, 11–12